Introduction

There is little doubt now that micro-electronics will cause major changes in our lives, both at work and at home. The papers which have been selected for publication in this book show not only examples of the applications of micro-electronics, written in as non-technical jargon as possible, but also show some of the problems that may arise from their use.

Those applications described here are only a selection from the thousands of current uses. Already hard at work, microprocessors are helping to make safer, the mines beneath our feet and the aircraft above our heads. Very soon they will appear in motor cars, providing not only fancy digital displays but in-built safety checks and warnings. The scope in areas such as this is virtually unlimited.

It would not do, however, to move into the position of dependence upon microprocessors without careful planning. There are social and political pressures to be considered and to be balanced against the economic advantages. It must be hoped that the external pressures on companies to use this technology will push them into a new era of co-operation with their work forces, to ensure the survival of the company. What is lacking at the present, however, are suitable retraining facilities and information. The former will hopefully be greatly improved when governments consider the problem at a national level. Already in the United Kingdom the Department of Industry is sponsoring the MAP education and training scheme which is administered by the National Computing Center. The information is available, if you know where to look, and in this series (Topics in Microprocessing) it is hoped to both provide concrete facts and to whet the readers' appetite for more. At the back of each book details of the abstracted magazines and journals will be found together with suggestions for further reading.

Clearly a great deal of work must be done if we are to adapt to this new environment. Engineers will need not only to learn about the new hardware but about system and software design. New techniques in fault-finding and maintenance will have to be developed. Companies stepping into this environment must be prepared for more than just new products. Before a product is put into production the necessary test and maintenance facilities will have to be designed. There will be no point in a product that cannot be satisfactorily tested or maintained, and microprocessors cannot be analysed with just an oscilloscope.

The current state of the microprocessor market is an interesting one. Very popular and successful at the moment are a group of processors whose common feature is the length of the internal logic field. This is known as the word length and the popular range currently uses 8 (binary) bits. The longer this word length, the more complex and powerful the device becomes. The next step is to 16-bit machines, although some have been with us for a while. In simple devices, even the power of the 8-bit microprocessors is wasted and simple 4-bit machines are available, geared towards uses in mass markets.

Although the popular press is eagerly awaiting the new 16-bit machines, just released or imminent from the manufacturers — Intel, Zilog and Motorola — these, effectively, minicomputer processors on a chip, are probably going to be more applicable as replacements for minicomputers rather than substitutes for 8-bit microprocessors. Time will tell.

The current generation of 8-bit machines are improved versions of ranges that have been with us for some years. Not only have these processors been improved, but there is a whole new range of supporting products. Improved development aids are available, providing elaborate facilities for preparing programs and de-bugging them. These systems now take the designer right through to the prototype stage by providing a substitute linkage for the prototype processor which is then emulated by the processor in the development system. This complex procedure, when properly used, enables a product to be tested or analysed in a way not possible before.

System design is becoming easier with the increasing availability of devices that sit alongside the microprocessor and do much of its work. Support chips to carry out complex mathematics, handle communications links or control displays are all available and compatible, more or less, with the current range of microprocessors. Now manufacturers are not only supplying chips but complete computers on a board. A whole range of circuit boards is produced and they can all be plugged into a standard chassis to make system building even easier. This market has been recognised by other small firms who are now supplying their own ranges of boards, in some cases at lower costs than the manufacturers.

Increasingly the manufacturers are moving towards supplying complete systems and the developments expected in the early 1980's should confirm this trend. It is also likely that the technology will look increasingly towards base materials other than silicon for mass storage of information. The prospect of bubble memories has been with us for some time and other even more novel technologies are being considered. The prospect for the future is an exciting one and will remain so as long as the suppliers find a market for their products.

Here we are concerned with the application of microprocessors and as the following diagram shows, the range of possibilities is immense. Microprocessors are applied in different ways and present different problems according to the particular market area. In mass markets, the final product is expected to be finished and the included software must be proven beyond all doubt. The maintenance of such systems must also be reduced to unplugging modules and testing those under automatic control.

Low volume markets can be supplied at a lower level of certainty as the supplier usually remains in touch with the customer who may well have technicians or even programmers on hand. The customer will also be paying for a large proportion or even all of the software effort.

In between these two, there are market areas where systems are made up of selected software run on standard hardware and others where both hardware and software are constructed from modules.

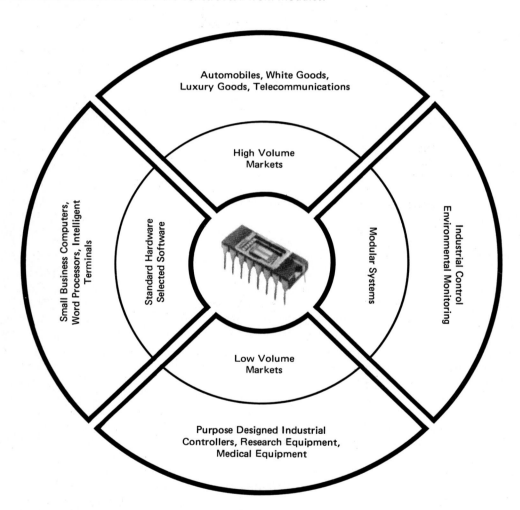

Throughout all market areas the question of software dominates. The reliability and efficiency of this essential component is one of the main concerns of both supplier and customer. Close liaison between electronics designers and programmers is needed to produce a good system. This co-operation is the responsibility of the project manager and is no mean task. Software design is now tending towards modular structures, making the job of testing and changing systems much easier. The task of the small business system programmer is also eased by supporting software that helps in the creation and handling of both data and program files. The appearance of such operating systems on these machines has been a major advance. Soon facilities for handling integrated pools of data (databases) will be available.

Micro-electronics have so far caused a ripple in industry; soon this ripple is expected to become a tidal wave. Whether a business or an economy is swamped by that wave or floats to the surface again, will be entirely dependent on its own efforts to apply this technology to suit its requirements.

Contents

Section 1

Introducing Micro-electronics, Microprocessors and Microcomputers

This section provides a broad introduction to the field of micro-electronics. It gives a brief history of the development of the microprocessor and an explanation of how microprocessors function, in a manner which can be easily understood by those without specialist training.

The Brainstorm Technology

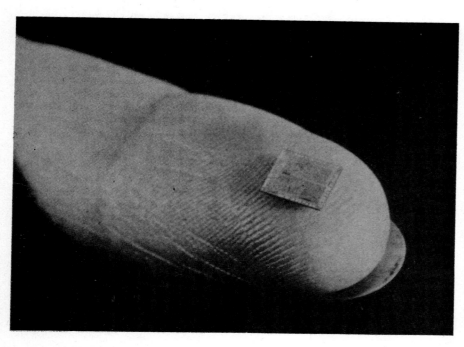

for micro computers went last summer to see a leading British manufacturer of cars, who said it was all up to the electrical components supplier. So the software house went to see the components company, which said it was all up to the car manufacturer. Yet in America Ford has just announced the largest ever order for ICs.

The articles that follow concentrate on the effect of the little chips on computers and telecommunications. But the effect on many other industries will be just as big.

There is another reason to take this industry seriously. Its success has lessons for a general problem in modern industry: the slowdown in technological innovation.

Seeds of change

Technology is losing steam in many industries. Production in American industry as a whole is rising less fast than in the 1950s and early 1960s. One leading American technologist has even predicted that the problem for the 1980s will be not to increase productivity but to prevent it falling faster than it would otherwise.

Another comment:

> I don't hear many of my industrial colleagues talking about exciting new discoveries that they think will shake the world.

When Intel was being founded, several hundred new technology-based firms were launched on the New York stock market each year; in 1975, there were only four such launches. Too many so-called innovations are me-too products, or minor evolutionary changes, rather than radical departures.

Some of the reasons for this decline in innovation—other than in the electronics industry—may be inevitable: increased pressure to improve the quality of life, rather than the quantity of goods; trade-union resistance to change; and the increased share of national product taken up by services.

But there are also lessons that government and industry could learn from electronics.

First, research and development. Of the five top R and D spenders in America two are in electronics, IBM

You are looking at the central brain of a computer. Little chips like this are going to make computers as commonplace as paperclips. They are called integrated circuits, and this one contains 15,000 transistors. It was made by Intel, a Californian company that turns them out by the bushel at a cost of around 50 cents a chip. Intel was founded in 1968. Last year it made 100 times more transistors than had been used in the entire world up to 1968.

Integrated circuits (ICs) are the quantum jump that is about to make a profound technological revolution possible. The nineteenth century was the age of steam and steel. The industrialised world is now entering the age of electronics. ICs will multiply all over offices, factories, homes, shops, aircraft, cars, what have you. They will control factory machines, enable you to turn the oven on by telephone before leaving the office, minimise your car's fuel consumption and exhaust emission,

automatically debit your bank account when you go shopping, and end the day by playing poker with you. They consume practically no energy, and their basic raw material is silicon, i.e, sand, the second most abundant element on earth. They will extend man's brain power the way most earlier technology has extended his muscle power. The IC is going to transform the product lines and manufacturing techniques of most industries. To ask what the applications are is like asking what are the applications of electricity. One firm has identified 25,000 of them.

Take any product, say, vending machines. ICs will make it easier to give exact change and no hardship at all to change the prices. They will reduce the number of parts that break down and they will make a better cup of tea. Any manufacturer should be examining his product line to see what effect ICs will have. Few are.

The leading British software house

($1 billion a year) and Bell ($800m a year). A third is partially so, General Electric. The other two make cars, where half the research budget goes on meeting government rules. Seven industries account for over four-fifths of the total R and D budget of American

Texas style

Texas Instruments makes ICs and IC-based products. It aims to grow from $1bn sales in 1975 to $10bn in the late 1980s, and without using the soft option of buying other businesses. How?

A major danger identified by management is the tendency to kill a revolutionary idea by thinking of all the difficulties. This is particularly true in consumer goods, where there is no major customer the idea can be tried out on.

So at Texas Instruments four steps have been taken: individual scientists can ask any of 30 managers for up to $25,000 to test a new concept, without anyone risking his career if it does not work; departments are asked to set aside up to 10% of their research budgets for high-risk programmes; bright young innovators are sent to the corporate engineering centre in rotation, and there given free rein to develop new ideas; and the whole emphasis has been redirected towards riskier projects, often ones unconnected with any of the firm's existing products. Add to all that, Texas Instruments' progressive stock ownership scheme.

The company also has a timetable of of when its research activities are expected to lead to new products. That is nothing special; but, whereas most firms would be putting the screws on to get research that will pay off in the short term, the main pressure in Texas Instruments is to get more products that can be launched 10 years hence. The company began work on silicon circuits in the early 1950s.

Slashing prices boosts sales

How one firm saw the calculator market in 1971...

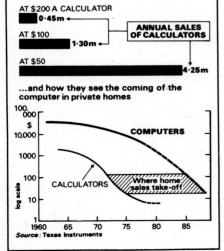

...and how they see the coming of the computer in private homes

industry, while four industries account for four-fifths of the spending on basic research. A similar picture emerges in Britain, but not in Japan. High R and D spenders grow fastest.

The difference in electronics companies is that the aims of R and D are more ambitious. They are looking for radically new products.

Look, for instance, at Texas Instruments (see box). Look at Univac's recent development of a mini computer for car dealers to use: instead of getting its computer scientists to scale down their existing designs, the firm bought in a fresh team to start from scratch. The result is cheap, flexible, and easy for the layman to use.

American electronics learnt a hard lesson in the 1950s, when Japan took over the lead in transistor manufacture, because American firms were too pussyfoot about exploiting a competitor to their existing, obsolete products. Now innovation is so fast that what seems the latest product can be obsolete before it is launched.

Investing in knowledge

	R and D as % of sales, 1975*
All US industries	1.8
Computers	
IBM	6.6
Burroughs	6.0
Mini computers	
Data General	10.8
Digital Equipment	9.1
Micro computers	
Fairchild	11.9
Intel	10.6

Excluding R and D paid for by government

Source: Investors Management Sciences

Patent rustling

Another striking thing about electronics is that the patent system works rather loosely, which encourages a free flow of technology. There is plain pinching, extensive cross-licensing, and a grey area in between. A new IC-based product can have a dozen imitators almost as soon as it is launched. Computer software is not even patentable.

Would there be a modern electronics industry if Bell, which is only interested in telephones, had retained the sole right to manufacture transistors? Indeed, the development from early transistors to modern ICs involves 100 inventions by a dozen firms. If they had all been dog in the manger, none of them would have had anything to eat.

One reason why a loose patent system works well in electronics is that electronic innovations need less capital investment to exploit them. As a general rule, industry needs about $10 of launch costs for every $1 of R and D. Thanks to

reductions in manufacturing costs, the ratio in electronics is often nearer 1 : 1. Thus, Burroughs could recently change almost its entire computer range within 14 months, and reckons that, without its research into manufacturing technology, computers would cost 20 times as much. Intel manufactures some of its products on the same machines it designs them on. Consequently, it can more easily introduce risky, revolutionary products, whose market is relatively untested.

No rules, OK

Another reason why electronics innovation is so fast is that there is hardly any government regulation. Such regulation as exists is aimed, rather crudely, towards encouraging competition. Even the Bell system's monopoly is less rigid than that of its overseas counterparts (and it was the government that forced Bell to make electronic patents generally available). In electronics, the free enterprise system still works, warts and all, the main wart being the oligopolistic strength of IBM.

Yet neither patents nor high cost of entry are the major weapons for IBM they might be in other industries: it cost Itel of California (not to be confused with Intel) only a few million dollars to launch a range of computers that emulate IBM's medium-size machines, at much lower cost. Instead, IBM has to resort to pricing and "bundling" strategies.

To break up IBM, as the justice department proposes, would be extremely hard. An alternative threefold counter-strategy to IBM has been suggested by some: a constant watch on pricing and bundling policies; force IBM to make all its products easily plug-compatible; and, more controversially, get it to use some of its multi-

"She's charming, witty and attractive, dear, but can she programme?"

billion dollar cash reserves as a trust fund to provide venture capital to other firms.

Most significantly, however, the electronics industry does not expect the government to solve its problems. When the department of commerce canvassed the idea of exploiting electronics know-how chauvinistically, the way Arabs exploit oil, the industry was just not interested. Just after Mr Carter's inauguration we asked a dozen electronics firms what difference the new administration would make. The typical response was, "Should it make any difference?"

Growth by getting smaller

The secret of electronics' success is cost reduction. Other companies' finance directors may justifiably ask nasty questions about investing in a new process that cuts costs 20%; they are frequently silenced in electronics, where the cost saving is often 90%. Furthermore, lower prices are nearly always rewarded by an even bigger increase in sales.

It began with the computer industry. When computers were first invented, one major industrial company forecast the total world market would be only 20 computers, and therefore was not worth bothering about.

Computing costs fell about 20% a year, and the market grew. The cost of ICs falls even faster. One firm makes 10 times as many logic circuits as in 1970, with the same labour force. And ICs have grown from being clever but rather expensive circuits looking for customers to becoming what is today called a computer-on-a-chip, a tiny pea-sized knot of circuits that combines memory, processing capability, and software programmes, all on one chip.

The manufacturing of these chips is

concentrated about 30 miles south of San Francisco, around Santa Clara, in what is colloquially called Silicon Valley, after the raw material of the industry. ICs were invented in 1958, the inventor of the key patent being Mr Robert Noyce, who was then with Fairchild, but who moved down the road to found Intel.

The first commercial ICs were launched in 1961, but they were more expensive than ordinary transistors. Acceptance was slow. They could not do all the tasks performed by conventional circuits. The answer, the industry's classic ploy ever since, was to lower the price by standardising on a few circuits that fitted the technology. This has worked so well that cost per circuit has decreased several thousandfold, while complexity has doubled every year. No other industry is within a mile of such productivity gains.

ICs are very reliable—they employ no moving parts—and the smaller they get the more reliable they become (though one firm did issue a pocket calculator that always got some of its sums wrong). But cost matters more than performance. If the price is low enough, it does not matter that the chip does not exactly match the customer's needs: he can afford to use extra chips, or chips that are redundant a lot of the time. This priority for price is very hard for a high-technology firm to achieve: the pressure from scientists is always in favour of the cleverer product. But, in electronics, clever means cheap.

A few years ago, the industry got stuck in a rut again. Complexity of chips was growing fast, but the range of functions they could perform was limited. The answer was to build a standard chip with stored programmes in memory, so that the customer could have a choice of uses. Put the chip in one gear, and it would be a pocket calculator; put it in another, and it would play video ping pong. So was born the microprocessor, and, now, the complete computer-on-a-chip (in practice, most complete micro computers are built on a board the size of this newspaper).

Mr Fred Bucy, president of Texas Instruments, likes to say of cost reduction:

> We must not aim at the moon. We must get there.

In most industries, such talk would sound pie-in-the-sky, but the IC industry is far from reaching the ultimate limitations on its technology, which are things like the speed of light and the difficulty of determining the precise position of an individual electron. If Mr Bucy did not get to the moon, he would be out of business. The industry's target is 1m circuits on a chip by the first quarter of 1979, and the great

Look, intelligent salami

thing is that, in principle, it costs not much more whether you have 1,000 circuits on a chip, 10,000 or a million.

The key to achieving this complexity is manufacturing technology. Research done by equipment suppliers is especially important in determining an industry's productivity. The IC industry has developed its own manufacturing technology. But it is a moot point whether the most dramatic breakthrough will in future come from Silicon Valley, or from what used to be its largest customer, the computer industry. IBM has an idea for a machine that could match the complete world output of chips.

The world of the electron

Chip manufacture is done in speckless conditions, mostly by women. The initial stage is to melt silicon and extract a tiny seed crystal, which is drawn out to make something about the same diameter and shape as a stick of salami. The salami is then sliced into wafers, and on to each wafer about 400 chips are printed, like photographs, using miniature glass masks that have been reduced from large-scale drawings of the chip's intended pattern. The pattern is etched, and impurities added; then more layers are put on by further processes. A device called a laser zapper is used to make corrections on the mask itself, but with a complex chip you may still only get 40 usable chips out of the

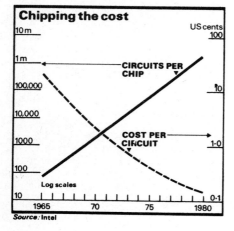

Chipping the cost

Source: Intel

Why chips switch

Very broadly, they work like this. Silicon has the same structure as diamond: each of its atoms has four electrons. Electrons bind the silicon atoms together, thus:

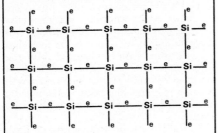

Now, if you replace a silicon atom with an atom of phosphorus, which has five electrons, you have an extra electron, free to wander round, and set up a flow of current. Phosphorus is called an n-type impurity, the letter n standing for negative charge.

Next insert an atom of boron into the silicon. Boron has only three electrons, so this time there is an electron missing. An electron that binds two of the silicon atoms can jump over and fill the gap. Boron's absence of an electron gives it positive charge, so the boron impurity is called p-type.

On the surface of a chip, the impurities can be layered: p-type on top of n-type, and n-type on top of p-type. The chart below shows part of one circuit out of several thousand on one kind of chip. Different electrical currents are applied to the different layers. The difference between the currents enables the circuit to be used to process computer information.

Surface of chip

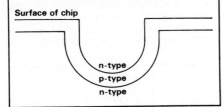

400 on the wafer.

Many of the design aims conflict with each other. If you want the chip to work fast, as computer manufacturers do, you need to make it smaller, so that the electrons have less far to travel; but then the power density goes up, and the chip overheats. Honeywell is overcoming this partly by micropackaging up to 100 chips on a substrate, the chips being joined by a plastic film. The density of a chip is not much greater, but the chips are closer together. The aim is to get synchronicity of signals in different parts of the system. But, with conventional air cooling you get a disaster if the fan stops, so Honeywell is also using liquid cooling of chips. Another development is a matrix shifter that can shift a stream of incoming data in any direction.

For the denser integration of chips now being talked of, involving a further 100-fold decrease in feature size, electron beam lithography is the coming technology. This is needed to make devices smaller than the wavelength of light: the wavelength of the electron being much smaller than that of light.

Another tool for making chips is the ion implanter, a miniature version of the particle accelerators used at places like CERN. This is a fast method of firing impurities on to the silicon. Magnets bend the microscopic impurities in the right direction. One implanter in use now can, in half an hour, process 50 wafers, each with between 150 and 1,000 chips. This step in making chips used to take many hours. One prediction is that the semiconductor may become, in a sense, the first machine that can replicate itself.

Whereas technology usually lags far behind basic science, electronics is helping to push forward the barriers of basic knowledge. To work at tiny dimensions that make hair-splitting look like chopping logs, IBM had to go into the business of inventing new microscopes. The industry is one of the few that thinks basic science too serious to be left to the universities.

One fruit of this is a chip called a charge coupled device (CCD for short). On these chips you set up wells in the silicon, in which a charge is stored, and can be moved from one well to another. This is equivalent to moving information through the silicon. One application of this is to take photographs in the dark: the camera senses electrons, instead of photons. Fairchild sells such a camera for use in missiles, which, before exploding, transmit a film of the battle-field back to the missile launcher. In computer memories, CCD will replace discs for some functions, because of its fast access time.

CCDs will also be used in a new technology called surface acoustic waves, in which elastic waves are converted to electric energy and back again. This was used on the Jupiter-Saturn space flight to reject signals from neighbouring radio channels: interference can be reduced by five orders of magnitude. In the future, surface acoustic waves will be used in telecommunications to get more channels on a given range of frequencies.

Another fruit of basic research is something called bubble memory. This is a thin film of magnetic material, in which the north and south poles are reversed relative to the surrounding material. IBM has worked at a density of 40m bubbles to the square inch. There are no moving parts to wear out, and you do not lose the memory when

Little grey cells

the power is turned off (rather important in, for instance, motor cars). Bubbles are the first type of computer memory with the capacity for not just storing data but also rearranging it.

Another new breed of chips, but with application limited to enormous computers, like those used in weather forecasts, is something called a Josephson junction. Two films of superconducting metal are separated by a layer of very thin insulating oxide that electrons can tunnel across. The switching speed is 10 trillionths of a second. This is another IBM development. Watch out, Silicon Valley.

David v Goliath

A tense battle is beginning between the Davids of the IC industry and the Goliaths of ordinary computing. On David's side, let us take two examples that demonstrate the enormous capacity, at low cost, of the micro computer:
● Television games. The market for these in 1977 is forecast at 7m games, over a third of them being programmable sets (ie, computers). Fairchild sells a basic unit, costing $170, that can be plugged into an ordinary television set. This has the raw computing power of an IBM 701, which sold for $1m in 1954. For $20 a time, you can buy extra cartridges, each with up to four games, including ping pong, football, shooting

gallery, blackjack, baccarat, random maths puzzles, the equivalent of Master Mind, and the facility to draw colour pictures on your television screen. By 1980 the video games market may consume more bits of memory than the whole computer market.

● Process control. For under $300 you can buy a micro that will run almost any machine tool. Today, almost every process has enormous safety margins, using excess materials, time and energy. Sensors run by micros can do anything from blood analysis to marijuana sniffing. They will make the process control of 1977 look like blacksmithing. An entire new industry is going to be based on the use of ceramics as a structural material, and this could be the first industry whose creation is dependent on micros to do process control.

The obvious question is, why not string a lot of cheap micros together, and save yourself the trouble of getting a $1m IBM machine? At present, however, micros have drawbacks.

A major use of computers is to do sums in minutes or hours that would once have taken teams of mathematicians days or years. Most of the IC industry's present products are too slow for such jobs. Consequently, computer manufacturers are designing their own circuits, and the big research budgets they can afford mean they will compete with Silicon Valley in the invention of new technology. Indeed, IBM is possibly the largest chip maker in the world, though it does not sell any chips outside IBM.

Another drawback of micros is that nearly all of them can currently only add and subtract, not multiply and divide. Also, they are unattractive for handling large data bases. And you can at present write only short programmes into them.

The Goliaths' real confidence is based on distributed processing, in which vast data networks will be linked by telephone. Big computers at present have indigestion. Because 90% of the transactions involve only 10% of the data, it makes sense to get most of the data out into the terminals, often into micros. Yes, concedes Goliath, micros will be littered all over the place (often made by Goliath), but they will be linked to central computers, in a system designed by Goliath.

Micros will therefore expand maxi sales. Put micros in cars, and they will generate data on the cars' performance that will be fed to the garage's mini, which will in turn generate data to the big computer that keeps track of what is happening to all cars.

Furthermore, Goliath's customers are very loyal, partly because they are stuck into Goliath's programmes, and partly because Goliath maintains a worldwide sales and service force to keep them happy, with vast software libraries, and field engineers to keep the system running 24 hours a day. When some stupid computer manager gets into trouble, he can always blame it on Goliath. For all these reasons, Goliath says he feels secure.

Infant prodigies

But this may be a false security. Goliath's scenario describes the contest in about round-two of a 15-round fight. The micro is currently 10 years behind the computer, but is moving twice as fast. It is in its infancy, and to judge it by what it can do now is like judging the computer by what it could do in 1950. For example, there is no logical reason why the micro should not be taught to divide and multiply.

Most of the problems computers handle can be broken into sub-tasks that micros can handle, and, because of the micro's low cost, you can afford to be prodigal in its use. As some computer people admit, in five years' time the micro will probably do all the things the maxi can do.

Furthermore, the ability of Goliath to sell a complete system is being undermined. For one thing, users are getting more sophisticated, more willing to take responsibility for choosing a mix of suppliers. For another, field engineers will become less important: hardware will become so cheap it will pay to throw a faulty part away and plug in a new one (a micro computer will tell you which part to replace).

The speed with which computer firms can respond by launching better products is severely limited by the danger of eroding their existing rental base, which is one reason why they are moving so tentatively into minis. Because minis and micros are all sold outright, model changes are four times as fast. And another reason why Goliath cannot make his small systems as attractive as he might is the fear that the customer won't bother to buy the larger machine. Another handicap of the giants is that the financial strength of some of them has been weakened by their failure to make consistently good profits.

A vital issue is how successful Goliath can be at making his maxi incompatible with David's micro, so that the user is forced to buy only from Goliath. Yet Texas Instruments itself uses an IBM central computer, with its own micros attached. That makes it much easier to sell to IBM customers products that can be plugged into IBM systems (using IBM software, of course). Intel offers a memory that competes with an IBM 370/125. According to Intel, IBM does not provide enough memory, so Intel offers twice the 125's memory, saving the customer from having to upgrade to a larger IBM computer.

A significant decision was taken recently by the computer committee of the American National Standards Institute. The committee voted—by 33 to 8—in favour of accepting an IBM system as a standard interface for the the industry. This will make it much easier for users to shop around for any mix of suppliers they want.

An important point is that Silicon Valley got into computer manufacture

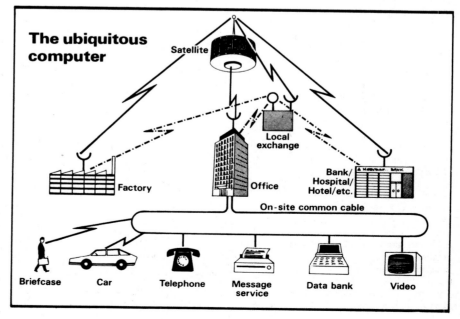

The ubiquitous computer

Satellite

Local exchange

Factory

Office

Bank/ Hospital/ Hotel/etc.

On-site common cable

Briefcase   Car   Telephone   Message service   Data bank   Video

almost by chance, as a spin-off from its main business. If it lost the entire microprocessor business, that would have little effect on its turnover. But the micro represents a big threat to the revenue of the old computer manufacturers.

Nevertheless, Silicon Valley does face a problem. Its firms are traditionally component suppliers, selling cheap hardware by reducing frilly overheads. Computer manufacturers have defined problems and designed solutions; the IC industry is about hardware looking for problems to solve. The big test will be software. This is the strategic bridge that must be held by whoever wins the computer battle.

Software's the hard sell

Software has not yet enjoyed a revolution in productivity like that in hardware. Whereas hardware design is 100% scientific, software is still 50% artistic. The result is that half the cost of running a computer is software, and often 90% for a micro.

Yet a computer is pretty dumb. It has a memory with numbers stored on it, and it pulls these down on to registers to do simple arithmetic, very fast. The clever things done with computers are the result of ingenious software, developed by the human brain.

Till the late 1950s, the computer's instructions were laborious. If you wanted to add 10 numbers, you went through many dozen steps. Then came so-called "high-level languages" that enabled you to write a brief formula that would then create all the other instructions inside the machine. But there has been little progress since.

Such progress as there is probably came more from Burroughs than any other single company. Evidence confirms that Burroughs' customers are loyal, which tells its own software story.

Burroughs has largely designed the hardware to fit the software. And this is what Silicon Valley is doing by writing the software options into the intricate wiring of the chip. Indeed, the Valley sometimes takes the computer industry's investment in software and adapts it to micros. It does not even have to steal directly from Goliath, because you can buy software from consultants. Thus, Fairchild has developed a chip that can use software designed for Data General's minis, and Texas Instruments arranges software exchange between its customers. As such practices are still in a minority, a British software house, CAP Microsoft, has been developing ways to

make it easier to write programmes for a micro than a maxi: for example, a programme written for one micro is instantly portable to any other model.

The development of micro software is likely to be similar to that of minis in the 1960s. Digital Equipment Corporation, the largest mini firm, also began as just a hardware supplier, but now half its research staff are doing software.

Another trend that will benefit micros is that computer customers are increasingly having to settle for standard programmes, instead of custom-tailored ones, because of the high cost of software. One user reckoned a tailor-made solution would cost $200,000. Then it found a standard programme that could be adapted for $25,000. By 1984, hardware and software combined may cost $25,000. Standard programmes are what micros are best suited for.

But there is one drawback of micros that some people think is here to stay. That is that their small size limits the length of the instructions they can be given. But, once again, software houses are looking for cheap solutions.

The computer industry is at last beginning to show more results from software research. One now realistic aim is for everyone, even the housewife or schoolboy, to be able to talk to the computer, in human language. The natural language shows up on a video screen, and the user is given a list of things the computer can do. He can tap the option he wants with a special electronic pen, and, hey presto, the computer translates the English (or Japanese) instruction into its own hieroglyphics. One company has cut the time taken to train soldiers to use a computer from six months to two days.

The day seems to be coming when women will carry computers in their handbags, men on their wrists, and businessmen will use computers as freely as telephones.

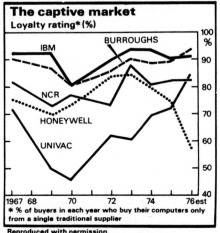

The captive market
Loyalty rating* (%)

BURROUGHS
IBM
NCR
HONEYWELL
UNIVAC

1967 68   70   72   74   76est
* % of buyers in each year who buy their computers only from a single traditional supplier

Reproduced with permission.
Copyright, 1977, by International Data Corporation

As common as paperclips

Paperclips? That may sound fanciful but it is going to be so, because computing power is becoming cheap and portable. Take a typical office. Some 40m west Europeans are office workers. But the average spent on office equipment is $100 per head.

IBM aims to make the telephone a much more efficient tool, using ICs, of course. It has designed a telephone that takes messages, sends memoranda to people, files documents, automatically tries numbers again if they are busy, and generally acts as a secretary.

Telecommunications and computing are coalescing. A word processor is a typewriter attached to a computer, and is supposed to save enormously on typing costs. If word processors become common, the next thing is to connect them together, so the mail can be sent electronically.

A third stage is dawning in which the computer can be taught to recognise speech. The basic nature of speech is now understood quite well by computer scientists, and it turns out there are relatively few features of speech that it is vital for the computer to recognise.

Once an executive has a cheap computer terminal on his desk, there is no end of things he can do with it. He can start his own electronic filing system, and access that of other executives. He can ring up data libraries for information his own company does not file. Once the data is easily accessible, he can pull averages and comparisons out of it. Computer terminals are going to become as common in offices as pocket calculators.

Similarly, the computer is entering the home. Over 50,000 American homes already have them, and there are over 300 shops for computer hobbyists.

What on earth will you use them for? For tax returns and household budgeting. For remote control of domestic appliances. For keeping central heating bills down. For access to data banks. Or for just fun.

Every technology brings drawbacks as well as benefits. Some proposed applications of computing are merely frivolous; some will raise the ogre of infringement of privacy; some will prove less economic than their promoters claimed (among other ways by provoking working men to resist them through strikes or overmanning); and others will be rightly accused of making life more impersonal but will be adopted all the same, because of economic pressures. Many others will, like paperclips, carve out a lasting use.

Microprocessors — A Primer

Theodore J. Cohen, PhD

A sophisticated electronic device known as the microprocessor will shortly have a profound impact on our way of life. Within a year or so, this device, about half the size of a matchbook, will be incorporated in a variety of consumer products ranging from automobiles to digital watches.

What are microprocessors? Why are they important? How do they function? And how will they be used in consumer products? These are the questions answered here.

The Heart of a Computer System

All computers consist of five basic sybsystems:
- An input device through which instructions and data are entered into the computer;
- A central processing unit (CPU) which controls the computer's operation;
- An arithmetic logic unit (ALU) which performs mathematical operations;
- A memory, in which instructions and information are stored;
- An output device, through which processed data leave the computer.

The heart of this basic computer system, which consists of the central processing unit (CPU) and the arithmetic logic unit (ALU), can be incorporated on a single integrated circuit (IC) chip, and this chip is known as a microprocessor.

While early microprocessor-based computers required a considerable number of IC's (30 or more) to recover data from memory, second-generation microprocessors permit the construction of computers having as few as two chips. Thus, it is not unusual to find that the microprocessor is often referred to as a "computer on a chip."

A New Electronics Era

Despite the rapid advances which have been made in electronics since the introduction of the transistor some 30 years ago, many consider the development of the microprocessor as heralding the beginning of a new electronic era. The reasons for this are many. For example, some arithmetic and computational capabilities available in today's microprocessor-based systems would be impractical to duplicate using more conventional circuitry. Then, too, the use of microprocessors results in drastically-reduced product design time, reduced product complexity, and hence, lower product cost. Finally, microprocessor-based products can be programmed to execute a sequence of instructions, and thus can control, or interact with, a variety of instruments, machines, and systems.

In short, the capabilities inherent in microprocessor-based products represent a significant advance in computational and control circuit design.

The Microprocessor as a Circuit Element

As already seen, a microprocessor can form the heart of a computing system . . . the heart of a microcomputer, if you will. Here, the microprocessor, together with such additional components as read-only memories (or ROM's, which are used to store the microcomputer program), random-access memories (or RAM's which are used to store data) and interfaces for peripheral devices, is so connected as to perform computations and to make decisions. The microprocessor determines what external devices should provide or have access to data, performs calculations using the data provided, and makes decisions based on these calculations and upon timing constraints which may be imposed by the user. Looked at another way, the microprocessor, which is only one component of a microcomputer, coordinates the activities of the memories and the input-output devices, and

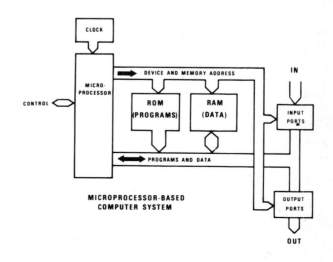

MICROPROCESSOR-BASED
COMPUTER SYSTEM

Intel's 8080 microprocessor, a popular second-generation device, contains the equivalent of 5000 transistors as well as most of the basic operational features found in present-day minicomputers. The chip itself is about 1 cm² and 0.1 mm thick. It is mounted on a plastic package called a DIP (Dual In-Line Package) about 5 x 1-1/2 cm. The MPU is dwarfed by the other discrete components (resistors and capacitors) on the PC board.

performs logical or arithmetic operations on the data stored in RAM. Used in this manner, the microprocessor makes it possible to incorporate decision-making and data-processing capabilities in a variety of products ranging from automobiles to watches, and from calculators to television receivers.

There's a Microprocessor in Your Future

If you drive an automobile — and most of us do — there's a microprocessor in your future. The need for more dependable, fuel-efficient vehicles makes the automobile a prime candidate for early applications of microprocessor technology. Through the use of an on-board microcomputer, it will soon be possible to monitor such diverse parameters as engine speed, ignition timing, engine temperature, compression, and emission, and to determine automatically that point where fuel economy and emission control are optimized. It will also be possible to determine more accurately when shifting should occur, thereby minimizing transmission damage. Even diagnostic analyses of critical engine functions will give the driver advance warning of impending breakdowns.

While the on-board microcomputer is monitoring your vehicle's performance, it will also be watching out for you, making your ride smoother and safer. Don't worry

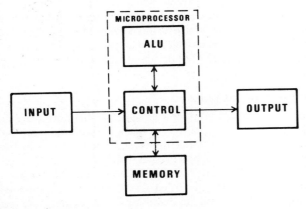

A BASIC COMPUTER SYSTEM

about your doorlocks; the computer will lock the doors for you once your car's speed exceeds 5 m.p.h. The microprocessor-based computer will also monitor your braking system (to prevent lock-up), and your speed (to warn of excesses). The onboard computer will even be able to provide anti-theft security by disabling the ignition control system when your car is entered without a key having been used.

Now that your appetite is whetted, consider how microprocessors will be used to improve the performance and capabilities of the following products:

Digital Watches

Engineers are already working on microprocessor-based watches that will include a calculator, an alarm, and an interval timer. It may even be possible, someday, to own a watch which provides personal physiological monitoring.

Hand-Held Calculators

While mature, the calculator market is certainly not saturated. Newer more complex units will soon be available, and some may even be able to monitor such body functions as blood pressure or pulse count.

Television Receivers

Microprocessors will permit the expansion of today's television receiver into a comprehensive recreational and entertainment center. Through advanced technology, it will be possible to play a wide variety of games, either against an opponent or against the microcomputer itself. Liberal use of color will make video games more exciting as will the generation of more realistic game sounds. It will even be possible to play games which provide a challenge to players having a wide range of skills; in this way, users will not lose interest as their skills improve.

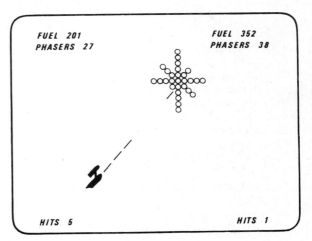

An Electronic Revolution

A revolution is upon us! Developments in microprocessors are changing the electronics industry at an unprecedented rate. As a result of the changes, a new generation of "smart" consumer products will soon be available . . . products which are not only more capable, but which are also designed to analyze data and to make decisions which permit a variety of tasks to be performed in a highly efficient and dependable manner.

Portions of this article appeared in "Microprocessor Technology — An Electronic Revolution," T. J. Cohen, *Sea Technology*, March 1976.

Microcomputers in One Easy Lesson

PHILIP G. DORCAS

A microcomputer (as small computers are sometimes called) is based on a microprocessor. This Central Processing Unit (CPU) gives a computer its incredible logic capability. A microprocessor operates according to instructions contained in a program and with data contained in the computer's memory.

The word size (or data width) is the number of bits of information the computer processes with each instruction. There are many types of processors with data widths of 1, 4, 8, 12, 16 and 32 bits. Most small computers use 8 bits. Some more expensive computers use 16 bits. They are perhaps a little faster, but not enough to make a difference in most applications. Generally, an 8-bit processor can do what a 16-bit can, but the program will probably require more instructions.

Most popular processors are 8-bit types — the 8080, 6800, Z-80, and the 6502. The 8080 is by far the most popular and has become standard in many cases. The Z-80 is like an 8080 with added instructions. It also operates faster than the 8080.

Memory

Memory can be of several types. There is RAM (Random Access Memory), ROM (Read Only Memory), PROM (Programmable Read Only Memory) and a few others. Data is written into and read out of memory by addressing specific memory locations. The amount of memory a computer can work with is determined by the number of address lines controlled by the processor. Most processors have 16 address lines which can address 2^{16} or 65,536 words of memory. In some cases the amount of memory is limited by hardware or the power supply.

Input/Output devices

A computer is not worth anything unless you can talk to it. Getting information into and out of a computer is called I/O (input/output) and is usually done with a keyboard and either a TV monitor or a printer. CRT terminals are perhaps the handiest as they have both a keyboard and a TV monitor as well as the necessary electronics to interface to a serial port. Sometimes the I/O device is built into the same cabinet as the computer.

Input/Output ports

Interface circuits — either a serial or parallel port — are required for communication between the processor and the outside world. In a parallel port, the data moves along parallel lines so that all 8 bits in each word are sent at the same time. In a serial port, the bits of data all move down the same line, one after the other. Parallel ports are normally used for printers and keyboard inputs. Serial ports are normally used for CRT terminals. Two common electrical standards for serial ports are the RS-232 (voltage level) standard and the 20 ma current loop.

Glossary

ASCII — American Standard Code for Information Interchange. The ASCII code is the standard binary representation for numbers, letters and control characters.

Assembler — A program that translates assembly language programs, written by humans, into machine codes which the computer understands.

BASIC — Beginners All-purpose Symbolic Instruction Code. BASIC is one of the easiest-to-learn computer languages. It is used in most small computers. BASIC runs efficiently in most computers and requires less memory than many other languages.

Binary — Number system based on 2. All binary numbers consists of only 1s and 0s.

Bit — One binary digit. The smallest unit of information. A 1 or 0.

Byte — 8 bits. Most small computers process information 1 byte at a time.

Bus — A communication line used by many parts of the computer. S-100 and SS-50 are two common standards for computer bus structures.

Clock — The computer's timing circuit or "heartbeat"

Compiler — Translates a high level language such as BASIC (written by humans) into machine code which the computer can understand.

CPU — Central Processing Unit. The "brains" of the computer. Also called MPU (Micro Processing Unit).

CRT — Cathode Ray Tube. A video display tube like a TV screen.

Debug — To remove errors from a computer or its programs.

DMA — Direct Memory Access. Transfer of data between memory and peripherals without using the CPU.

Firmware — Software programs that are built into the computer and contained in ROM or PROM.

Floppy Disk — A flexible magnetic diskette used to store large files of information, approximately 70K or 250K depending on which of the two sizes you get. Information can be transferred at a very fast rate.

A Look at a Typical System

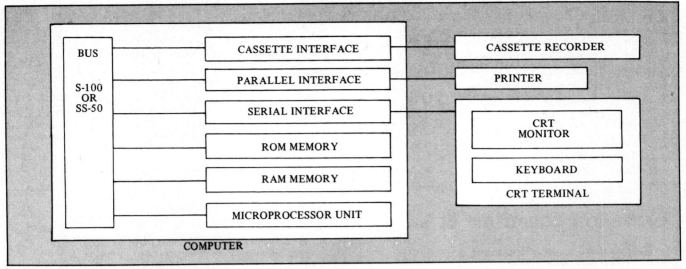

A typical system (with SS-50 or S-100 bus) is shown here in block diagram form. This flexible, expandable system can be upgraded. It will accept more memory, more peripherals, or whatever the application might demand.

Bus structures

Most small computers (the ones that are expandable and flexible) have a bus structure to carry the data, address, control and I/O information to the various parts of the computer.

The most popular bus configuration is called the S-100 bus. Most 8080 and Z-80 computers use this bus. S-100 bus computers (Processor Technology, Cromemco, Altair, IMSAI and so on) allow you to add memory, interface ports, battery back-up boards, music system boards and so forth simply by plugging in the circuit boards. Many manufacturers support the S-100 bus.

The second most popular bus is the SS-50 bus used by 6800 processors. It has 50 pins rather than 100 because of the way data and I/O are handled.

Storage methods

Programs and data can be saved for future use by several methods. The most popular method is using regular audio cassette tapes, which require a cassette interface to convert digital data to audio tones and vice versa. This low-cost technique is popular with home computers. The most popular standard for storing information on tape is called the Kansas City Standard.

Paper tape is another way to store data, but not quite as convenient or popular as cassettes. Data is stored on the paper tape via punched holes.

The fastest but most expensive means of data storage is the flexible magnetic diskette or "floppy disk". These disks come in two sizes, 5-¼-inch or 8-inch diameter, and look like 45 RPM records. The surface is a magnetic substance similar to that found on magnetic recording tape. Special disk drives and interfaces are required to operate a disk system.

Floppy disks are used primarily in businesses where the extra speed is worth the extra cost. A program requiring over 10 minutes to load from cassette tape can be loaded in a fraction of a second with a disk system.

System monitor

Many computers have a system monitor in ROM which contains the program necessary to operate the system. This allows you to examine the data in memory, enter data, run programs and save or load data from tape.

Software

A computer is useless without programs to make it run. Software comes in a variety of forms. It can be a machine language program that runs in the computer "as is", or it can be in a high level language program that must be compiled or interpreted to machine language that the computer can understand.

Most small computers have a BASIC interpreter. BASIC is a very simple, easy-to-learn language that lends itself to many applications. It can be used for personal computing, business, industry, education and science.

Other high level languages are also available. Some hobbyists enjoy programming in assembly language, then using an assembler program to get the machine code.

You can buy software on cassette, disk or paper tape. You can get program listings from books or magazines, enter them into the computer via the keyboard, then save the programs on cassette tape. You can also write your own programs and save them for future use.

Home Systems

The computer in the home can be useful as well as entertaining. It can be more enjoyable than watching TV because it is an interactive process which is also educational. Useful functions for the home computer include checkbook maintenance, household budget, recipe file, diet and menu planning, shopping lists, record keeping and education for all members of the family. Many experts predict that home computers will become popular at an increasing rate until they are commonplace by 1985.

Here are two typical home systems:

Typical Home System 1	kit	assembled
Sol-20/16 (16K RAM, BASIC-5)	$1850.00	$2095.00
9" monitor	175.00	175.00
Total System Price (less recorder)	$2025.00	$2260.00

Typical Home System 2	kit	assembled
SWTP MP-68 computer (w/4K)	$ 395.00	$ 495.00
4K RAM additional	100.00	150.00
CT-64 w/CT-VM monitor	500.00	700.00
AC-30 cassette interface	79.95	120.00
4K BASIC	4.95	4.95
Total System Price (less recorder)	$1079.90	$1469.95

Hobby Systems

The computer hobbyist is often interested in using the computer with another hobby, such as ham radio, model railroading, chess, music, computer art, astronomy, robotics, or speech recognition and synthesis. Many hobbyists have some electronics experience and are willing to build their own computer from kit form. This typical system uses a TV set for the video display and a cassette recorder for program storage:

Typical Hobby System

SWTP MP-68 computer kit (with 4K RAM)	$395.00
Percom CIS-30+ cassette interface kit	79.95
CT-64 Terminal kit (less monitor)	325.00
Pixieverter kit (for TV set)	9.25
Total Price (less TV and recorder)	$809.20

Education, Science and Industry Systems

Small computers have made a tremendous impact on education, both at home and in the school. The computer can be used to help students in almost any subject. Computer Aided Instruction (CAI) can teach a student on a one-on-one basis according to a programmed lesson, enabling the student to progress at his best rate.

Computer science departments are becoming decentralized by the small computer, adding efficiency and reliability to department operations. In the past, when the big central computer went "down", the entire computer department was "down". With several independent small computers, malfunctions are less common. When they do occur, only the system at fault is down. The other students can still do their work. The convenience of interacting with a small computer means time saved.

The small computer provides ready computing power in the lab. The scientist or engineer can use the mathematical and analytical capabilities of computers to aid in research and design. Having a computer handy saves time. Without one, the scientist usually has to perform calculations with a pocket calculator or get involved with interdepartmental procedures to use the big computer.

Small dedicated computers in industry provide fast and accurate control of production line operations. Gauges, heat sensors, motors, relays and heaters can be read or controlled by computer to increase efficiency and reduce waste. The small computer can also be used for fire and smoke detection, perimeter systems control, maintenance control and alert, and environmental/energy control.

Business Systems

Business is perhaps the most obvious application for small computers. Many businesses can now afford computers. Only a few years ago a business computer cost $100,000 or more. Now, the system hardware usually costs less than $10,000.

A home computer by itself is normally not suitable for business use. A business system needs to be very reliable. It needs to have a floppy disk memory system and usually a printer. Floppy disk systems usually come with two drives, allowing more storage capacity and the ability to copy from one disk onto another disk.

Small businesses with limited uses for the computer can often meet their needs with the small disk or "microfloppy". These disks are 5¼ inches in diameter and can store 80K or more per disk. For full business functions, you need a full size floppy disk system. These disks are 8 inches in diameter and can store 250K or more per disk.

Printers come in a variety of sizes and speeds. For light use such as occasional printing of reports, the Centronics Micro-1 ($595) is a good buy. For medium use, such as printing mailing labels, payroll checks, and weekly or daily reports, the Centronics 700 is good. Heavier use, which demands constant use of the printer, means speed is the most important factor to consider.

Business applications include payroll, cost accounting, inventory control, accounts receivable and payable, general ledger, word processing, sales analysis, mailing list maintenance and market survey tabulation. If that's not enough work to justify using a computer, you can also program it to do work scheduling, bid estimates, financial planning and analysis, real estate and loan evaluation, tax calculation, appointment calendars, stock market analysis, personnel records and trend analysis.

Software is the key to a successful business system. Most businesses underestimate the role that software plays. There are several ways to get software for a business. You can get an independent systems analyst to look at your needs and produce the software. You can sometimes get ready-made programs to do what you want. However, most businesses require their own unique software because they want their own kind of reports. It is usually better to get the computer hardware and software to fit the business rather than try to change the business to fit the computer.

Service is an important factor in considering a business system. The system must be easily maintainable and have factory authorized service available.

The following systems are typical business systems with varying capabilities. Other systems are also available. These systems are all assembled and tested. They all include dual drive floppy disks with power supply, cabinet, floppy disk operating system (FDOS), disk BASIC, system controller, and interface.

Mini Business System

Computer, Southwest Tech 6800 (MP-68)	$ 495.00
Memory, 32K (M-16-A)	758.00
System ROM, SWTBUG	19.95
Terminal, CT-64, CT-VM	700.00
Floppy Disk System, MF-68	1200.00
Printer, Centronics Micro-1	595.00
Parallel interface, MP-L	65.00
Printer cable and connectors	35.00
	$3867.95

Good Business System

Computer, Sol-20/32 (with 32K RAM)	$2395.00
CRT monitor, 9″	175.00
Floppy disk, iCOM FD2411-46 (5¼-in drive) with FDOS and Disk Extended BASIC	1505.00
Printer, Centronics 700 (60 cps)	1520.00
Printer option, 2 channel vertical format unit	125.00
Printer option, rear tractor paper feed.	100.00
All required cables and connectors	45.00
	$5865.00

Better Business System

Computer, Sol-20/32 (with 32K RAM)	$2395.00
CRT monitor, 9″	175.00
Floppy disk, iCOM FD3712-60 (8 inch) with FDOS and Disk Extended BASIC	2650.00
Printer, Centronics 700 (60 cps)	1520.00
Printer option, 2 channel, vertical format unit	125.00
Printer option, rear tractor paper feed	100.00
All required cables and connectors	45.00
	$7010.00

Becoming acquainted with the many aspects of a micro before you buy will help you avoid costly mistakes in selecting a computer to suit your needs.

Common questions & answers

Q. How much memory do I need?

A. To run programs in machine language, you might get by with 4K or 8K of RAM. For BASIC you need memory for the BASIC interpreter, then more memory for the program. To run small programs with the Southwest Tech 4K BASIC, for example, you need 4K of RAM for the BASIC and perhaps 4K more for programs. That's 8K total. Using the Southwest Tech complete 8K BASIC with longer programs, at least 16K would be required. For home and hobby use, most people start with about 8K of RAM. For other applications such as business, 32K will support most needs. Keep in mind that you need the capability to add more memory with S-100 or SS-50 memory circuit boards. These circuit boards are available from many different manufacturers.

Q. What do I need to know about computer bus structure?

A. The S-100 bus is the standard bus configuration for 8080 and Z-80 computers. Computers with the 6800 microprocessor normally use the SS-50 bus structure. If you buy a computer that uses one of these standards, you can be assured of having a system that is flexible, expandable, easily serviced and compatible with most other small computers on the market.

Q. What are the main differences between different brands of terminals?

A. The main differences are quality of display, number of characters presented on the screen, number and type of keys on the keyboard, quality of the keyboard, and the speed of data transfer with the display. Don't buy a unit with a keyboard before you try out the keyboard. It should feel comfortable and should operate smoothly. The speed of data transfer is called the baud rate. The terminal should have adjustable baud rates up to at least 1200 baud. Some keyboards have a numeric keypad at the side which is handy for business use.

Q. Don't some computers have BASIC in ROM?

A. Yes. If BASIC is in ROM memory, you don't need to load BASIC every time you turn on the computer. But keep in mind that you lose lots of flexibility, because you cannot change the program in ROM. If you have RAM memory, you have the choice of running BASIC, machine language, music systems, chess programs and possibly other high level languages (FORTRAN, APL, COBOL, etc.).

Q. How can I add things like printers, other terminals, etc.?

A. It is not difficult to add printers or other peripherals if you have the proper serial or parallel interface on your computer. For example, if you want to add a printer, you need a parallel port. If you don't have a parallel port handy, you can get one that plugs into the S-100 or SS-50 bus.

Q. How do I store programs and data for future use?

A. You can use cassette tapes, paper tape or "floppy disks". If your system has a cassette interface, find out what kind it is. The Kansas City Standard type (one of the most popular) is quite reliable. Some computers use two types of interfaces, the Kansas City Standard and their own (which is usually faster). If you're thinking about getting a disk system, be sure the price includes the disk drives, cabinet, power supply, floppy disk operating system (FDOS), disk extended BASIC, interface circuitry and the disk controller — all needed for a disk system to operate.

Q. Are all BASICs the same?

A. Not exactly. There are some slight differences between the BASIC languages offered by the different manufacturers, but these are usually very small differences. Some computers offer a full BASIC and a smaller BASIC to save on memory. For example, Southwest Tech has both 8K and 4K BASIC. The 4K version does not have string variables or trig functions. They also have a disk BASIC, which is the 8K BASIC plus disk commands. Processor Technology has disk BASIC, 8K BASIC and BASIC-5. Some manufacturers claim to have BASIC, often in less than 4K, which is really a micro-BASIC. These "tiny" BASICs are better than trying to program in machine language, but they fall short of the tremendous capabilities of a full 8K BASIC.

Q. Why do some brands of computers have lots of switches and blinking lights on the front panel?

A. These lights certainly add to the cost of a computer, but the final effect is that the unit simply looks more like what a computer "ought" to look like. I give up, why do they?

Best Business System

Computer System: Processor Technology Sol System III, with Sol-20 computer, 50,176 bytes of memory, BOOTLOAD personality module, Helios II Model 2 disk system (769,000 bytes), Extended Disk BASIC, PT-872 video monitor, PTDOS, and documentation $5995.00

Printer, Centronics 703 (180 cps) with rear tractor paper feed	2805.00
Printer option, 2 channel vertical format unit	125.00
All required cables and connectors	45.00
	$8970.00

This article appeared in *Personal Computing*.

INSIDE A MICROCOMPUTER

About programming languages

There are so-called "higher level" languages, such as BASIC, FORTRAN and COBOL. There are also "fundamental" programming languages referred to as "assembly language".

Regarding any programming language, the most important point to understand is that a programming language is a programmer's convenience. A programming language is an artificial creation, designed to make your life as a programmer easier. Whatever language you decide is best for you, the computer still demands that it receive the program as a sequence of numbers.

Now the computer will, itself, take care of converting the program from the form in which you, the programmer, write it, to the form in which it, the computer, can understand and execute it. In order to make this conversion, the computer executes another program — a program which someone else wrote for you.

A program called an "assembler" converts programs which you write in assembly language into programs which the computer can understand and execute.

A program referred to as a "compiler" accomplishes the same conversion task for programs which you write using a higher level language.

Assemblers and compilers treat your program as data; they read in data (your program) and convert it to another

---

Technologist Arthur C. Clarke once said,

"Any sufficiently advanced technology is indistinguishable

from magic." If computers seem like magic to you, this article

may shed some light on their inner workings.

This article appeared in *Personal Computing*.

form of data (the computer-executable version of your program).

We refer to a program in human readable form as a "source program". That is to say, a source program is a program written in a programming language. Once the program has been converted into its computer readable form, it is called an "object program". An object program is nothing but a sequence of numbers.

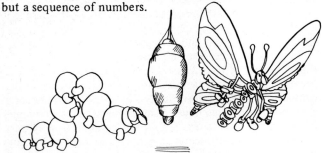

Source Program Conversion Object Program

Thus assemblers and compilers read in data (your source program) and convert it to another form of data (an object program).

In reality there are two types of compilers. One type of compiler takes your program, converts it into a computer readable form and saves the computer readable form. Subsequently the computer readable form is loaded into memory for execution. This may be illustrated as follows:

Step 1 - The Compiling Step

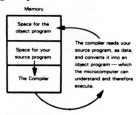

Step 2 - The Execution Step

Another type of compiler never saves the computer readable form of your program (i.e., the object program). This type of compiler is called an "interpreter". When you use an interpreter, your whole source program resides in memory along with the interpreter, for as long as the source program is being executed. This may be illustrated as follows:

The interpreter converts your source program into object

code as needed. This may be illustrated as follows:

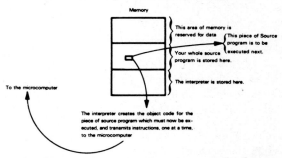

The illustration above shows an area of memory being set aside for your whole source program. You might be misled into thinking that the amount of memory set aside for your source program puts an upper bound on the size of source program which you can execute. In fact, you can execute much larger programs so long as the larger program can be broken into blocks, where no one block overflows the available source program memory space.

Compilers and interpreters are themselves object programs which someone else wrote for you.

We can explain the difference between a compiler and an interpreter in non-technical terms by thinking of the ways in which an actor may learn to deliver lines in a play. Think of the source program as the actor's script; object program instructions going to the microcomputer are equivalent to the actor delivering his lines to an audience. If the actor learns his entire part, then throws away the script and delivers his lines, what he has done is equivalent to compiling a source program. But suppose the actor does not learn his entire part; suppose the actor keeps the script and has a prompter display his lines one at a time using prompting boards. He is now delivering his lines in the fashion of an interpreter.

BASIC is the most popular microcomputer higher level language; it is also an interpreter language.

In summary, we can divide most programming languages into "higher level" languages and "assembly" languages. Higher level languages are converted into object programs by compilers and interpreters. Assembly languages are converted into direct code by an assembler.

The principal difference between higher level languages and assembly language is the fact that higher level languages are designed to represent problems, whereas assembly languages are designed to represent the computer. Thus a computer views a higher level language source program as a very alien thing and a compiler has a big job converting the source program into an object program. In contrast, an assembly language source program can be converted into an object program quite easily; an assembler is therefore a relatively simple program. Let us now compare higher level languages and assembly language in order to more clearly identify differences between the two.

A comparison of higher level languages and assembly language

We will first look at the advantages of higher level languages.

Higher level languages are easier than assembly language to use; that is because higher level languages represent the problem rather than the computer. For example, a simple addition would be written in this self-evident form using a higher level language:

SUM = VAL1 + VAL2

VAL1 and VAL2 are names you assign to an augend and an addend – which can have any values. SUM is the name you assign to the sum. Assembly language presents you with a definition of your computer – in a human readable form. Thus the addition illustrated above would be programmed in assembly language as follows:

```
LXI    H, VAL1
LDA    VAL2
ADD    A,M
STA    SUM
```

VAL1 and VAL2 are no longer names you assign to the augend and addend. VAL1 and VAL2 are now addresses – they identify memory locations in which the augend and addend are stored. Thus the augend and addend must each be small enough to fit within one memory location. SUM, likewise, is the address of the memory location where the sum will be stored – providing it will fit into one memory word.

The assembly language definition of the addition is by no means self-evident.

There is another important advantage associated with the fact that higher level languages are "problem oriented". What we mean by "problem oriented" is that the language is not designed with any computer in mind. Therefore if you write a program in a higher level language, you can convert this higher level language source program into an object program that will run on any computer – providing the computer has a compiler (or interpreter) for your higher level language. Suppose, for example, you write a program in BASIC. You can execute the BASIC program on your computer, and all of your friends can execute your program on their totally different computers – providing their computers also have BASIC interpreters. This may be illustrated as follows:

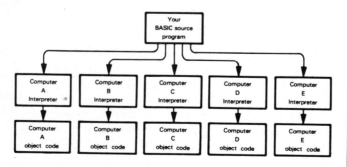

Assembly language, on the other hand, is a human representation of the computer you are using. Thus, every single computer and microprocessor has its own, unique assembly language; and a program written in one computer or microcomputer's assembly language is totally unintelligible to any other computer or microprocessor. If you write an assembly language source program for your microprocessor, only people with microcomputers containing your microprocessor will be able to assemble and run your source program.

In theory it would be possible to write a program akin to a compiler that would take a source program written in one microprocessor's assembly language and convert it into an object program for another microprocessor. In reality few people do this, since another microprocessor's assembly language is as strange and hard to deal with as a higher level language.

With all the advantages that accrue from programming in a higher level language, why would anyone bother with assembly language? Assembly language also has advantages.

In the first place, assembly language generates much shorter object programs than higher level languages. This is because the assembly language for each microprocessor or computer is designed specifically for that microprocessor or computer. In fact, an object program created by a compiler from a higher level language source program is usually 2 to 4 times as long as the same object program created by an assembler from an assembly language source program. This is because the compiler must, in reality, write an assembly language program to represent the problem as defined in the higher level language. But whereas a human programmer can write an assembly language program using human judgement, a compiler must do the job by fixed rules.

Consider an everyday analogy: you must give someone directions to drive from one point to another in a city. If you know the exact source and destination, and the exact city, you can define a very direct route.

Now try to create a set of general-purpose instructions which you can string together in order to define the route to be driven between any two points in any city. These instructions, if they are to be interpreted by a machine, can leave nothing to the imagination. Thus there must be some fixed number of instructions such as:

Turn left
Turn right
Test for a one way street
Test for a dead end road
Test for a 45° turn
etc.

You cannot include instructions that assume you know whether or not a street is one way, since one way streets are subject to change. You cannot include instructions that simply define the number of blocks to travel in a straight line, since there may be barriers in the road preventing such travel, or in cities with steep hills such as San Francisco, a road which appears to be continuous in reality has a 100 foot (i.e., 30 meter) precipice dividing it at some point.

Once you start devising a set of general purpose direction rules that take into account undefinable contingencies, you will have some idea of the problem faced by a compiler. The compiler does not know what the peculiarities of any specific computer may be; therefore it must generate programs that take into account the strangest possiblities.

Higher level languages have another problem. The compiler which converts a higher level language source program into an object program is itself a large program. A compiler program may be eight times as long as an assembler program. Thus until your microcomputer system is quite large you cannot use a higher level language, since your microcomputer system will have insufficient memory to hold the compiler.

If you have an interpreter, then the interpreter must always be in memory, together with the program you are executing. This difference between a compiler and an interpreter was illustrated earlier in the article.

The fact that higher level language source programs generate longer object programs also means that the object program will take longer to execute, since there are more instructions to be executed. If your application is running into speed problems, you can speed things up by a factor of 2, or more, by simply rewriting your program into assembly language.

Even some of the advantages associated with higher level languages are not all they appear to be. For example, higher level languages are supposed to be portable; that is to say, one higher level language source program can be compiled and executed by many different microprocessors. This is not always true. Frequently you will find that there are minor differences in the way one computer's compiler expects the source program to appear, as compared to the next. However, even in the worst case, the changes you would have to make to a higher level language source program, when going to a new microprocessor or computer, are tiny compared to the problems associated with completely re-writing the program in the new microprocessor or computer's assembly language.

What then is our conclusion?

If you are going to use a microcomputer simply as a vehicle for executing programs, you should go to higher level languages as quickly as you can. If, on the other hand, you plan to get inside the microcomputer itself, building your own, changing it, extending it, or otherwise playing with its components, then you should learn assembly language as quickly as possible, and you will probably stay with assembly language.

Microcomputer functional logic

The object program you create determines the functions that will be performed by the logic of your microcomputer.

Functionally Figure 1A illustrates the logic of a microcomputer; this is the logic which we are now going to discuss.

It does not matter what the microcomputer is going to do — ultimately the task consists of these three steps:
1) Bringing data into the microcomputer.
2) Modifying the data.
3) Transmitting the modified data back out from the microcomputer.

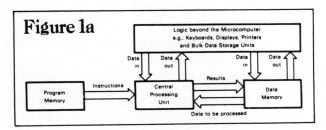

Figure 1a

Logic beyond the microcomputer (which consists of physical units) is used to enter information, receive results and store large quantities of data. Data that is in the process of being operated on is stored in data memory, which is fast ac-

cess, read/write memory. Therefore, steps 1) and 3) above are handled by the shaded microcomputer logic shown in Figure 2.

Physical units transmit information to and from the microcomputer via appropriate interface logic. With reference to Figure 1B, this may be illustrated as follows:

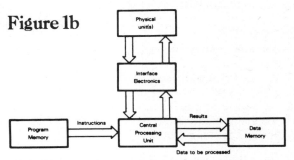

Figure 1b

Operations which are actually performed on data are performed by logic within the Central Processing Unit. These operations are defined by a sequence of instructions which, taken together, constitute a program. The program is stored in program memory. Thus step 2) of the above three steps is handled by the shaded microcomputer logic shown in Figure 3.

Program memory can be read only memory, or it can be read/write memory. Program memory can be read only memory because instructions are transmitted from the program stored in program memory to the Central Processing Unit; but instructions are usually not transmitted from the Central Processing Unit to program memory. Program memory does not have to be read only memory. It is common practice in microcomputer systems to separate programs from data, as shown in Figure 1A, and in many industrial microcomputer applications, programs are held in read only memory to ensure that the program is never accidentally changed or lost.

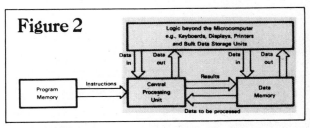

Figure 2

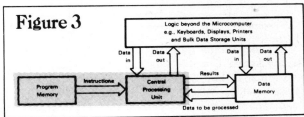

Figure 3

But program memory and data memory could be one and the same memory; moreover, it is possible for one part of a program to treat another part of the program as data, in which case the program changes itself. As you might expect, programs which change themselves can become very complex; so at least while you are a beginner, it is wise to think of program memory and data memory as separate and distinct entities.

The fact that you do not have a good understanding yet of how program and data memories work is unimportant. Program and data memory chips can store information in a computer-readable form. For now that is all you need to know about program and data memory.

Information Paths

Let us now consider the various information paths shown in Figure 1.

When the Central Processing Unit is modifying data, it usually fetches the data to be modified from data memory, and it usually returns the results to data memory. Therefore there are paths in both directions between data memory and the Central Processing Unit:

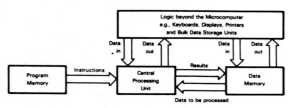

New data entering the microcomputer travels from external physical units to data memory via the Central Processing Unit. Results being output travel from memory via the Central Processing Unit to external physical units. This may be illustrated as follows:

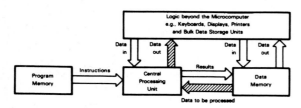

High speed information transfer between floppy disk and data memory frequently occurs directly between these two devices, bypassing the CPU:

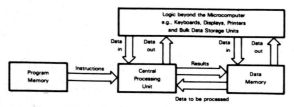

The data path illustrated above is referred to as Direct Memory Access. Direct Memory Access is usually referred to by its initials: DMA. While memory has to be at one end of the DMA data transfer, a floppy disk need not be at the other end, even though it frequently is. Any external logic may provide the other end of the DMA data transfer.

Whenever the Central Processing Unit is doing something — moving data or modifying data — a stream of instructions transmitted from program memory to the Central Processing Unit controls Central Processing Unit operations. Thus there must be a unidirectional path for information to flow from program memory to the Central Processing Unit:

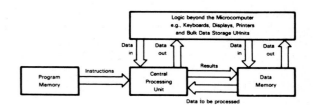

The central processing unit

Central to all microcomputer logic is the Central Processing Unit. The Central Processing Unit is the electronic logic which actually performs all operations on data; that is to say, in various other parts of the microcomputer system you can move data from one location to another, but only within the Central Processing Unit can you actually change data. The Central Processing Unit is usually referred to by its initials: "CPU".

Serial Logic

In order to generate the versatility and power commonly associated with computers, Central Processing Unit logic must be capable of performing a large number of different operations; and that is indeed what the Central Processing Unit can do. However, the Central Processing Unit can only perform one operation at a time. Consider the addition of two numbers; when two numbers are added, they are called the Augend and the Addend. The Augend and the Addend are summed via the following serial sequence of events:

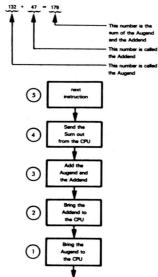

Each event is identified by a number 1, 2, 3, 4, etc. The CPU performs each event as a single operation. Therefore, in order to perform the addition illustrated above, the CPU performs event 1, then event 2, then event 3, then event 4.

During the first step the Augend is brought to the CPU. During the second step the Addend is brought to the CPU. During the third step the Augend and Addend are summed by electronic logic within the CPU. During the fourth step the sum is transmitted out from the CPU. These four steps are essentially identical to the four steps via which you will add two numbers using many older hand-held calculators.

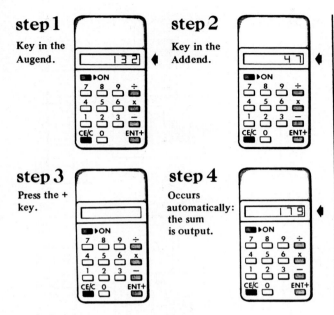

step 1
Key in the Augend.

step 2
Key in the Addend.

step 3
Press the + key.

step 4
Occurs automatically: the sum is output.

Now you know why calculators used to make you do things awkwardly; they were forcing you to use computer logic sequences. This cut the cost and complexity of the calculator.

More recent calculators use more complex logic which lets you work in human sequence:

During step 1 you key in the Augend.
During step 2 you press the + key.
During step 3 you key in the Addend.
Step 4 occurs automatically: the sum is output.

We can use the four hand-held calculator steps (either version) via which you add two numbers to illustrate the concept of a serial device, since a hand-held calculator and a Central Processing Unit are both serial devices; each can perform just one operation at a time. This is simple enough to understand in the case of a hand-held calculator; you cannot, for example, simultaneously key in the two numbers which are to be added. The two numbers must be keyed in serially, one after the other. In the case of a Central Processing Unit, you cannot simultaneously bring the Augend and the Addend to the Central Processing Unit; each number must be fetched via an independent step, and the two steps must occur one after the other.

Serial Logic Step

The next problem that we are going to run into is determining what a single "step" consists of. In the case of the hand-held calculator, this is not a very important consideration. When you enter the number 132 via the keys, does entry of the entire number constitute one "step"? Or does each keystroke constitute and individual "step"? Frankly, for a hand-held calculator, this question is inconsequential. But what if you have to write down a sequence of instructions which someone else must follow? You could write down the following single step:

1) Enter 132 at the keyboard.

You could break up the one step into three separate steps:

1) Press the 1 key.
2) Press the 3 key.
3) Press the 2 key.

Consider an even more mundane example; eating a piece of cake.

Suppose a piece of cake can be eaten in ten mouthfuls; is eating this piece of cake a ten-step process? Perhaps, but perhaps not. Eating a single mouthful of cake may itself consist of these four steps:

1) Separate a piece of cake with your fork.
2) Impale the separated piece of cake on the end of your fork.
3) Transfer the separated piece of cake to your mouth.
4) Chew and swallow the piece of cake.

It would be easy to nitpick these four cake eating steps, creating any number of additional smaller steps. The same is true of single Central Processing Unit steps. Some Central Processing Units perform operations in relatively big steps; others sequence events as a series of relatively small steps. But for every Central Processing Unit, every step is clearly and unambiguously defined as an "instruction". There is nothing vague about an individual instruction, or step, that can be executed by any Central Processing Unit.

Every Central Processing Unit responds to a fixed number of instructions. These instructions, taken together, are referred to as an instruction set. Typically a Central Processing Unit will have from 40 to 200 different instructions in its instruction set. Every instruction is represented by a unique number, which when transmitted to the Central Processing Unit at the proper time, causes the Central Processing Unit to execute the operations associated with the instruction. For example, our addition sequence may be illustrated as follows:

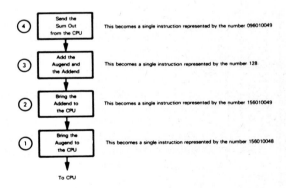

Central Processing Unit Local Data Storage

The four instructions shown above illustrate a logistic problem associated with the CPU.

The CPU has storage space to hold the data that it is about to operate on, and that is all. This may be illustrated as follows:

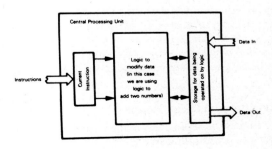

You cannot expect to leave the Augend, Addend and sum in the Central Processing Unit data storage space, because you will almost certainly need this space for the very next operation which the Central Processing Unit performs. The Augend, the Addend and the sum must therefore have permanent storage locations somewhere beyond the Central Processing Unit — for example, in external read/write memory. That is why steps 1, 2, 4 are present.

Program Memory

In order to perform any operation, such as the illustrated addition, you must create a sequence of instructions, which taken together constitute a program. The program is a sequence of numbers. This sequence of numbers is stored in a fast access memory, which we call program memory. Using arbitrarily assigned number codes for the addition instructions, the addition program may be represented conceptually, as shown above.

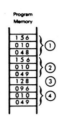

Memory is being likened to a ladder of "pigeon holes"; each pigeon hole represents an individually identifiable and addressable location.

Whenever a number is transferred from the CPU to memory, one "pigeon hole" will be filled. When a number is transferred from memory to the CPU, the CPU receives the contents of one "pigeon hole".

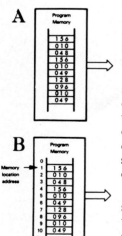

Memory Locations and Addresses

Each "pigeon hole" is called a "memory location". Every memory location is individually identifiable via a unique memory address.

We are not going to concern ourselves with how you create the memory address which identifies any individual addressable location within memory; therefore the addition program sequence illustrated above will be represented occupying an undefined sequence of program memory locations as in A.

Without discussing memory addressing at all, we could illustrate the addition program instruction sequence occurring in the first ten addressable locations of program memory as in B.

Data Memory

The information which is used by a program while it executes is referred to as data. In our simple addition example we are going to handle three pieces of data: the Augend and the Addend which are to be added, and the sum. These three pieces of data will likely be stored in local, fast access data memory.

Addition Program Event Sequence

The process of adding two numbers may now be illustrated conceptually as follows:

Step 1: Fetch the Augend.

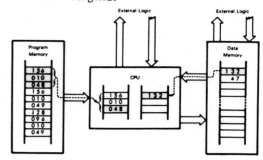

Step 2: Fetch the Addend.

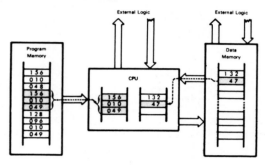

Step 3: Generate the Sum.

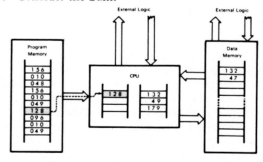

Step 4: Output the Sum.

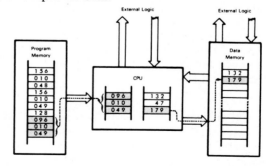

For each of the four steps illustrated above, the first event to occur will be the transfer of an instruction code from program memory to the CPU. In each step the instruction code is the shaded number in program memory. The CPU cannot know what to do until the instruction code has reached it. Once the instruction code has reached the CPU, operations required by the step actually occur. Operations are self-evident.

Note that in Step 4 the sum is arbitrarily shown being written back to the same data memory location from which the Addend was fetched. Thus the Addend will be lost.

Section 2

Microprocessors in Business

The articles selected for this section discuss how microprocessors may be used in the business world, both to increase efficiency and reduce costs. The low price of microprocessors and microcomputers means that these devices can be used effectively even in small businesses.

DO-IT-YOURSELF MICROCOMPUTERS

by M. HEALEY, M.Sc., Ph.D., C.Eng., M.I.E.E.

In 1977 the American journal *Byte*, a well produced glossy aimed specifically at the amateur computer enthusiast, conducted a survey of its readership with most interesting results. First was the staggering figure of over 100 000 circulation. Secondly, from a random sample of 2163 readers, 35% owned their own computer, which, with a crude estimate, implies around 50 000 installed systems by now. In the UK, growth has been less spectacular, but companies such as Computer Workshop, Computer, Comart, Haywood etc. are importing both complete systems and kits. Computer Workshop and Sintel are now manufacturing in the UK, and there are numerous other 'minimum' systems appearing. There is, however, an intriguing side effect for the professional engineer. These systems can be of industrial quality, and systems backed up by floppy discs make cost-effective program development systems. There is also a good range of interfaces available, so that they can well be used in process control applications

The microprocessor as a system component is by now an accepted tool. It is not, however, a computer. A US company, MITS, now part of Pertec, with great foresight, designed a small computer around an Intel 8080 microprocessor and marketed it as a kit, rather as Heathkit had done in the past with hi-fi. With great courage, it defined from the outset a standard bus system, now known as the S100. It is rather liberal on pins and therefore relatively expensive, and, as such is subject to criticism. This is indeed churlish since *any* standard is a boon in the notoriously 'I-can-do-it-better' computer industry.

Any computer is only as good as its software and peripherals, so that the MITS computer, called the Altair, had to offer some ideas outside the traditional professional computer concepts if the home enthusiast was to be trapped. Thus, techniques were developed for audiomodulators for storing programs on standard cassette recorders, a keyboard with a character and video-signal generator to plug into the domestic t.v. to give a visual-display unit as well as adaptations of old electric typewriters and the like. The other move of significance was to produce a Basic interpreter, of surprisingly high quality, which was virtually given away with the computer. Here was a real break from professional computing where hardware is sold to help sell software; in the amateur world simple quick access to the computer's facilities was an essential feature if acceptance was to be gained. Basic is still the normal software system of which there are many variants available from the commercial-standard disc-based Altair package, from multiuser teaching versions down to the incredible Tiny-basic, which runs in about 2 kbyte of memory!

There is no point in dwelling on the enormous success of the d.i.y. computers, which now sell in tens of thousands a year even through retail shops. They have become the latest craze following radio hams and hi-fi. A number of journals have been established specifically for this amateur market, e.g. *Byte, Doctor Dobbs* etc. *Byte*, for example, is a high-quality journal, which has a circulation over 100 000 a month! Most noteworthy among these journals is the publishing of detailed program listings. *Byte* recently conducted a survey of their readership and produced the quite staggering statistics that 35% of them spent over $2000 a year on home computing.

The success of the Altair machine led to a large number of competitive products. Many of these have adopted the S100 bus, e.g. Imsai, Polymorphic, Cromenco etc. They also use the 8080 except for Cromenco who have moved into the higher performance field of the Z80 (4 MHz). The major alternative product is produced by South Western Technology (SWT) which uses the Motorola 6800 processor with a much simpler bus than the S100. Altair also produces a 6800 system with a simplified bus, so that, rather unrelated to processor performance and more to the bus structure, the marketed 6800 systems are cheaper than 8080 systems. With the definition of the S100 bus and the vast market potential, there are numerous companies making cards to fit the Altair microcomputer, particularly memory cards, input/output cards and floppy disc controllers – plug-

1 **SWTP Motorola 6800-based system, now manufactured in the UK by Computer Workshop. This system is one of the cheapest available using a general bus for the (wider) central processing unit and memory cards with a narrower, decoded plane for input/output cards. It is normally available with up to 32 kbytes of memory**

Martin Healey is a member of the IEE Control & Automation Divisional Board. He is with University College, Cardiff CF2 1TA, Wales

0013-5127/78/0367-0201 $1.50/0
© IEE: 1978

'. . .the evaluation-board concept has a lot to answer for in the problems many people face. . .'

compatible peripherals for microcomputers, which should give IBM some consolation! You must be warned, however, that various add-on products pick up unused S100 pins for a specific use that can clash with somebody else's product. Most machines have only a simple display, power on/off and reset control buttons, relying on the reset button to activate a programmable-read-only-memory based monitor to begin communication with the system. The more expensive machines, however, have full front-panel systems, with switches and light-emitting-diode displays for detailed control.

Rather belatedly, but not suprisingly, Heath have announced two Heathkit microcomputers. One is 8080 based, the other is a quite different approach and uses the DEC LSI-11, the Western Digital microprocessor. Heath have defined their own 8080 bus, a 50-line system, with tristate line driver/receivers on all lines to avoid noise and loading problems. The H11 uses the standard DEC LSI-11 processor board with the 38-line bus: it is also supplied with the older DEC paper-tape software system, and users are eligible for membership of the DEC users association, Decus.

One further innovative feature of these microcomputers is the method of providing power supplies. The main power packs provide rectified and smoothed voltages to the bus, which are individually regulated on each card as required. This has the effect of constraining the cost of regulation to an 'as-required' basis and reduces problems of instability. Nevertheless, you are warned to ensure that the main power packs have sufficient capacity for all the boards plugged in: do not assume that there is sufficient power for use of all the slots provided.

Although the d.i.y. microcomputer originated as a specific minimum computer system, the component parts bear comparison with the card products of the microprocessor manufacturers. I feel that the 'evaluation boards', which were the first packaged products, are now outdated in comparison with the cost and expansion potential of a d.i.y. computer, although they are still the cheapest unit of all. Indeed the evaluation-board concept has a lot to answer for in the problems many people are facing in professional appli-

2 To keep costs down to home-enthusiast levels, cheap input/output devices as well as computers were needed. Here a keyboard unit provides a video output that will plug into a t.v. aerial socket, although a cheap monitor is actually displayed

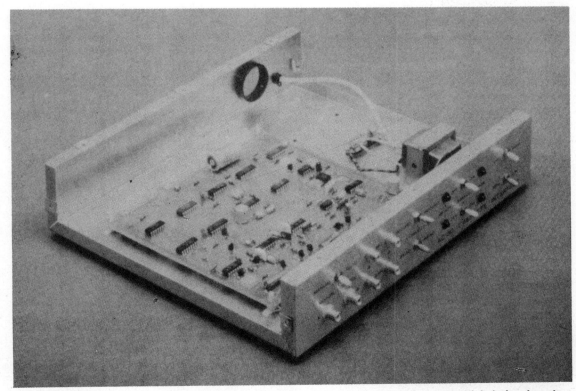

3 As well as input/output, cheap program storage is also needed. A simple box encodes digital signals onto a continuous audio signal that is recorded on a conventional mono cassette recorder at 30 Hz (120 Hz is now available)

cations, as they lead to the misconception that anyone could start designing systems with an outlay of £500 or less. Practice dictates that one needs program-development systems with file storage, assemblers, compilers, printers etc., with costs of £5000 the more reasonable starter. Thus microprocessor development systems (m.d.s.) appeared with v.d.u.s for input, floppy discs for storage, a printer to produce listings in reasonable time and sufficient memory to give efficient assembly etc.

There exists a marked similarity between say an Intel m.d.s. and an Altair 8800b with floppy discs. The latter is cheaper and has a wide range of alternative cards. Both offer the prospect of using similar cards to those in the development system as production units, allowing cost-effective use in low-volume situations as opposed to specially designed production systems, which are only cost effective in bulk. The main difference lies in software. M.D.S. provide assemblers as the main program-development tool; compilers are available at extra cost, e.g. PL/M, PL/Z and Coral. Some of the monitors are quite good, and the disc-operating systems (d.o.s.) good enough for program development, although they can stand improvement. There is at long last a trend towards producing decent real-time operating systems, e.g. Intel's RMX/80, to combat the growing criticism of the low standard of microprocessor software. The d.i.y. computers do provide adequate d.o.s. software, but they are essentially Basic oriented. The Altair disc Basic is in fact good enough to use as a commercial data-processing system, but there is relatively little to help in more general-purpose applications. This is changing now, and assemblers are available and monitors can easily be transferred. Executives, for real-time applications, however, and compilers are going to take more time to establish. The challenge to the highly skilled amateur is very real, however, and software products of high quality will emerge. One welcome trend is versions of Basic with real-time features that will prove extremely useful in relatively slow applications.

One further feature of a microprocessor development system is a p.r.o.m. 'blaster' for transferring

'There is at long last a trend towards producing decent real-time operating systems'

4 32 kbyte Altair 8800b with twin mini-floppy discs sits alongside an 'official' development system, the Intel Intelec 8/MOD 80. The Altair, with video-display unit and printer, is used for assembly-language program development for word-processing and process control systems

5 S100 bus, demonstrated on this Altair 16 kbit random-access-memory board. Note the ample transformer and the on-card voltage regulation. 32 kbit memory boards are now available for £800, assembled and tested. A wide range of S100 cards from a variety of suppliers includes Z80 c.p.u.s , p.r.o.m.; serial and parallel input/output; disc controllers; timers; analogue-to-digital and digital-to-analogue convertors; multiplexers; and optoisolated and relay-driven process-control input/output

developed programs to p.r.o.m. These are available either as peripherals connected through input/output ports or as S100 bus devices.

The standard cards produced by the microprocessor manufacturers use bus structures that are incompatible with everybody else. There is some attempt to establish the Eurocard standard, but everybody seems to want to go their own way (they all know better) and argue, possibly correctly, the superiority of their bus over S100. You only have, as a user, to witness the range of S100 plug-in devices now available to appreciate the importance of a standard. If now, with hindsight, a better standard could be produced, it would still not outweigh the practical advantage of S100 unless it was universally accepted.

Although d.i.y. computers have used either the 8080 or 6800, thereby adopting the unavoidable software growing pains, the interesting alternative, particularly from the professional view, would be to use complementary metal-oxide semiconductor microprocessors equivalent to the DEC PDP-8. The limited instruction set of this machine is hopelessly outclassed by the 8 bit microprocessor, and, in principle, has no place in modern computing (unless one needs the low power consumption of c.m.o.s). There is, however, a vast wealth of PDP-8 software; indeed existing PDP-8 installations can be used as development systems. In fact they have not appeared on the d.i.y. market.

It is most unlikely that the home computer craze will sweep the UK yet as it has done in the USA, owing to the relative financial climate. It is as a professional tool that I see the major interest arising in the UK. Obvious examples are as computers in schools – far better and cheaper than a Teletype dial-up link to a sympathetic local-council computer – and as small business systems. Here I want to consider industrial applications. I should, however, point out that in May 1977 Online Conferences Ltd. hired the IEE facilities at Savoy Place and put on a 1 day introductory conference with invited speakers, which attracted 600 delegates, so that interest in the UK is certainly not insignificant, if on a much lower scale than in the USA. Online is currently asking for participants for a follow-up event in June 1978.

Potential industrial controller

MITS and the plug-compatible-card manufacturers are obviously not unaware of the potential of the d.i.y. computer as an industrial controller. Already the standard process-control devices are available, e.g. digital and analogue input/output cards, timers and interrupt subsystems. Quality is obviously the key word. The high quality of the basic components of the d.i.y kits was one of the first pleasant surprises of my association with these systems, employing good quality printed-circuit boards and components from reputable manufacturers. Stripped down chassis are also available, i.e. without front panels, and one manufacturer at least supplies a standard rack mounting for S100 cards: I must, however, reiterate my warning to ensure that the power supplies are adequately rated.

Standard cards provide serial input/output to EIA standards, and 20 mA current-loop convertors are also available. T.T.L. compatible parallel input/output ports are also mounted on cards, in various combinations with serial input/output ports. Altair provide an excellent process digital input/output card with eight outputs via reed relays and eight inputs via optoisolators. A variety of manufacturers can supply multiplexed analogue-digital and digital-analogue S100 compatible cards. It is in this latter area that I feel most problems could occur, and microcomputers still leave us with the real-world problems of contact bounce, noisy signals, matching of logical signal levels etc. Thus these devices are very cost-effective tools in the hands of a professional control engineer, but induce some rather disastrous under-costed 'solutions'

if the overall problems are underestimated.

In many situations, the d.i.y. computer used by independent process-control and software engineers can provide a distinct challenge to solutions offered by the more traditional companies like Foxboro, Honeywell etc., and to the newer systems offered by Bristol Automation, Negretti & Zambra etc. This is particularly so since the process engineer can deal in one-off situations, without crippling hardware development investments. One can never ignore the continuing problems of reliability and maintenance. D.I.Y. computer cards are readily available, and thus offer cheap hardware maintenance on a plug-in basis. It is, however, my opinion that the microprocessor has spawned a whole new set of maintenance problems, despite an overall improvement in reliability, in the differentiation between hardware and software faults. I feel that the problems of software reliability, self checking and the like are not adequately solved. Further, as cheap hardware makes microprocessors suitable for lower-level control problems on a wider scale, the problem becomes more severe.

One area in which the d.i.y. computer can well find application is in machine controllers. There are many manufacturers with production runs of under 100 a year making relatively high-cost machines that incorporate cabinets of relay controllers, timers etc. costing over £2000. Much of the logic can be replaced by a microcomputer, although the cost effectiveness has yet to be firmly established as power relays, indicators, setting dials etc. are still needed. The potential for major cost savings lies in the possibility of tailoring the logic to suit a specific machine, particularly prevalent when the machine is offered with optional attachments. There are unfortunately many stumbling blocks to be overcome. Aside from the above mentioned maintenance problem and the specific operator-controls' interfaces, there remains a major problem of human communication at design level.

The relay logic is traditionally designed on a trial and error basis, despite the teaching of Boolean algebra and specified on a 'ladder diagram'. The engineers involved have no experience of computer programming, nor is the smaller company likely to invest £5000 in a development system until he is sure he can profitably use it. The alternative of a terminal to a time-shared bureau hardly helps either. Research and development establishments, software houses etc. can possibly provide solutions if the utilisation by industry can be encouraged enough to provide sufficient customers to enable a cost-effective service to be offered. The universities can help in these early phases. However, this raises yet another problem of an acceptable method of specifying requirements. It is possible to program from a ladder diagram, but this does not seem right since the machine designer would still have to sort the logic out beforehand. There is thus an educational exercise required in producing formal statements of machine requirements in a form that can be readily converted to a p.r.o.m. program, e.g. flow charting or state diagrams.

In conclusion, the d.i.y. computer has provided a hardware system at much lower cost than traditional minicomputers. They make it quite practical to employ microprocessors in one-off jobs as opposed to the big production runs previously required to offset development costs. They provide a cost-effective alternative to the cards supplied by microprocessor manufacturers with a much wider choice, particularly of compatible devices. In many ways they 'dangle a carrot' to open whole new application areas, but these are as yet fraught with pitfalls of human communication between disciplines and the introduction of software into traditional hardware enviroments. Development-aid software for d.i.y. computers is far below that of the specialised development systems, but real-time Basic may prove a winner with many simpler, low-speed control applications.

PCW Small Business Case Study

BORIS SEDACCA

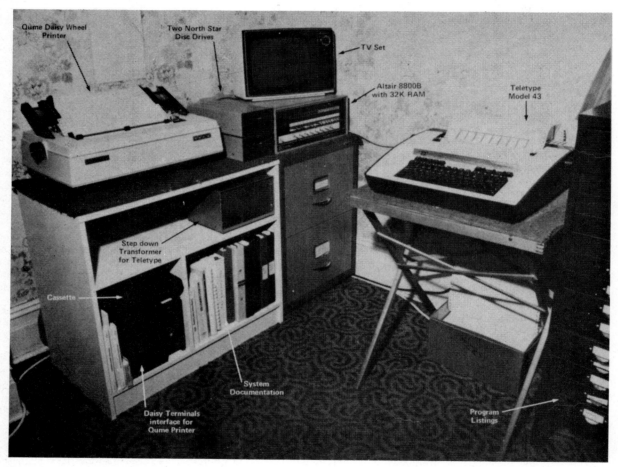

The System
The note on the wall contains a list of instructions on how to switch on and run the computer. This is for the benefit of Brian Crank's children, should they wish to play games in his absence.

The Company: Brian Crank Associates
The Business: Technical public relations
The Background: Brian Crank Associates was formed three years ago. Growth has since been steady and the bulk of the company's turnover comes from about half a dozen large accounts.

The System:
Altair 8800B microcomputer with 40K RAM
Special interfaces (see diagram)
Twin North Star mini-floppy disc drives
Teletype 43
Qume 40 Daisywheel printer 40 cps and controller
Television and Polymorphic VTI board for video output
Cassette drive
A similar configuration at current market prices will cost in the region of £7,000 (Compelec Electronics are sole

UK agents for MITS Altair). Brian Crank assembled the machine himself from a kit and added peripherals as the system developed. The audio cassette machine might appear somewhat superfluous and, indeed, this is now rarely used. However, it was invaluable in the early stages because in the beginning, it was the only bulk storage device in the system.

The Altair is something of a legend, it is the fore-funner of personal computing. It is manufactured in the USA by a company called MITS which has now been taken over by another company called Pertec, a manufacturer of magnetic storage peripherals. This takeover has been beneficial because the Altair can now be interfaced to 1OMB hard disc drive, (not in DMA mode however) which makes it particularly attractive to a business user whose storage requirements need

Reprinted with permission from *Personal Computer World.*

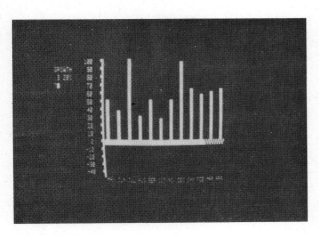

Sample Bar Chart

upgrading to a larger capacity.

Since it inception in 1974 many developments have taken place. Perhaps the most significant is the creation of a separate company called Microsoft Inc, set up to market and further develop the Altair BASIC. Microsoft Inc BASIC interpreter software is becoming increasingly popular on microcomputers, particularly those based on the Intel 8080 microprocessor.

An alternative is however available from a company called North Star which is preferred by some users because it supports hardware floating point, and because of some differences in features offered by North Star BASIC.

Perhaps more significant from the hobbyist's point of view is the creation of the S100 bus which is something of an industry standard nowadays and used extensively by microcomputer manufacturers, even those who make use of microprocessors other than the Intel 8080.

Brian Crank left the RAF some 11 years ago to begin a career with "Wireless World" as an electronics engineer. He later joined the editorial staff and wrote various technical articles describing equipment of his own design. Among his articles published was the design for a very limited digital computer for educational purposes made up of discrete components (about 400 transistors!). He then became deputy editor of "Wireless World".

"I feel that one important design project in which I involved myself in those days is what I then called the 'Logic Display Aid', which I believe to be the forerunner of today's logic analysers offered by companies such as Hewlett-Packard", says Brian. "Hewlett-Packard's equipment has more bells and whistles, of course, but my design featured all the basic principles. It would display the Karnaugh Map, Truth Table or Venn diagram, on a convential oscilloscope, of any combinational logic circuit. It was described in a series of articles in 'Wireless World' during 1969."

So Brian was not green as far as electronics was concerned. However, he had no previous experience of programming at all when he first bought his computer. Learning the commands was easy enough, but the production of really efficient programs was another matter, and the first programs which he wrote were more exploratory than functional in nature.

Today, eighteen months later, the picture is quite different. The configuration is quite impressive and Brian has managed to apply sound management principles to what was originally no more than a few boxes of components and diagrams.

"The machine's operation is quite simple, really. I have modified North Star DOS (the disc operating system) so that BASIC is loaded automatically and comes up running as soon as 'RUN' is selected. A file directory is printed automatically.

"I use the teletype's keyboard in simplex mode, thereby isolating its printer. I then have the choice of three output peripherals: the teletype printer which produces print of matrix characters; the QUME Daisywheel printer which operates much faster with high-quality print, or, if hard-copy (paper) output is not required, the information may be displayed on the television screen. These peripherals are accessed by simple commands."

Brian Crank's software (using North Star BASIC) comprises four main applications suites: financial transactions; word processing; price lists; and analysis of reader reply cards.

One minifloppy diskette contains one year's financial transactions. "When I first developed the software for the financial applications, I had to update files with separate runs of the various programs comprising the suite. This was a tedious job at times so I decided to apply database management techniques in order to achieve file independence and integration. I got hold of a book called 'Principles of Data Base Management' by James Martin and this helped me no end. It is an excellent book and I thoroughly recommend it to anyone who wants to develop his own database management system."

Once the database program has been loaded into memory from the diskette the following options are displayed on the screen:
1) Enter details of new invoice
2) An invoice is paid
3) Enter new expenditure
4) Call editor
5) Change program

If option 1) is selected, details of a new invoice are entered interactively with requests for information appearing on the screen and data verified at each stage. More specifically, the first request is for an invoice number; this begins with an alphabetical character which identifies the client, then a number for the invoice itself, and at the end of the number, an alphabetical character again which gives the income category to which the payment will be posted.

The rest of the details are entered in the same way and if anything is entered incorrectly the program will automatically go into editing mode for amendments to be made to the record number, the invoice details, date of purchase or for a search through the records by month or customer.

When payment is made against an invoice, the cashbook is automatically updated together with the customer's account in the ledger; a feature of the database software.

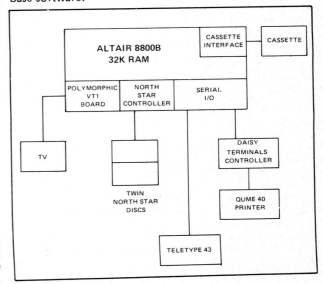

When a new client is entered, this is done by entering a new invoice number. The system does not recognise the new number and interactively asks for details. From this, a new chain is created for future file searches. "Customers are now changed on-line. Previously I had to change the program itself when I wanted to enter a new customer, but I overcame this by introducing a program module to deal with this."

At the end of the accounting period, typically on a monthly basis, reports may be produced by calling up the following menu onto the screen:

1) Amend the database (calls the database management program)
2) Print cashbook — expenditure
3) Print cashbook — income
4) Print client statements
5) Call the anlysis program
6) Print list of suppliers

A report of the expenditure by suppliers of which there are about 75 each identified by number is selected by keying in 2). This will display in chronological order each item of expenditure as it is incurred during that month, according to the following headings; supplier, VAT, Total and analysis. Analysis refers to type of expenditure such as freight and delivery, postage, travel expenses, stationery, telephone, photography, etc.

Income is listed by client with details, of invoice number, VAT, and invoice totals. Clients statements contain similar details plus date of invoice and age (days outstanding).

The analysis program collects figures from the database on a monthly basis. Categories which can be analysed include billings, income, expenditure, monthly cash flow, accumulated monthly cash flow, profitability, billing analysis and expenditure analysis. From this, one may elect to have the financial figures displayed numerically and graphically, or graphically only, by means of bar charts.

The word processing suite is used for occasions when invitations are sent out for events, exhibitions, press conferences, etc. Variables such as date, name of venue and address are entered, together with the time of the start of the event, the date the letter is to be sent, the name of the client and, finally, details of what the client will announce.

"Names and addresses of the people to whom invitations are to be sent are held on a disc file. The system automatically generates letters of invitation on standard letter headed paper, evelope labels for posting, and a list of invitees from which I may then follow up with an invitation. I also use the system for the printing of address labels for press releases and for captions to accompany photographs. For this latter activity, costs are automatically calculated and stored on disc. At the end of each month the file is passed to another program which automatically generates the invoices."

The computer and the Daisywheel printer form an excellent combination for handling price lists. In Brian's system, software has been written to handle product price lists. Such details as device type, description and price are sorted on disc in a base currency. The details of each form one disc record and there can be any number of records since the software will accommodate lists which occupy several discs. The editing section of the program allows new lines to be inserted, others to be deleted, and line to be altered at will.

Price lists can be printed out on the Daisywheel printer in any currency as long as the conversion factor between the base currency on disc and the desired currency is known. Price list pagination is automatic and page numbers and headings are printed. Page length can be changed at will to suit any stationery format. If carbon ribbon is used in the Qume, the output is so good that it can be used as camera-ready copy for bulk off-set litho printing or photo-copying.

The main advantage claimed by Brian for this system is the elimination of tedious proof-reading. Once the price list data has been entered and checked, it is only necessary to proof-read any changes that are subsequently made. Brian believes it is in this sort of application that the small computer is a real asset.

The suite for reader replies divides products into groupings. The number of cards received is input to the system, and for each product category the number of editorial mentions is counted. The average number of enquiries per mention is then calculated and compared with the actual enquiries per magazine, and on this basis the system allocates points and produces a scoreboard.

"Then, of course, I also have a number of games, including most of the usuals: 'Lunar Lander', 'Hunt the Wumpus', 'Market', 'In Out' (a word game for children), 'Stars', 'Weight Watching', 'Bio-rythm', 'Star Trek', 'Mastermind', and the 'Game of Life', all of which my daughters play from time to time. The 'Star Trek' program is quite interesting in that it is written in Palo Alto Tiny BASIC — an excellent small interpreter.

"A Heuristics Speech Lab has recently been added to the system, but the possibilities offered by this have not yet been investigated.

"I feel that the value of the microcomputer to the smaller business is incalculable and I would offer the following advice to the directors of small companies who cannot, as yet, write programs. The best way to learn is by experience. Take the plunge and buy a system. I did and have not regretted it."

PCW Review:
Research Machines 380Z

Mike Dennis

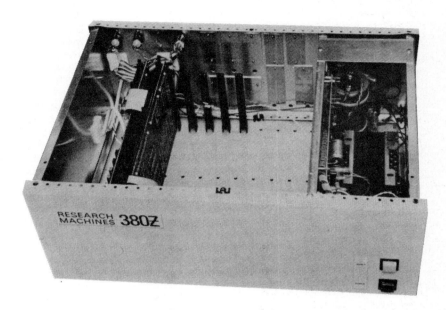

About the beginning of 1977, various advertisements appeared under the Sintel banner for the RML 380Z microprocessor systems. In fact, it was not until August 1977 that the first prototype machines went out and December 1977 that the first production models were despatched. The prices ranged from about £400 to £1400 depending on facilities and memory size and it was the grand-daddy of the range with 32K of RAM that I was given to review.

Originally I was to have it for only a week but I must have smiled nicely for Research Machines (RML) were quite happy for me to have it for a much longer period. In fact, I wholeheartedly endorse the editor's comments about the interest and assistance offered by this firm. Such attributes are all too often non-existent in larger organisations.

Appearance can be deceptive!

Surprisingly, the 380Z is much lighter than its' size suggests. It weighs only about 25lbs. in a cabinet the size of a small suitcase. No wonder, really, as when you open up the case all that you see are two PCB's, a power supply and a lot of air! (See photograph 1).

The 380Z was designed to be modular in construction, which is good. What this means is that fault finding is greatly assisted and spare boards or power supplies can be swiftly changed and thus reduce your downtime. What I didn't like was the use of Lucar connectors on some wires which were far too thin to carry the relatively heavy weight of the connectors. There are many other more suitable connectors on the market and so to use this particular type is sloppy. The general standard of construction inside was, I felt, more adequate than elegant. For instance, odd pieces of perspex sheet were stuck together in layers and then stuck to the inside of some of the panels presumably to stop them from rattling. The actual fixing flanges in the internal panels distort permanently with use as the screws are tightened up. You can see this in the photograph. Generally, in the professional equipment one doesn't normally find this. Surprising, too, was the lack of

Serial Number or other means of individual identification.

The power supply has been mounted well out of the way to give plenty of room in the case. More space has apparently been saved in this area by using a transformer designed by RML. All mains connectors were suitably protected against 'fairy fingers'. The mains input itself is via the detachable new IEC connector and comes ready to go with a mains lead of decent length and 13A plug. I must take RML to task, though, for not fitting a fuse of lower rating in the plug. I would have thought that one at 3A was more than ample and not 13A! (Dear reader, are all *your* plugs correctly and, therefore, safely fused?)

Beautiful PCB's

Another grey mark is the lack of protection for the two PCB's. They rest on the bottom of the case directly and although they are free to slide up and down, they are still vulnerable to shock or impact through the bottom panel. Perhaps if RML agree they could fix some form of foam plastic to the bottom of the case to rest the boards on? The PCB's themselves are *beautiful* — there is no other word for it. Of German manufacture, they are double sided and have about 1400 plated through holes *each*. The pair that I had were slightly spoilt by solder splashes which can cause intermittent faults. RML say that they hadn't been cleaned properly and certainly other boards that I saw were much better. In any case, I am really nit-picking as since the boards are mounted vertically then any solder splashes that fall off shouldn't have any catastrophic effect.

The physical size of the boards is 10" x 5½" and that's the nearest that RML get to the S100 bus — the same width! Provision has also been made for mounting a shorter six inch board. I think their bus technique *particularly cost effective.* They make use of connectors similar in style to Scotchflex but made by ITT Cannon. Essentially, they consist of a male (female?) half mounted onto the PCB and the other half crimped onto a flat ribbon cable. Extension leads with any number of plugs/sockets can be made up in order to connect up the various busses to any extra boards. Mind you, as the CPU board can accomodate *up to 32K* it would be some time, probably, before you needed any extra boards for memory! It was a pity that no indexing was provided as in theory it is possible to insert the plugs either way round. In practice, the physical layout and wiring prevents you from doing this. You can do it, though, with the dc supplies which is potentially disastrous. You could end up with a very expensive mistake on your hands. Take note!

Connections to the outside world are by a seven pin DIN socket and two sockets for a visual display. RML supply one DIN lead and one co-ax lead for connecting up. Provision has already been made both in the wiring, hardware and software to couple up two cassette machines via a suitable splitting box to the DIN socket (see later). I was not supplied with any of this but have seen a working system. Clearly, an indication that RML are continuing to expand the system, which is to their credit.

Signals

Although both sockets for the VDU were Belling Lee type co-ax, only one socket is fed by the UHF modulator. In practice, there was sufficient stray oscillation coming from the second socket to provide another UHF signal for a second TV. However, under these conditions it is possible that some TV's could interact between themselves to produce inferior pictures. RML never intended it to be operated in this way but nevertheless you *could* get a small bonus.

I tried feeding the UHF signal into a colour set and had great difficulty in tuning in the signal. Now most, if not all, colour sets have an AFC circuit which you disable when you tune in a station. When a similar technique was tried with the 380Z, as soon as the AFC was enabled again, it pulled the set off tune and so produced a bad picture. But if the AFC was permanently disabled by going inside the set, the problem then ceased as one would expect. On investigating further, the modulator was giving out a signal of about 10mV! More than enough to swamp any normal AFC circuit and so cause the de-tuning that I had experienced. The simple cure is either to use an aerial attenuator (available from any good TV dealer) or use a black and white set. However, this high signal level is rather naughty as the frequency of the modulator was about 592MHz or Channel 36 and so outside the broadcast band. There are other users around this frequency and so at signal levels of this amplitude it is conceivable that interference could be caused by the 380Z to any authorised users of this band.

The second socket is for a line-fed monitor and as such should have been fitted with the proper socket for the job i.e. a BNC (readily available from RadioSpares). Belling Lee co-ax sockets are definitely *not* professional for this type of work and in any case necessitate a convertor lead for use with any monitor. Murphy's Law applies when looking for this lead. Again, the video output level is a non-standard one of 0.15v pk-pk of syncs and 0.4v pk-pk of video. (If your system measures differently then this is due to production tolerances). I measured these when the signal was terminated (as it should be) in 75Ω. Leaving the signal unterminated increased the amplitude but made the characters look a bit ragged, which was expected. The definition in the monitor was, of course, much better than that obtained from the UHF feed. This is generally the case and I wish that better modulators were readily available.

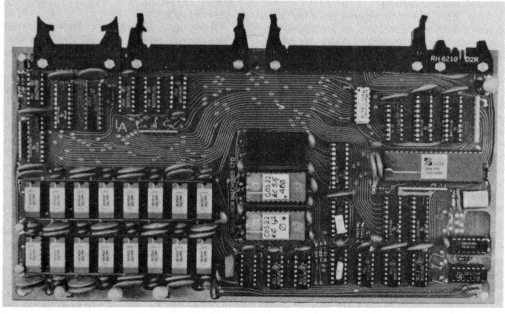

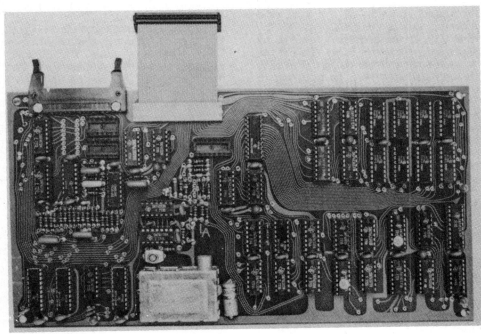

3

Hardware

Talking of volts brings us conveniently to a brief look at the actual hardware used, as I expect that some of you may be particularly interested in this aspect. As can be seen from the photographs 2 and 3, there are remarkably few IC's for so versatile a machine. There are approximately 45 ic's per board together with their respective sockets. I could write an entire article on the various and neat design aspects of the 380Z but suffice to mention just a few points.

1) 16k x 1 350nS dynamic RAM's were provided. They are NEC/Nippon devices and similar to the Mostek 4116 etc. As such, 4k x 1 dynamics are a direct replacement fit and provision has been made for this.

2) Thick film resistors have been used where any pull-up and pull-down resistors are required.

3) An 8MHz crystal is used for the system clock and divided down to provide a 4MHz clock of equal mark-space ratio.

4) One Wait state is put in all Memory Request (MREQ) cycles at the factory. Should you wish to run at a slower rate then the user can re-arrange on-board wire links to insert a Wait state in each M1 cycle.

5) Much use has been made of LSI devices such as the 74LS393 (two 7493's in one package). There is a liberal sprinkling of 74LS157, 158, 241, 244 and 374's. The majority of these are comparatively new devices to the TTL family and many have been designed with the microprocessor in mind. If you are at all interested in designing your own system then I can only urge you to buy an up-to-date TTL Data Book from one of the distributors. They make fascinating bed-time reading!

6) Liberal decoupling means *good* noise performance. RML have spread tantalum capacitors and 0.1uF's around like confetti and the result has been very little noise on any of the dc lines. Most commendable. Even the 3A regulator which is situated away from the CPU board by a very long wire seemed perfectly able to cope. In fact the 380Z only uses about 1½ of the available 3Amps which again allows ample expansion.

7) The COS (Cassette Operating System) lives in two 2708 ROM's and there is space for an optional

ROM be it user programmed or as, in my case, supplied by RML (more anon).

8) I spied a couple of other ROM's on both boards. On the CPU board were both a 74S287 (256 x 4 bits) and a 74S288 (32 x 8 bit) ROM. The 287 is used to decode which block of RAM is being addressed and there are four versions available depending on what type of memory you have (eg. 2 x 16K, 2 x 4K etc.). Should you win the pools or strike lucky at the finance meeting and wish to install more RAM, then all you do is swap the 287 and plug in another RAM. Slight alterations to one pin have to be made depending on whether you are using 4K or 16K RAM's and these are done on wire-wrap connections. Should you have 8K of RAM and wish to update to a 16K version then rather than supply a separate board as originally advertised, RML will buy back your 8K of RAM and sell you a 16K block. Any extra cost doing it this way will be absorbed by them.

One output of this ROM connects up to the 'S288 as an enabling signal and indicates that the lower 8K bytes of memory are being addressed ie up to 1FFF. This and address lines A9-A12 inclusive are then sufficient to decode the three ROM positions, the ROM data buffer, VDU memory select signal and 'I/O' port select signal. This latter when NANDed with A2-A8 inc. provides a low when locations 0FFC-0FFF are being addressed. However, I/O is really a misnomer as the IORQ signal from the CPU is never used as these particular I/O ports are memory mapped. 0FFC is either the keyboard in the read mode or Port 0 in the write mode. The pattern of bits written into this port control various functions in the monitor. 0FFD is a counter used for the software single step and reset. 0FFE is Port 1 and dedicated to the cassette/program storage facility etc. and other misc. functions. 0FFF is a user port and has even been provided with a buffered octal latch.

So with only two ic's, RML have decoded all of this whilst still maintaining a high degree of flexibility. A really good example, I think, of what a fresh approach can do in a situation like this. That really sums up the CPU board.

The VDU board contains both VDU and enough interface for two cassette recorders. Again, ingenious use had been made of two ROM's ('S287s again). These, in conjunction with their respective line and field counters, provide all the sync and blanking waveforms, reset signals etc. required by the VDU together with *all* the addresses required by the display RAM's and charactrer ROM. This is the first time I have seen such a clever design. The sync width is a little non-standard (4uS as opposed to 4.7uS) but in practice this should make very little difference.

Any calls to output an alphanumeric character to the screen occurs in Field Blanking. In order to use graphics in an interactive mode a faster rate is required. One sub-routine in COS uses line blanking (24uS) to output one character per line. Now, 24uS is not long, even with a 4MHz clock so if you wait for line blanking to arrive before beginning your o/p routine then you soon run out of time. However, since this output routine consists of a known length of machine cycles and hence time, you can anticipate the lineblanking signal and use a pulse of earlier timing. Because RML have done their sync generation the way they have, the line blanking ROM quite conveniently has just such a waveform with the right timing!

One design point that I personally dislike is the software conversion of capital O to □. This is necessary because the Texas 262 character generator used doesn't discriminate between capital O and zero. I personally prefer O and ø.

Note from the photograph (2) the conspicuous lack of any UART's (a UART is a large 40 pin ic that can convert 8 bit parallel data into serial data and vice versa). This is because about 256 bytes of COS has been used to record and replay a cassette tape to CUTS standard. At 2708 prices this costs very approximately £2.50 whereas two UARTs could cost together about £10 — clearly a good example of an economical software/hardware tradeoff. However, this is only the half of it as with the option ROM supplied there is a fast cassette option of 1200 Baud. Bear in mind that their cassette file handling is also *very sophisticated.*

Recording
To record a programme on tape you either type D for Dump or SAVE depending on whether you are in the COS system or have BASIC loaded in. Either prompts you with a request for a file or programme name. In COS, this can be up to six letters long; in Basic, ten. The system then prompts you with a request for the first and last address of the data or programme and also the start address. The programme is then parcelled up into either 128 or 255 (yes, 255 as in order to save bytes in the monitor, RML use the zero count for end of data block) byte blocks. Each block has the programme name attached to it.

Loading
To load a programme from cassette, select your recording speed (300 or 1200) if necessary, enter the program name and then replay the cassette. The COS system reads in all the data blocks and echoes the name at the beginning of each block on to the VDU screen. When the name coming off the tape matches the programme selected by you, the monitor loads the programme at the correct address. Since each block is named, either you or the 380Z can search through an entire tape for a specific programme. All that you need to do after entering the programme name is to fastwind through the tape, periodically stopping and replaying a short section of tape to see in which programme you are in. Likewise, by using cassette recorders (such as the Hitachi loaned by RML) with a remote pause means that the 380Z can load a block of data into its Assembler (ready soon!), then pause the cassette while it digests the data. Of course, this latter facility is only provided by their Cassette File Handling Programme which is supplied free with the more expensive versions. This programme can also be used, so RML say, for loading tapes recorded to other standards such as the INTEL format. An interesting side effect of the basic COS system is that

programmes recorded in this fashion have a certain (I admit, not fantastically great) security against easy pirating.

I used the cassette system quite extensively and, at first, had one or two failures. This prompted a visit from RML with various spare bits but we were unable either to reproduce the fault or to explain why they had occurred in the first place. Certainly, some failures can be put down to my lack of familiarity with the cassette machine. This is one of the few cassette machines that has both volume and tone controls on the output. Most cassette machines have neither but, in this case, it was necessary to adjust them correctly. One annoying feature of this cassette player was that connecting the DIN lead mutes the internal speaker. Personally, I like to have the volume up a bit so that I can hear what's going on and so if this too is your preference then this is not the cassette player for you.

A more annoying feature was the automatic return after the sixth letter in the name when loading in COS. If you make a typing mistake in the sixth letter, then you have to either *Reset* the 380Z or ignore the mistake, replay some tape and then hit Control C. (This is because you cannot return to COS if the tape isn't running. This is one drawback of using a software cassette interface in this way.) With either you have to go through the whole loading procedure again.

Mind you, hitting the Reset isn't as disastrous as it could have been had RML not had the forethought to do it carefully and keep the refresh going for the dynamic RAM's during reset! However, you've got to remember to reset your fast tape option, if necessary, after reset, otherwise you'll enter your name, start the machine and then have to start all over again! This is because COS 'fails' to normal tape speed after a reset. A better way would be a 'fail' to 'fast mode in' as most programmes will be stored on tape in this way.

One nice feature of the COS loading is that should you get a read error then the machine won't abort completely, unlike some. You have the option of either aborting deliberately or of rewinding the cassette a bit, typing 'L' and the programme will be reloaded at the start of the next block, and hopefully go in OK the second time round. I noticed that you couldn't do this when Saving a Basic tape.

I tried playing back pre-recorded cassettes made on various cassette machines and had no compatibility problems. I measured the "dynamic range" over which the COS would load and save tapes satisfactorily and found the system was still coping at a level of 20dB below peak recording level. What this means is that you should have no need to worry unduly about what level to record at when saving programmes. Obviously, when using the high speed option, tolerances regarding drop-out etc. on the tape are that much tighter and RML quite sensibly recommend the use of high quality tapes.

One possible problem with some cassette machines is that the output is 180° out of phase with the input. RML have thought of this and provide a pre-recorded programme called "TSTCS" or Test Cassette. This enables a check to be made both for optimum replay level (assuming you have control) and for phase. This is all fairly well documented in the literature and any out of phase machines can easily be cured by using a 1:1 transformer suitably wired.

Software

Any system, no matter how good the hardware, must stand by its firmware and software and it is here that the 380Z scores. In particular, the 'software front panel' is one of the clearest and most versatile that I have met (see photograph 4.). Briefly, it displays in the upper unscrolled 20 lines of the screen, the contents of all the main registers, stack pointer and programme counter. Those registers that can be paired up are and the resultant 16 bit address thus derived is displayed alongside. The contents of the memory location thus addressed by each pair is *also* displayed together with the contents of several locations on either side, the actual location being pointed to by the arrows. Personally, I would have preferred the display of these locations to stand out from the rest of the display (bright-up?) as it was often difficult to remember where each one was. The contents of the registers and programme counter can be altered at will.

The data display, of course, will alter as these registers are changed and so the effect on the system of any changes can be instantly seen. The stack pointer cannot which could possibly prove annoying at a later date. Neither the I nor the R registers are shown. It is possible to switch to the 'other' registers. Another good point is the ability to single step through a programme. Pressing 'Z' causes an NMI into the single step routine. The programme counter, stack pointer and registers all change before your very eyes and one can really appreciate the effects of the various instruction code, stack pointer manoeuvres etc. *I can't recommend this feature strongly enough for anyone involved in teaching micro's.* Go and see for yourself. A nice touch is the actual printing of the various flags when set e.g. Z and C if both the zero and carry flags are set.

All this display is contained in ten lines. The remaining ten lines are taken up by a separate memory pointer. The address of this can be entered by the user following an 'M' command. The pointer will alter and 32 bytes of data on either side of this new pointer will be displayed. The pointer can also be incremented or decremented by either 1 or 8 bytes. Data can be written into memory directly and this is how a hex programme would be keyed in. The bottom four lines of the screen echo keystrokes and scroll.

Another nice feature is the 'Memory Shift' command. This works out the best way to move the memory blocks so as not to corrupt the data should you wish to move one block to an area that, in fact, overlaps part of the original block. Many other monitors eg. Zapple will corrupt the data under certain conditions.

One or two minor bugs were: —

1) any non-hex character acts as a terminator and in one case caused the system to lock-up necessitating a 'Reset'. This means that the monitor is not very forgiving and that if you make a typing mistake, COS will not let you correct it! One man's meat . . . though, as RML say that some people prefer a system this way because you *don't* have to always hit CR to terminate. You pays your money . . .

2) Confusion due to choice of keys for certain commands eg. 'Z' in 'frontal panel' single steps (a Go type signal) but 'Control Z' in Basic halts the programme!

3) Good though the single step facility is, it would soon get pretty tedious stepping through a loop with a count of 255. RML have thought about this and included the provision for setting break points. What can happen is that the breakpoint is never reached. The keyboard is then locked out and so the only resort is 'RESET'. Unfortunately, as this wipes the registers, tracing the bug can prove difficult. What is needed is some form of "time-out" facility to return to the monitor. Not many monitors do this and unfortunately COS is no exception.

COS resides at 0000-07FF (see memory map). Beware, there be dragons, in the form of the restart vectors. RML have used these to great effect. Four are jump outs into RAM for user control. One is the

normal reset to 0000, one is used for break points and another for simulating RELATIVE CALLS. (see later). By far the most ingenious, however, is F7 which is a Trap Call and is a two byte instruction equivalent to a 'CALL'. The second byte following F7 contains the trap code of the desired target sub-routine. If all the commonly used sub-routines eg. Get keyboard character etc. are routed through as 'transfer vectors' using this Trap Call, then the number of bytes saved by not having to use a 3 byte Call every time will more than offset the bytes needed for the Trap Call routine. As Trap Call only uses a few vectors, you the user have well over a hundred left! Space does not allow me to do justice to, what to my mind, is one of the carefully thought out and refreshing (no pun) monitors that I have seen for a long time. Drawbacks? Well, often programmes are designed to run at this address so you'll have some relocating to do. The other drawback is slightly greater execution time.

The relative call simulation is used to great effect in the PIC or Position Independent Code. The Y index pointer is used in conjunction with this to enable any programme written with PIC to run elsewhere in the system. The range is limited to +/− 128 bytes but by writing in extension routines within this range it is possible to extend the range to anywhere. Many RML programmes are written in this way and when loaded are automatically loaded at the top end of the available RAM (stored as HIMEM in COS). HIMEM is then altered to its new lower value and if desired another programme could be loaded ad infinitum (well almost). Each programme then uses PIC to find out where its been put!!

Yet another facility is the Page mode should you wish to address >48K of memory. Of course, you'll need a Memory Extension Board plus more RAM/ROM but that's a small price to pay and of little consequence. The main point is that RML have provided for you.

One cannot end this exhaustive (and exhausting) review without mentioning their 8K Basic which is good, very good. There are many extra facilities, in particular the Line Editor, which one would normally find in Extended Basics of greater length. This Basic is also very fast — look at the Table in John Coll's article in Vol 1 No. 1 of *PCW*. It isn't the fastest but its times are still very respectable. How do they do it? Well, for a start all the Basic command words like 'Print', 'If' are encoded as each line is entered into a one byte code with bit 7 set. This means that you can save on memory space, and speeds up programme execution time as each programme is part compiled. They are continuing to refine their Basic and, in fact, are up to Basic which has graphics to: —

1) **Plot x,y,z where x = 0-79 else error**
$$y = 0\text{-}47 \quad ,, \qquad ,,$$
$$z = 0 = \text{dot off}$$
$$1 = \text{dot on dim}$$
$$2 = \text{dot on bright}$$

2) **Graph 0 = Normal scroll**
,, **1 = Clear top 20 lines, scroll bottom 4.**
,, **2 = No clear, 4 line scroll.**

Another facility is to execute 'Control S' before executing the programme or listing command as this stops the scroller. Each 'Control A' then scrolls one page and then stops the scroll and programme. 'Control Q' restores to normal operation. It is very easy in this mode to wonder why the programme has stopped (you've forgotten to press CTRL A) and so RML give you a clue by switching the cursor off.

Personally, I think it would be better to blink it on and off. Another minor irritation is the carriage return automatically on character 40 and not 41 as one expects.

During a visit to RML, I was shown their new Assembler and Text Editor in a working system with twin cassette machine floppy disc and TTY. The software also caters for paper tape. Again space and time did not permit a thorough examination but it looks as if it is very powerful, very flexible and very good.

The summing up

Obviously, many of my criticisms were purely personal and should be taken as such. Technically, the product was excellent (the boards really are a work of art!) and there were many innovative and ingenious design features. Much though has gone into the design to make it as flexible and easy to interface to as possible. The styling is a bit functional and the general construction could be tidied up. The monitor ROM and software backup are *excellent* and

continually being updated and improved. Existing customers can get either free or at cost the fast scroller, fast tape I/O, Intel loader and TTY routines from RML. I just have the slightest unease about the lack of consistency between some of the characters used for commands and terminators. There is a hint of illogicality about some of them — probably as a result of this 'fine-tuning' to the system. And don't forget, you don't need to take out a second mortgage. You can buy a 280Z version which consists of CPU board and VDU board fully built and tested (soak tested for two weeks as are all their machines) for £400. If I was on a tight budget, then this is the version that I would buy. Otherwise any businesses, firms, institutions, schools etc considering buying a good all-rounder could do a lot worse than take a long hard look at any of the RML versions. And don't forget, you aren't necessarily tied to buying any extra memory from Research Machines.

To conclude, a few quirks but in general an excellent machine. I was sorry to see it go.

MEMORY MAP

FFFF		
Cooo	User RAM	48k bytes of user RAM possible without paging
8000		
4000		
3000		
2000	Assigned	May be used for ROM etc.
1000 / 0E00	Control ports	
0800	VDU	
	COS Monitor	
0000		

4100	Start of user RAM	
40FF	Monitor stack	
	I/O vectors	256 bytes
4000	Monitor variables	
3FFF		
	Unassigned	
2000		
1FFF	Can be used for ROM	
1000		
0FFF / 0E00	Control ports, KBD, User I/O	512 bytes
0DFF	Memory mapped VDU	1½K bytes but physically only 1K
0800		
07FF		
	COS monitor	2K bytes
0000		

How to build big the little way

Microcomputers are creating literally hundreds of new business application areas. Their low cost is bringing down the price of computer power so that you don't have to be a big company to take advantage. This article explains how small firms in the construction industry can compete on equal terms.

THERE is a very real need for the use of computers in the construction industry to improve the flow of data and to handle the increasing complexity of calculations and regulations even apart from the more exotic areas of computer-aided design.

Much work has been done in this field over a number of years. For example, two of the authors designed and developed a very large integrated system for West Sussex County Council in the early 1960s which covered many aspects of the design, production and construction data for buildings.

So much was excluded

All the work was done on large mainframe machines—IBM 360 and 370 Series with a light pen input/output device (IBM.2250).

The cost of the hardware and the software for such a system meant that this work was developed only in large organisations with large resources. As the construction industry is largely made up of small professional firms and small contractors, the major part of the industry was excluded from most of those developments.

Not only that, but some of the large organisations which developed large computer systems suffered the alienation of the user from the computer. Because the computer and its programming staff were often remote from the user and outside his control, time and resources were allocated only according to someone else's behest.

Even the best systems were often dogged by the "us and them" syndrome. Further, some people became worried about the power they were handling over to departments outside their control.

While the team recognised those problems at a very early stage, there was nothing to be done about it until the cost of computing dropped dramatically.

Initiative and enthusiasm

The microcomputer created this opportunity. One member of the team is a microcomputer hobbyist and it was his initiative and enthusiasm which helped to put together the first configuration working with a conventional colour television set. The original equipment and its cost was:
- Microprocessor with 12K memory £514
- keyboard £248
- cassette tape interface £70
- two cassette tape recorders £30
- colour television set.

With that equipment it became obvious that a great deal of the work could be done on the microcomputer if the systems were scaled down and the configuration enhanced.

Reprinted with permission from *Practical Computing.*

The original equipment was, therefore, enlarged by the addition of

- four direction cursor controls with joystick
- graphical symbol display
- increased display capability
- colour board
- floppy discs
- an extra 8K memory.

At that stage the biggest problem in transferring a system for a large IBM computer to the microcomputer was to stop thinking complex systems. The tendency with large machines is to design so that the maximum amount of work can be processed in the minimum time.

With a system such as the micro-computer we can afford to process work a small step at a time. The only problem with this is that without the overall control normal in a complex program one's steps may be in the wrong direction, therefore the philosophy of programming design has been to keep it simple.

In that way the user has been provided with a reasonably fast response to a series of mundane processing tasks. This means all the programs are written as simple, straightforward processes, often with data input in a conversational manner.

There has been no attempt to double-up the functions of programs the user can initiate another slightly different program for a slightly different task—for example, file creation versus file printing. This approach is thought to be valid because the decision-making of a user who knows the system is bound to be more effective and accurate than that of a program, however complex.

Separate entities

Design and construction in the construction industry are separate, as opposed to most other industries where they are part of one organisation, and, therefore, a convention of communication has to be established. The language of communication consists of:

Symbols which are put together as drawings to indicate the location and type of work to be performed. The drawings are not visual representations of the work to be performed but an amalgam of established symbols. For example, the following symbols are known to everyone in the industry although they do not look strictly like the object.

Manhole	*External wall*	*Door*

Unfortunately, the symbols leave a great deal open to misinterpretation and therefore need further definition.

Considerable repetition

That additional definition and specification is given in alphanumeric terms. The symbols and descriptions are recorded every time as though the situation had never been seen before, whereas in fact for most architects and contractors, there is a considerable repetition of many items.

The rules for manholes are laid down clearly and there are few needs for variation. Similarly with brick cavity walls and so on. A personal range is often used while someone else may have his own different personal range.

Therefore if one prepares one's own set of, say cavity wall types, this can be related to the symbol and given a suffix of A, B or C type or 1, 2 or 3 type. The symbol for cavity wall can be called up on the TV screen and, by means of the joystick control, a plan produced showing where the walls are required. The type of wall can be entered by

- typing in description;
- typing in suffix
- using colour as a selector
- using speech input.

Volumes from heights

If heights are given as the plan is developed, the computer will be able to calculate volume. Therefore it is possible to build up data files which can be manipulated to provide a wide range of outputs. For example, values can be attached to each of the following symbols:

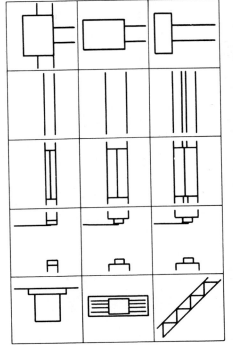

The following values are an example:

- a quantity surveyor's normal unit
- quantity
- the material content
- the manpower content
- the activity content;
- the plant content
- heat loss characteristics

Even taking those few simple items of data, it can be seen easily that simple algorithms can produce a bill of quantities for the 'drawing' on the TV screen; the material, manpower and plant requirements and activity content; critical path networks with outputs under those headings; the total heat loss of the building and from that the quantity and cost of energy input.

They are only some examples of possible usage. It is, of course, possible for a contractor to update his files as often as he wishes, to give himself an up-to-date cost. For example, if each symbol is related to material, manpower, activity and plant files, when any item within those files is updated the computer will update the value for each symbol. Only profit has to be added.

If files are kept on manpower—usually for PAYE purposes in any case—then they will be linked to the symbol description. Therefore, if bricklayers' wages increase, the computer will look for bricklayers throughout the file and update these, similarly with materials.

In that way the up-to-date cost of any building can be produced as it is drawn, to which profit is then added. It is obvious that a variety of designs can be tried and the comparisons between capital cost and running cost carried out quickly. Similarly with other resources.

Two problem areas

The building system has two main problem areas as far as data is concerned:
The size of the database is beyond the capacity of the twin floppy discs. Thus it is envisaged that the user will take the approach of separating information into smaller groups and performing multiple passes against different diskettes. That has the advantage that programs which break down infills into component materials, activity, manpower and plant are run in several passes, giving shorter run times and greater opportunity for control.
Some of the information used in the building industry is very volatile (rates) as opposed to other information which is fairly static (activity times, quantities). To speed processing, this volatile information has been separated from the files of non-volatile information. This means extra processing and easier file-handling in the long run.
The use of speech on this system was developed to ease communication.

With the drawing joystick and keyboard, he has too much to do with his hands. Thus, a vocabulary has been developed so that he can further describe his symbols (the suffix) with speech.

The vocabulary has been paged. The first page contains:
● colour specification
● command words for picture
● manipulation
● page selection for spelling mode
● room description entry.

The analysis and correlation program is written in machine language as an interrupt routine.

Basic the language

The building system is intended to be used in architects', quantity surveyors' and contractors' offices. The computer system demonstrated would need a printer as well as the keyboard and TV display. No office could process Bill of Quantity information without having a hard-copy facility.

It is only budget limitations which have prevented the addition of one to this system. It is felt that a matrix printer is the most suitable type, because the dot matrix characters could then be used in the same way as on the screen to produce hard copy of plans.

Basic is the computing language of the system and has been found to be very easy to write and debug. Only in two cases has machine level programming been used—speech input and screen reading. In both those cases, speed is of the essence and so the Basic interpreter is not satisfactory.

The file handling of the disc operating system was also found to be rather limited. In a commercial situation it is also very necessary to have a rounding function. This could usefully be incorporated in the SWTPC Basic.

It is possible that this type of work may have some significance for the future. The public in the past has found little opportunity for involvement in the design of its own environment because the design/evaluation process takes so long that a commitment has to be made at initial sketch stage. Also enormous resources have been expended by the time a tender and other evaluations are available.

The technique described can be developed to give direct user interaction with his design. Further, with the advent of Teletex and Viewdata, it may be that details of materials and prices could be produced at a national level on the TV screen while using the microcomputer for manipulating the data at a personal level.

This could mean that the small firms of professionals and contractors would be able to compete with the large organisations, having mainframe systems; those larger organisations could break down the size of their units; the ordinary man may be able to become involved in his environment, if not to design some of it for himself.

The Microcomputer in the Construction Industry, by John Paterson, former deputy county architect, West Sussex, now principal of a private practice; Joanna Firth, former systems engineer with IBM and now a researcher at Reading University; and Ted Cogswell, architect in private practice and lecturer at Southampton College of Higher Education.

Owner's Report
THE TRS-80
A.J. HARDING

The TRS-80 is one of the first of the new breed of microcomputers which is now becoming available to the home and small business user, known as "appliance" systems because they are delivered complete with a built in firmware language and are ready for use immediately the power is switched on.

The TRS-80 is manufactured by the Tandy Corporation, an American company which trades as the "Radio Shack" in the United States. The first 200 units arrived in England in April 1978 and I understand that this first batch was sold very quickly. Various articles have appeared reviewing the computer but it was thought that one which relates an owner's experience of it may be of assistance to people who are considering its purchase.

In England, the TRS-80 (Figure 1) is delivered complete as four separate pieces of equipment: the keyboard, which also contains the computer board itself, a video monitor, a cassette tape recorder for programme and data storage and the power supply. In the United States

the monitor and the cassette need not be purchased, enabling the user to save money by using any such equipment which he already owns. Although this may be possible in England, there is no doubt that, at least initially, the sales drive is towards selling the complete system.

Although it is rather paradoxical in an appliance system to buy only parts of the system, there is little doubt that the monitor is over-priced. In the U.S. where 12" portable televisions can be readily bought for under $100, it costs $199.96, so substantial savings can be made. It is not known whether Tandy will go the separate route in England but if it does, it is certainly one which should be considered. The other side of this particular coin of course, is that one of the advantages of buying all of the parts together is that it is *guaranteed* as a system. What Tandy's policy is when, say, only the keyboard is purchased and a fault develops in it which may be the result of a malfunctioning cassette already

Reprinted with permission from *Personal Computer World*.

owned by the customer, one hates to imagine! In any event, so far as I know, the piecemeal approach is not available here as yet, so the point is academic.

As a matter of interest the prices in the U.S. are: TRS-80 complete is $599.95, the keyboard including the computer is $399.95, the cassette is $49.95 and the video display is $199.95. Hence the customer saves about $50 by buying the complete unit, as compared to the sum of the individual prices. In England the price of the system is £499. At an exchange rate of $1.90 to the pound, this means a differential of about £180, which is not as bad as some in this day and age, when it is not uncommon to see the same figure price on both sides of the Atlantic for the same article, even though one is in dollars and one in pounds. If it is any consolation, the price differential between the U.S. and Canada is roughly $300, which is large when one considers that there is only about 12% difference on the different dollars.

The system comes in three cartons, one containing the cassette, the second the keyboard and finally one containing the video monitor and power supply. Also included are all necessary connecting cables and an Operating Manual. For some reason best known to Tandy, at least one of the cartons had been flown to England from the United States *via* a stop in Belgium but despite this somewhat circuitous route no transit damage was evident, no doubt due to the entirely adequate plastic foam packing used. Interconnection between the four parts of the system proved to be no problem at all. Even without the manual instructions it is fairly obvious where everything goes.

It is a pity that Tandy have sought to economise in the type of connectors used. Five pin DIN plugs are used for the three connections to the keyboard unit (Figure 2) and if Murphy's law is to be believed, someone, sometime will insert them incorrectly. Probably exchanging the tape and video connections would not do much harm but connecting the power supply to the video output might well cause some trouble! However, at least these connections are firm and instil some confidence in the user but unfortunately the same cannot be said of the connections to the cassette. As a normal production audio cassette is used, the 3.5 mm and 2.5 mm miniature plugs usually associated with lower cost cassettes are incorporated. The smaller plug is the remote connection to the tape, by which the computer switches it on and off.

On my unit the connection is intermittent and the plug has to be in just the right position for a proper connection. Unfortunately, this is the plug which has to be removed and reinserted when it is required that the tape be manually rewound, a function which the computer cannot perform. This results in the troublesome plug being frequently in use. Checking that proper con-

tact is being made every time that a rewind is performed, is to say the least, inconvenient. The solution is the small modification shown in Figure 3 and consists of a miniature toggle switch which takes over the job of the jack switch, which is activated when the plug is inserted or removed. One word of warning however, the installation of this switch probably voids the warranty on the cassette, although one would hope, not on the rest of the system.

To install the switch remove the back of the cassette by unscrewing the three obvious screws plus the two hidden away in the battery compartment. The printed circuit can be removed but it is not essential because if you look along an inch or two from the set of jacks, two white wires will be seen connecting to the component side of the board. One goes to a ground island on the printed circuit pattern and the other to a lug, the other side of which is connected to a yellow wire. An SPDT switch is used for the modification. Before mounting the switch, remove the yellow wire mentioned and solder it to the centre switch lug. Drill a hole in the plastic case and mount the switch with about four inches of fine wire attached to each outside lug of the switch. After mounting, one of these wires is soldered to the point from which the yellow lead was unsoldered and the other goes to the ground island. The switch will now take over the action from the jack switch and it is no longer necessary to remove the remote control plug at all.

A better modification of course, would be to install the switch as described and then *permanently* wire the three leads which go to the cassette and do away with the plugs and jacks altogether. Tandy are going to introduce a disc storage system to replace the cassette however, so if it is anticipated that this will be purchased, the permanent modification on the cassette would mean that it could not be used as an ordinary cassette later.

Whether or not a user likes the four individual system parts, as compared to other computers, such as the PET, wherein everything is one enclosure, is purely a matter of taste. The interconnecting cables can be a nuisance but on the other hand, the single enclosure is inevitably quite large and cumbersome for desk use. Personally, I think that the advantage of being able to move the keyboard aside easily to make room for the inevitable scribing chores associated with programming, far overrides any aesthetic considerations. Incidentally, a spot of emery cloth rubbed over the rubber feet on the keyboard bottom, works wonders for its stability.

Once one has re-checked the interconnecting cables and plugged into the mains, after changing the U.S. and Continental plugs supplied over to 13 amp ones (but using 3 or 5 amp fuses), the system can be switched on. Neither the switch on the monitor nor the one on the keyboard disconnect the transformer primary from the

mains, so it is better that all mains connections are made to switched outlets, in order that the outlet switch may be used to totally disconnect power, when the equipment is not in use. Otherwise the transformer will be continuously warm and, of course, a small amount of power will always be draining away. The same remarks apply to the cassette. After the application of power the word "READY" will appear in the top left hand corner of the monitor screen together with a prompt sign and the cursor underline. This means of course, that the BASIC is immediately available and the machine is, as it says, ready to go.

Although such efficiency and convenience is to be admired, it does have one very great drawback, namely that there is no way of dropping into machine language *before* the BASIC interpreter takes over. Parenthetically, what a hard to please lot we are! Ever since home computers became available we have complained (or rather some of us have) about manipulating machines with toggle switches in machine language, or having to load paper or magnetic tapes before we can use a higher level language. Now it is all laid on and the first thing I comment on is that machine language is not available!

It is not the purpose of this article to take the reader through all of the specifications of the TRS-80. These are available from Tandy or from previous review articles on the computer which have appeared in various magazines. However, a brief outline is necessary, so that we know what we are talking about.

The TRS-80 in its £499 version is supplied with 4K of ROM, mainly taken up with the BASIC interpreter and 4K of RAM, of which only 3583 bytes are available to the user for programming. At the present time, the RAM can be increased to 16K by the purchase of an additional 12K for £229. Also an improved BASIC, called Level 2, will be available in July 1978 for £79. The Level 1 BASIC supplied is similar to Tiny Basic and contains only the barest bones of the language. There is no doubt that Level 2 is almost essential for serious work. For instance, although two string variables (A$ and B$) are allowed, they cannot be manipulated in any way. It is a pity that at least a comparison of them is not included in Level 1; in other words the command IF A$ = B$ THEN ..... is illegal and results in an error. Most of the other important BASIC commands and statements are included. One array is available and 26 numerical variables.

An important trade off, bearing in mind the amount of RAM available, is that a Shorthand Dialect is permitted for most commands and statements, so that PRINT becomes P., GOTO G., NEXT N. and so on. In a fair length programme this can add up to a saving of many hundreds of bytes. Consequently if a decision of whether Level 2 or more RAM should be purchased arises, the user would be well advised to opt for the Level 2 first.

Unfortunately, nothing is yet known about Level 2 and Tandy are unable to supply even a list of the commands and statements included. As they insist on a deposit in order to assure delivery in July, this seems a little unfair and can be likened to buying a "pig in a poke". The market is certainly a seller's one at the moment! Local managers of Tandy (at any rate certainly mine in Eastbourne) are *very helpful,* within their capabilities in a new field, but apparently experience difficulty in extracting information from Head Office. It must be said in fairness however, that at least the TRS-80 *has been delivered to the market place.* If this necessitated some details getting lost on the way, then it is preferable to simply being on a waiting list! In the U.S.A. waiting lists of months are not uncommon for new micro computers.

The video display has a 12" screen (30 cm diagonal) which is a nice size and is preferable to the 9" screen which some micros have. The characters are legible al-

though sometimes some judicious spacing is advisable. Automatic scrolling from the bottom only is provided. It is regrettable that only one cursor shift direction (backspace) is supported by software at this time, but presumably this will be rectified in Basic 2. The TRS-80 is not as strong on graphics as the PET and other micro computers such as the Apple. Almost any graphic is possible but they are carried out by an instruction to "light" one of 128 horizontal by 48 vertical small blocks, each made up of 2 dots wide by 8 high. The command SET lights a specified block and RESET extinguishes it. This is not too bad with iterative designs. For instance the following programme will draw 22 vertical lines on the screen and can be written in under 60 bytes:

```
10    FOR X = 0 TO 26 STEP 6
20    FOR Y = 0 TO 47
30    SET (X,Y)
40    NEXT Y
50    NEXT X
99    GOTO 99
```

The everlasting loop in the final line ensures that the prompt sign does not appear on the screen. If however a non-iterative design, say the picture of a dog, is the subject of a programme, it gets to be a tedious business!

Incidentally, although the Manual does not mention it, the cursor controls, although not as yet effective in moving the cursor in three directions, may be used in their Shift position in PRINT or INPUT commands to draw arrows on the screen, in any of four directions. The text consists of 16 lines of 64 characters. Tandy say in their sales literature that this is software selectable to 32 characters per line, which presumably would result in larger characters but this is not mentioned in the Manual and despite a telephone call from the Eastbourne manager to Head Office, no information has been forthcoming.

The 233 page Operating Manual entitled "User's Manual for Level 1" will please some customers and horrify others. It is written in a "folksy, lets you me and the computer be friends together" style, common in the U.S. but which will surely grate on the nerves of some customers over here. It does however, succeed in its objective, which is to give a complete newcomer to programming a reasonable grounding in Basic. I personally found it instructive and amusing and am sure that it can teach someone with *no experience* of computers or programming, most of that which it is necessary to know, to get the most out of the TRS-80. Two and a half pages of Addendum are included and although it is a tiresome job, these mistakes should be rectified in the Manual before starting to read it. Unfortunately there are other errors but most of them are fairly obvious and a careful examination of a possible mistake leaves little doubt in the user's mind as to whether he or the manual is at fault.

One serious deficiency is the lack of an index. It is true that the mnemonics for the statements and commands are itemised at the back but they reference to chapter numbers rather than to page numbers. If this is intended to take the place of an index, then it is a poor substitute. One final criticism of the Manual is that the proportion of space allocated to one subject is not in balance with that allocated to another. For instance, over 10% of the Manual deals with the subject of graphics and yet only 8 pages deal with using the cassette for storage and 4 of these are said to be "optional" in that they deal with Data Files. Whilst it is true that due to the restrictions of ROM and the consequential shortage of BASIC commands used, the use of Data Files is very restricted, it is thought that they deserved more mention than an "optional" 4 pages in an Appendix!

In summary therefore, it is fair to say that the Manual does that which it is intended to do and a prospective buyer with no knowledge of computers or programming *can have confidence that it will enable him to use the machine;* but it could have been a lot better, and the student will probably wish to make an additional investment in one of the many books available on the subject of BASIC.

The keyboard, as previously mentioned, includes the computer "works". As might be expected from an appliance machine, the TRS-80 does not lend itself to the add-ons and other modifications so dear to the hearts of the hardware fraternity of home computer enthusiasts but there is a port at the back of the keyboard which gives access to the main board and mates with a 40 pad edge connector. The address, data and control buses are available at this port. Tandy and at least one other firm in the U.S. have brought out an expansion interface and an S-100 bus adaptor is also on the market.

The keyboard itself is of satisfying quality and is formatted in the standard typewriter configuration. Actually, there is only one valid criticism of the keyboard and that is that there is no protection between the keys and the printed circuit supporting them. Thus, when the user is typing he can actually see the copper side of the board through the spaces between the keys. If, like the author, you are prone to a scotch and soda whilst working, keep it well away from the keyboard! The same may be said of the sweat which beads the brow of most programmers from time to time. Any liquid spilling through could do serious damage to the whole machine. Surely even a piece of felt with cut outs for the key stems would have been preferable to nothing?

Perhaps the first programme which should be run and stored on the cassette for future use, is the Diagnostic routine contained in Appendix C of the Manual. This tests the functions of the computer and then tests the individual cells of RAM. As this programme takes up almost all of the 4K of RAM, it takes a while to enter and is certainly worth keeping on tape. I expected some trouble with using the cassette for storage as data dropouts, distortion and other horrors are not uncommon when using audio cassettes. With this unit however I have *not had the slightest difficulty.*

Tandy tell you to keep the volume control set between 7 and 8 but this does not seem to be particularly critical on my machine. On one occasion it was some days before I noticed that the control was around 6 and everything had been going well! Furthermore, one user in the U.S. mentioned a problem he had on the TRS-80 loading, which was cleared when the cassette tone control was changed. Mine works fine regardless of the tone setting. *One important feature* when using the cassette is that the uncertainty, associated with some machines, as to whether a programme is actually "playing back" properly to the computer, has been rectified by displaying two asterisks at the top of the screen. One is displayed when the computer encounters a programme and the other flashes on and off as each line is read. The length of time for which the flashing asterisk is displayed is directly proportional to the length of the line being read.

After a little use it becomes possible to almost recognise a programme by the length of the flashes and their pattern! I find this particularly useful as programme names, in the context of searches (REM of course is permitted) are not allowed. As the computer will read the first programme to which it comes, regardless of whether or not it is the one you happen to require, it is a good idea to have one, or at the most two programmes to a tape. Tandy say that they have 10 minute cassettes available but I have been unable to buy them. If others have the same problem a solution is to buy some "Cassette Salvage" cassettes made by **Bib.** These have no tape in them but do have a double length of leader tape in the cassette shell. Pull this out and cut it in the middle. Mag-

netic tape may then be spliced to each free end, thus making any length of cassette required. I made up several 6 minute tapes in this way and use them for programme storage. Obviously, if you have any cassettes for which you have no further use, these could be cut down to size. Whatever system is adopted the quality of the ferric tape used must be good. It is simply false economy to use cheap tape for computer applications.

As previously mentioned, only a few pages of the Manual are allocated to the discussion of cassette storage and this is why this article has been particularly concerned with the subject. Before we leave it there is one further omission that should be explained for the benefit of those who have no experience of computer languages. The commands to effect a storage and retrieval of a programme on tape are CSAVE and CLOAD. Obviously, a programme may contain letters as well as numerical values, as for instance when PRINT commands are contained in the programme. In the Appendix dealing with Data Files however, instructions are only given with regard to storing *numerical* values on tape and it may be thought therefore that it is not possible to store letters or words following the commands PRINT # and INPUT #, which are the commands used to store on tape information or data other than that in the form of a programme. *This is not so;* but letters, spaces etc. must be enclosed in quotation marks in order to store them:—

```
10    PRINT # "JOHN";",";"HARRY"
20    PRINT # "KATE";",";"JEAN"
30    END
```

And retrieved as:—

```
40    INPUT # A S, B S
50    PRINT A$,B$
60    INPUT # A$, B$
70    PRINT A$, B$
80    END
```

Resulting in the display, after RUN 40:—

| JOHN | HARRY |
| KATE | JEAN |

The above can of course be considerably compacted but has been listed in full to make the point.

Bearing in mind its price range, the TRS-80 can be called a medium speed machine. It will complete a 500 count FOR — NEXT loop in one second. If fifty randomly generated numbers between zero and one hundred are stored in an array, the machine will sort them into numerical order in about 2 minutes.

A few small further points are worthy of mention. The Manual recommends that "P.M." be entered from the keyboard, as a test, when switching the computer on. This is shorthand for PRINT MEMORY and displays the amount of memory remaining. If there is nothing in RAM (as when powering up) the display should read 3583. Sometimes on applying power and carrying out this check, a smaller number will appear, which as the Manual says "indicates that the computer has not powered up properly".

Actually, the problem is the power switch which is not debounced and can switch the poor computer on and off a few times before finally opting for "on", unless it is pressed firmly. After a while this test becomes superfluous as one gets the feel of the switch and knows when it made a hesitating contact.

The instruction GOTO XXX entered from the keyboard, that is, not as a programme line, is interpreted as RUN XXX and the programme pointer will go to line XXX and start running the programme from that point, exactly as it would when encountered in a programme.

In common with most micro computers, the TRS-80 generates a certain amount of radio frequency interference. A weak F.M. station, for instance Radio London received in Bexhill in Sussex, will be drowned out with hash when the receiver is in the same room as the computer, but reasonably strong F.M. stations will not be perceptibly effected. This is something worth bearing in mind when deciding where the computer is to be sited.

A Software Exchange for the TRS-80 has already been started in the U.S.A. and no doubt it will not be long before one is started here. Meanwhile anybody requiring the American address and membership details may obtain it from this magazine or the author.

Whilst this article was being written Tandy in the U.S.A. have announced the (hopefully) final form that their marketing of TRS-80 systems will take and on the assumption that these will cross the Atlantic in the same form, it was thought that a "preview" may be of interest. There are now five versions as shown in the list below. To get a rough estimate of what the systems may cost over here in pounds, divide the dollar amount by a factor of 1.25 but bear in mind that this is only a rough estimate and Tandy have not announced the actual prices, nor even that the equipment will be available in England.

System Name	Contents	U.S. Price
TRS-80 "Breakthru"	As described in this article	$599
TRS-80 "Sweet 16"	As above but with 16K RAM	$899
TRS-80 "Educator"	As "Breakthru" with a "Screen Printer" which reproduces the screen on 5-1/2" tape.	$1198
TRS-80 "Professional"	As above but with 16K RAM, a disk drive, an expansion interface and Level 2 Basic.	$2385
TRS-80 "Business"	As above but with 32K RAM, a line printer and two disk drives.	$3874

Just as "dog bites man" is not news but the reverse is, so it is necessary to realise that the many matters I have not mentioned reflect the computer *working well,* and are therefore not news. The TRS-80 is aimed at that section of the public, whether hobbyist or business, who are interested in computers but know little or nothing about their use. If they have any sense, they are not therefore about to spend thousands of pounds to find out whether they either enjoy programming as a hobby or whether computer usage is viable in their business. For these people the TRS-80 is *ideal*. It is not heavily orientated towards graphics nor towards data processing.

It is a truly middle of the road, general purpose machine at a (comparatively) low price. Within these parameters *it is to be recommended* and Tandy *are to be congratulated* on attaining precisely, what I imagine their design specifications directed them to achieve. In North America alone Tandy have 6000 shops, so by the law of averages, there are going to be an awful lot of these computers around, which has to be beneficial for all owners.

To Buy or Not to Buy: Is that the Question?

BY DAVID PRICE

You've heard computer horror stories before. The myriad computer fraud cases, for instance. Or the programming error that caused the destruction of a multi-million dollar satellite. They're not too hard to find.

If you own a small business computer (or are contemplating the acquisition of one), you'll want to protect your business from the devastation of such an incident. In fact, you'll probably need to be even more circumspect than your counterparts in the big-computer world.

Why? Because the microcomputer market has historically emphasized price competition rather than customer support. Which is all rather ironic, since the small business computer owner needs this support even more than his corporate cousins. Generally, small businesses cannot afford to hire expensive specialists, do not have the expertise in-house, and are less capable of absorbing the concommitant financial loss. In other words, it pays to be prepared.

The purpose of this article is to better equip you for this preparation process. Moreover, it will provide a jumping board from which you can develop your own evaluation criteria.

This article contains many questions, but very few answers, because *you* must consider and answer the questions as they apply to your situation. And you shouldn't be afraid of "undesirable" answers. Remember: you aren't doing yourself any favors by pretending a pitfall doesn't exist or by counting on it going away. Only careful, logical planning will eliminate potential problems.

The Suppliers

If the suppliers are not reliable, a multiple of problems can result. "Suppliers" refers to both the manufacturer and the retailer. They are almost always independent organizations, and both of them should be ready to back up what they sell.

First, consider the manufacturer: does he take pride in his products, or does he seem to be after a quick buck? How long has he been in business? Is his a national organization, or does he operate out of his basement? In short, can you trust him?

Fortunately, incidents of outright fraud are few and far between. What does occur with disheartening frequency are situations where the manufacturer starts with the best of intentions only to discover he simply cannot, for any number of reasons, deliver the product. (He might, for example, find himself unable to secure a certain scarce component.)

Another (infinitely more insidious and not uncommon) setup occurs when a company solicits orders for a product which, unknown to the buyer, doesn't even exist. Why? One explanation was printed in the November 1975 issue of *People's Computer Company*:

"Insiders in the computer world learned a long time ago that things aren't always what they seem. And it isn't just that products aren't always what the advertising says they are: sometimes there isn't any product at all. This can be deliberate. It has been known for a company to announce a new machine in glowing terms, although it did not exist, solely as a maneuver intended to inhibit potential purchasers from buying from a rival. Where this was a straight bait and switch ploy, deliberate intent is obvious. Sometimes the intent may be more honest although the effect is the same. Markets, by definition, are competitive and the timing of the announcement of a new product may be critical to its success. The electronics industry is particularly sensitive to this . . ."

How, then do you avoid getting burned? Here are a few common sense things to remember.

Read up on the product. Find out if it has been reviewed by a magazine, trade journal or club newsletter. Is the article an objective one? If it seems to consist mainly of the manufacturer's puffery, take its claims with a bit more than the proverbial grain of salt.

Ask other hobbyists about their experiences with the product — and the company. (Computer club meetings are excellent for this.)

Study the product manuals. If you can't borrow them from somebody, it might pay to buy copy(s). Most manufacturers will sell you their manuals separately. Find out how well written they are. Note whether they're professionally laid out and typeset, or if they were run off on the office copier. Product manual documentation often offers a clue concerning how conscientious a company is in other areas, as well.

Always remember, you should not be basing your decision on one source alone; gather information from a broad range of inputs.

Illustrations by Nancy Lawrence.

Reprinted with permission from *Personal Computing*.

The Retailer

Even after you're confident you're dealing with a dependable manufacturer, ask the same set of questions about the retailer. After all, quality equipment won't do you much good if your dealer isn't helping you use it properly.

Some people need more hand-holding than others — how much will you need? And how much can you get?

How many of your personnel will need training? Will the retailer you buy your system from train them? How will they be trained? Will they have to attend classes at the retailer's outlet? Will they have to study at home?

Consider durability. What kind of warranty backs up the various hardware components? The software? When the system needs maintenance, how will it be performed? Will you have to bring it in to the outlet, or can you get on-site service during office hours?

And what about preventive maintenance? How long will you have to wait for repair service? How long can you afford to have your operations disrupted while waiting for it to arrive? What will the situation be after the warranty expires? Is a service contract available?

Make sure you get a firm commitment from your dealer in terms of postsale support. And even though the prices

may be lower at the supermarket-type dealer, consider whether you might be better off in the long run by paying a little more for an assured higher level of support.

Evaluating Your Needs

Before you lay down your money for a system, make sure the one you've chosen fits your needs. If the system can't be integrated into your operations and do its job efficiently, it may become an underutilized, overrated, expensive nuisance.

Consider how much staff time will be spent collecting data and preparing it for input. How will this preparation and input be accomplished? Are the procedures workable or will you need to hire additional personnel? Can you see any bottlenecks forming as a result of time-consuming procedures or processes?

When justifying the existence (expense) of your proposed system, consider the output — just how useful will the information generated by the computer be? Will its

frequency suit your needs? What will you be able to determine from this information? To what extent will your short- and long-range strategies be affected by your analysis of it? And taking all this into account, do the benefits of the system justify its cost?

Also keep the future in mind — you wouldn't buy last year's car if this year's model got better mileage for less money. So consider the possibility of system expansion. Does your system allow it, or will you be frozen into one configuration? How easy is it to add to main memory, mass storage and other peripherals, such as input and output devices?

And your software is just as important as your hardware. How expandable is your software? Does the documentation give you the information necessary for later modifications? Can the manufacturer or dealer make these changes for you? At what cost?

The final question concerns the danger of obsolescence. That is, will peripherals, software and service continue to be available for your system? Is it extensively second-sourced? Does it use a standard architecture — such as the S-100, or Altair, bus design — which is supported by many manufacturers? If so, you're on much safer ground than if you commit yourself to an unpopular processor or a nonstandard bus structure. This should be pretty obvious: if your system uses a common architecture, and something happens to your original supplier (heaven forbid), you save yourself from the disaster of being stuck with a machine that *nobody* is supporting. Also, by using a widespread architecture, you wind up with a much better selection when it comes time to buy new equipment.

Don't forget your customers. How will they react to computerized material? Will they benefit from the system, will they be alienated by it, or will they even care? Do the benefits of the system outweigh the risk of depersonalization?

The Options

You don't have to buy a system even if you decide your company is ready. Consider the options available. Many dealers offer lease plans, for example. Timesharing, another alternative, lets you access a remote computer via phone lines, paying only for the terminal time, processor activity and memory space that you actually use. As the name implies, a timesharing system handles many users simultaneously; it responds so quickly, however, that for all practical purposes each user has the functional equivalent of an entire computer at his disposal.

Don't forget the possibility of an outside service bureau either.

All three of these approaches have two rather obvious advantages: first, your money is not tied up by a high initial outlay, and second, because you don't actually own the equipment you're using, you remain free to terminate your relationship with a particular vendor with relative ease.

To summarize: you must decide whether the system is well suited to your application, whether its resources are sufficient to cope with the demands of your application and whether it will disrupt or enhance your operations.

Privacy

Most business applications of computers involve record keeping. In fact, record keeping is usually one of the computer's primary functions. In this area you should think about a number of potential problems.

First, and most obvious, how reliable is your equipment?

A system is only as strong as its weakest link, after all. Does your main memory use some sort of error-checking scheme? Ditto for your mass storage devices: how reliable are they? Remember that no such device is 100 percent error-free; the best you can do is minimize the number of errors.

Current equipment designs have remarkably low error rates, though. Your primary concern should probably be the storage medium itself — the magnetic disks and tapes. Don't skimp on them.

Unless you're prepared for it, a power failure — even a quick brownout — can cause a great deal of harm. If they're common in your area (particularly during the storm season), make sure you're protected. Commercial systems frequently include special power supplies to protect the system from power fluctuations. And, in case of a total blackout, some go one step further and automatically shut themselves down, thus preventing loss of the data in memory (as well as damage to sensitive hardware).

But, in spite of all of your precautions, your records may wind up damaged anyway. The magnetic radiation from your janitor's vacuum cleaner could erase everything on your main disk. What then?

Once again, an ounce of prevention is worth innumerable pounds of cure. One useful practice is to maintain a "backup disk" (or tape). This simply involves creating duplicates of your disks, and storing the copies in a safe place. You might do this at the end of every day, for example. Then, if catastrophe occurs, it won't really be that much of a catastrophe at all, because the only information you'll lose will be that which was placed in the disks since they were last duplicated.

People Problems

Now that you're better protected against hardware and software failure, consider another possible source of error: people. How do you eliminate human error? The answer is, of course, you can't. But you can build safeguards into the system to minimize it.

The very best safeguard is a competent user. Who will be operating the system, or feeding it data? If they're familiar with the usage procedures, you're that much better off. If the general public is to use the system (via public terminals of some sort, or what not), make sure the usage instructions are easy to understand.

Consider the inputs that will be made: do the input-handling sections of the software have safeguards against invalid inputs? Here are a few typical examples:

1) An order number or transaction code. These generally have a fixed number of characters. One useful error-checking scheme would be to make sure that all such inputs have the proper number of characters.

2) Prices. It would not be difficult, in most cases, to define a range of values which would be accepted as valid. If a price outside this range was entered, the user would be asked to verify that figure (or correct it).

3) Dates. Unreasonable values for dates (such as the 32nd day of a month, or the year 1878) are easily caught. Once again, it is simply a matter of determining the minimum and maximum valid inputs.

Thus, you can see it's important to assume the user will occasionally make mistakes. But think about this — in *2001* (the book, not the movie), one of the boys with Mission Control commented, "We can make our systems fool-proof, but there's absolutely nothing we can do to protect them from sheer maliciousness."

Are the contents of your records potential targets for theft or tampering? They probably are. After all, what better way to cover up stockroom theft than to alter the inventory records. And what about payroll files and accounts receivable and . . . well, you know what I mean.

So far, of course, most computer-related crime has involved large financial institutions such as banks and insurance companies. But even though small businesses are a much less likely target, it's always wise to keep on your toes.

Conversion Time

Conversion time: That's the anxious period when the new system is being phased in and debugged. How long will yours take — a day? a week? six months? And to what extent will your operations be disrupted during this period?

In addition to breaking in the system itself, the phase-in period usually includes two more tasks: personnel training and record conversion. The first is self-explanatory. The second, as its label implies, is the process of converting your existing records into a format suitable for the computer. As you can see, both of these points are crucial for a successful conversion period.

Finally, don't forget to include your customers in your conversion plans. By this point, they should be aware of anything concerning the sytem that will directly affect them.

Don't be intimidated by all the suggested pre-purchase planning. I didn't intend to scare you away. On the contrary, the more thoughtful planning you do now, the more trouble-free your implementation will be, and the more rewarding your system will be in the future.

Distributed microprocessing enters the business world

The first electronic typewriter makes it easier for businesses to move toward distributed processing—decentralized computer power. And the typewriter itself uses distributed *microprocessing*—a master Z-80 controller and a pair of F-8 chips—to handle drive motors.

In its basic form, the typewriter, developed by the Qyx Division of Exxon Enterprises Inc., Lionville, PA, does far more than a standard office typewriter. Yet it goes for just $1390—not much higher than the nearest comparable mechanical machine (about $900).

The Qyx typewriter has 70% fewer moving parts than electromechanical typewriters, says Dan Matthias, general manager of Qyx. Microprocessors controlling linear motors replace conventional cables, pulleys, and gears.

The Z-80 microprocessor, from Zilog Corp. (another Exxon Enterprises affiliate), Cupertino, CA, handles overall system control and memory operations. A pair of F-8 microprocessors from Fairchild Semiconductor, Mountain View, CA, controls the linear motors that position the carriage and the rotary print head.

The Qyx typewriter can be expanded beyond its basic functions by adding plug-in boards and changing keyboards —without sending the machine back to the factory and without expanding the size of the typewriter itself.

Typewriter built in blocks

The Qyx Level 1 features dual pitch (either 10 or 12 characters to an inch) and proportional spacing (each character takes up only as much space as it needs). The rotary "daisy wheel" print head is coded for type format, so changing print heads automatically resets the typewriter.

The typewriter can even center a line of type automatically and automatically type columns of decimal numbers so that the decimal points line

up. Stock phrases and formats can be stored and called up to speed typing repetitive forms.

In addition, the basic typewriter has automatic erase backspace. A lift-off tape, like that used in the IBM Correcting Selectric, pulls an erroneous character off the paper so that a correction can be typed. According to Matthias, Qyx has developed the first daisy-wheel printer that can position its print head accurately enough for this function. This is accomplished by building the rotor of the linear print head-drive motor into the $25 print head itself and by feeding-back position information through a light-emitting diode and photodetector sensor.

With an optional $850 display module, a typist can read a line of copy as it is entered, then have it printed after it has been typed correctly. The red LEDs read out upper and lower-case

characters in a 5 × 7 dot matrix format.

The carriage itself rides on a linear motor that is controlled by one of the F-8 microprocessors. Instead of a rotary motor and a series of pulleys and gears, the linear motor can move and position the carriage correctly for character spacing.

Expand to word processor

By adding plug-in boards and modules for data storage, the Qyx typewriter can expand to perform most of the functions of a word-processing system, yet retain its physical dimensions.

An advanced model, the Qyx Level 2, adds store and edit features; add, delete, and move commands; and right-hand justification, when needed. Up to 10,000 characters can be stored in random-access memory.

The Qyx Level 3 typewriter adds a

The first electronic typewriter, from the Qyx Division of Exxon Enterprises, distributes computer-aided typing throughout an office while itself taking advantage of multiple processors—three µPs.

Reprinted with permission from *Electronic Design*, Vol. 26, No. 5 March 1st 1978   Hayden Publishing Co., Inc., 1978.

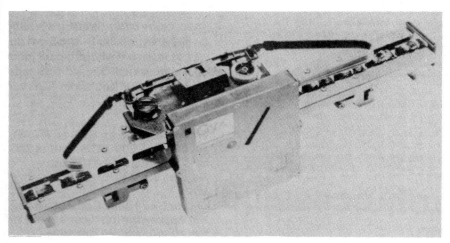

A linear stepper motor controls the position of the Qyx carriage, while a microprocessor controls the motor. The ribbon cartridge is mounted on the typewriter's case, instead of on the carriage, and flexible guides lead the ribbon to the lightweight carriage.

Change a phrase everywhere

The top-of-the-line Qyx Level 5, priced at $7750, includes two diskette 120,000 characters of storage, and features "global change." A word or phrase that appears throughout a manuscript can, with but one correction, be changed throughout the typescript each time it appears.

Any Qyx typewriter can communicate with another Qyx typewriter over standard telephone lines with the addition of a $500 communications module. The module incorporates the features of a modem and a data-access arrangement, so it can be tied to a telephone line directly. The numbers on the typewriter's keyboard can be used to dial the call, and communications moves at 1200 baud. The interface is proprietary, but "will soon be expanded to include communication with Vydec word processors and even to computers," says Matthias. Vydec is another Exxon affiliate.

All typewriters will be available in New York, Washington, and Philadelphia first, and other cities will be added later in the year, according to Matthias. With the typewriters, companies will be able to perform many of the functions of word-processing departments—like duplicate letters—at a secretary's desk, instead of in a separate operation. ■■

buried-media diskette drive to the Level 2 machine. This drive can store up to 60,000 characters.

In the Qyx Level 4, the diskette drive is accessible from the front of the machine and accepts standard 5-1/4-in. diskettes. The accessible drive is slightly different from the fixed drive, says Leon Staciokas, assistant general manager at Qyx, since the accessible drive must be able to position removable media precisely and the nonaccessible

drive must not wear out a semipermanent disc. Yet both use linear-induction drive motors and linear stepper motors to position the read/write head.

The diskette drives are about half as thick as commercially available diskette drives so that they can fit within the typewriter case. Qyx has no plans to offer the drive as a separate OEM product, according to Matthias.

The effect of the microprocessor on the small computer market

by Martin Whitbread

We are told that we are on the brink of a new industrial revolution. This will be caused by the impact of recent developments on microelectronics on all facets of society. For senior staff who are neither engineers nor computer staff there appears to be an information vacuum. It is the objective of this article to examine this revolution and show the effect that it has had on the small computer market.

The key element in the microelectronic revolution is the microprocessor. Its evolution can be traced back to the transistor, first produced in the late forties. After a false start using germanium instead of silicon as a basic material, the race began in earnest. First one, then a few transistor circuits were put onto a single piece of silicon. Later photographic etching techniques increased this number to thousands. What was being created were transistors arranged in circuits, to form large numbers of logic gates. Thus a particular device was designed to meet the needs of a specific application. Eventually an attempt was made to construct a microprocessor, a more flexible structure in the image of the classic Von Neuman processor that is used in mini and mainframe computers.

The two pioneers, Motorola and Intel now dominate the market for microprocessors. Etched onto pieces of silicon about 5mm square, micros do not look like the sort of stuff that revolutions are made of, yet, they are at the very heart of a technology which will tend to change our lives over the next few decades.

● What do they look like?

The silicon 'chip' containing the processor needs some form of mounting and wires connecting its external pins. The now familiar bug shaped component is formed, looking like an entymologists nightmare, the size of a large postage stamp with perhaps forty gold legs (pins).

Like this the microprocessor is a useful as a square wheel. It is a microelectronic component that needs other circuits, particularly interfaces, memory and power supplies. When these facilities have been supplied an operational microcomputer is formed. In line with the continuing trend for increased integration on the chips, microprocessors are now available with memory and interfacing circuits all on the same chip. Such single chip microcomputers will soon be marketed for a few pounds. The impact that these microcomputers will

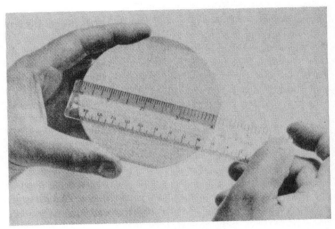

A microprocessor chip on a 4" diameter wafer.

have and are having on the traditional application areas for minis and mainframe computers is a matter for further discussion.

What differentiates between a mainframe and a mini is not just a question of computing power, but also of marketing. Thus the impact of the microcomputer should be examined with respect to both of these areas.

The first task is to provide some definitions. At the lower end of the range of mainframes, where our main concern lies, the small business computer is found; such as the Burroughs B80 or the IBM System 34. These are sold with 'cradle to grave' support; software packages, peripherals and maintenance all being provided. A true minicomputer is a small or medium performance, general purpose, digital computer. It would not be sold direct to the user but to a specialist customer (commonly called an OEM) who would tailor a system for the user. Here are found the DEC minis and the IBM Series 1. Full marks if you have just spotted that IBM is competing with itself or maybe backing both horses.

Small business machines are sold in the user market at the best price that the market will stand. The customer frequently has little computer expertise and the consequent heavy overheads which can be involved in providing support have to be paid for. Selling minis to a demanding OEM market is another

Reprinted with permission from *Management Services*, Vol. 22, No. 12.

matter. The price must be competitive and the technology up to date. Thus a company may buy PDP-11 minicomputers from DEC and use as the computing component in a system that it sells. The final system may be assembled from components from all over the market, printers from Centronics, discs from CDC and visual display units from Newbury Labs. The minis sold successfully in this market are generally those that can support large numbers of terminals. They can do this, not because they were designed to do so, which may seem strange, but because of their origin. These processors owe their origins to process control where the need to handle frequent real-time events is ever present.

In the OEM mini these real time events are signals from terminals. Another happy accident is the ease of interfacing a computer to various peripherals where the computer was originally designed to be linked to a whole variety of industrial plant. Thus the whole thing seems a bit like genetics. These features that fitted the mini for survival in one market have enabled it to thrive in another. It must have worked well, DEC became the number two manufacturer of computers in 1977, right next to IBM, who has responded with the Series 1.

Systems that are designed for real-time working do not often respond well to batch processing. The associated software and file structures may make sorting and merging by conventional means difficult or even impossible. In some cases a relatively small mini can handle an amazing number of terminals, using purpose designed files and programs. A good example of this is the Redifon Seecheck system that can handle over 20 terminals for key to disc operation. This is not a batch system although batches can be received by communications links and sorted with the other terminals maintaining operation, although slightly degraded. In direct comparison it is possible to get a system that will handle both batch and real-time, but the number of terminals that can be supported is down to four or less. Such a system is the Nixdorf 8870.

Before we leave the world of minis and small business machines and return to micros, the types of software support should be considered. The reason why many users turn to a small system when they already have a mainframe is the overload that operating systems can place on the mainframe. This burden is not carried lightly and can be expensive. It is to be hoped that it is a lesson learned, and the mini operating systems will not evolve in the same direction. They are better as an integral part of an application, orientated system. Rather than turn a mini into a poor copy of a mainframe, it would be better in many instances to buy two.

Not only are operating systems for minis developing in their

Nasco's NASCOM 1 Chassis

ability to handle real-time events, but they are also being mated with some very powerful file handling packages. TOTAL is now available on a number of operating systems and provides, along with Data General's INFOS, Hewlett Packards IMAGE and DEC's RMS-11 very powerful file handling and enquiry facilities.

It is enquiry systems that are contributing to the growing use of minicomputers; leaving the company mainframe to do the batch processing. With the type of software support that is becoming available, such systems need not be expensive in terms of hardware. At the same time features such as security, at record and field level are part and parcel of these systems. A user can be prevented from accessing individual records or the enquiry can be restricted to certain items within records. Perhaps even more intriguing is the use of mini computers to emulate mainframe communication protocols. They can also be used to emulate a mainframe peripheral, gaining access to the processor by a high speed if slightly unorthodox link. An interesting use of this ability to emulate, say IBM's 2780 protocol, is that it imposes a standard on different mini computer suppliers. So it is possible to make a direct link between two systems with very little difficulty. For example, a cash receipting system from Datasaab can transmit remote batches to Redifon Seecheck, using standard 2780 software on both systems.

The high performance Z2D Cromemco

A picture has been built up where minis are taking on some of the tasks that mainframes find a burden. They are doing this at a price considerably below that of additions to the central system.

Now that the microprocessor has entered the scene what effect will it have on the mini and small business machine market? Just as the mini must not be seen as a shrunk mainframe, the microcomputer is not a reduced mini. No one would consider towing a caravan with a baby Fiat even less with a moped. The situation with computers is the same the means must suit the ends.

The microcomputer market is more complex even than that for the mini. It is possible to pay from £200 to £10 000 for a microcomputer, based around the same microprocessor.

At the cheaper end are found the single-boarded systems, produced for hobbyists and experimenters as 'evaluation kits'. As an educational tool, properly supported with literature, like the ICS system, they are fine. For serious industrial use, unless the time spent can be written off, it would be better to give it to the engineer and tell him to take it home. For any kind of industrial development, think in terms of thousands, not hundreds. Something like the Cromemco Z2D with a visual display unit and printer will be needed.

Up market from the single board system, an unexpected

group of microcomputers are to be found. At first glance they appear to be key boards that can be linked to a TV set to display the characters typed in and also a domestic tape deck. Well they are that and more. Underneath the key board is usually found a large single board, sometimes acting as a backplane for smaller boards. These devices are complete microcomputers, usually based around the 8080, the Z80 or the 6502 processors (from Intel, Zilog and MOS Technology respectively). Examples are the Micronics Micros, the Tandy TRS 80 and the SOL. Printers Disc drives can be attached to them and they all have BASIC interpreters.

For anyone who is short of time and/or experience a high level language is a must and these systems provide one. Because the BASIC is interpreted, programs can be written or altered and run immediately. There are no complex compilation stages. Of course you cannot win all ways and the resulting programs will be slower than compiled ones, which are not only already converted to the machines code, but optimised as well. Purists will also say that it is more efficient to write in the machine's code directly. Well let them, then drop in and see them as the weeks pass by.

We are on the brink of some action. For around £500 These are 'Personal Computers' and do not present a challenge microprocessors. A few years ago no one would have believed that systems with such power could sell for these prices. By spending a little more one can achieve a great deal more.
Now we can examine three very remarkable machines; the much publicised Commodore PET, the Research Machines 380Z and the Apple II. These all have powerful versions of BASIC, including graphics and the ability to link in specialised subroutines written in the machine's code. Standard interfaces are available, particularly that known mysteriously as RS232 – V24. Using this they can link to minis or even mainframes. These are 'Personal Computers' and do not present a challenge to minis or mainframes but rather a new dimension in computing. They have applications in education, research and business. Most systems of this type have got, or are about to get, printers and disc drives. Software is available, mainly in the form of games or mathematics packages, but this will change. The next twelve months will probably see the introduction of business and industrial packages. With discs and printers the price will already have taken us to £1500 +. Beyond this there is a range of microcomputers that are effectively lower market end minis. They can be used in development projects for micros, for process control or many business applications, such as word processing. Large capacity discs and quality printers are available together with FORTRAN, COBOL and of course BASIC. Disc and real

time operating systems are already marketed. The similarity between these systems and minis is so close as to blurr the picture. In fact systems like the DEC LSI-11 which can run the PDP-11 software are just small computing systems, and we can ignore the 'mini' or 'micro' label.

Just as there are micros that have become lower market end minis, there are others that have become lower end business machines. These are built into desk fittings as a rule, and use a visual display unit, a disc drive and printer. The software is usually tailored by the supplier and unless it is written in say, business BASIC might well restrict the users future operations. The software in such a system must not be rigid, it must allow for tax or organisational changes and therefore must be easily understood. In the Table is shown a number of microcomputer systems, and, for a guide, the typical prices and the type of user who might start at a particular level. This table is only a guide and no doubt points could be argued.

Type	Examples	Typical Prices	Suggested user Entry Point
Single Board	SBC-80/04 Intel SDB-80E Zilog 6800-MDC Motorola COSMAC-VIP RCA	£150-200	Experimental Engineer, Educationalist
Chassis only	NASCOM 1 Nasco Sales TI-990/4 Texas Miproc 16AS Plessey	£200-600	Hobbyist Teacher OEM Designer
Personal (Boxed)	PET Commodore APPLE II Pers. Cmp 380Z Res. Mcns TRS-80 Tandy	£500-1100	Researcher Self-employed engineer or businessman
High Performance	Z2D Cromemco MCZ-1 Zilog Intellec Intel LS1-11/03 DEC F100L Ferranti	£1500-5000	Industrial Designer
Small Mini	1500 ICL-Singer PDP/11/10 DEC Nova Data General	£5000+	Engineer Small DP or Educational System Designer

DEC's digital PDP 11/03

A small mini computer – DEC's PDP 11/10

Up till now no mention has been made of a low market end, small business micro computer. These have been with us for some time and are often based on the Intel microprocessors. Some are marketed with an applications package that can be adapted to the users needs while others have software writing facilities. They are frequently built into a desk unit together with large capacity floppy disc drives, such as the Computabits System 8. There will be a vast market for cheap small business systems — 'there is more business in the desk top computer than all the mainframes have ever provided' — Computing P17 July 6 1978 quoting Alex d'Agapeyeff.

There are problems with the use of microcomputers. Software and interfacing present difficulties but these can be overcome. Software houses and consultancies offer services and the potential user need not feel naked and alone. Special development systems are available from the chip manufacturers, providing diagnostic and testing aids. Seminars are held by On-line, Infotech, BIS and others to help cover this ground and more. The magazines in the bibliography will provide some useful guidance.

My objective has been to show the effect of microelectronics on the small computer market. From where we stand now, it looks as though the effect will be dramatic. Prices have fallen and are continuing to fall, it will lead some say to an information or post-industrial society. Where ever we are going we had better be prepared.

● Bibliography

Electrical Research Association Report on Microprocessors 1977 Ref. ERA 77-1.

NCC Computer Hardware Record on Microcomputer Systems NCC Apl 78.

An Introduction to Microprocessors Aspinal Pitman 1977.

UK Monthly magazines: IPC Microprocessors, ECC Practical Computing Intra-Press Personal Computer World.

Section 3

The Implications of Automation and the Industrial Use of Microprocessors

There is an almost unlimited potential for the application of microprocessors to industrial processes. This section examines several case studies.

The Automated Factory—
A Dream Coming True?

The completely automated manufacturing plant, from numerically controlled machines to computer managed production and inventory control has been a vision of control engineers for at least two decades. This article walks you through one plant where it has all come true, though it has taken heavy government support. Controls range upward from programmable controllers, microprocessors and microcomputers, through levels of mini-, midi-, and maxicomputers. The plant is a paean to computer control, and a model for ultimate control capabilities in private industry. The author is a director and founder of the National Space Institute, and a technology utilization consultant to NASA.

NEIL P. RUZIC, National Space Institute, Washington, D.C.

Your first impression when you view the McDonnell Douglas parts fabrication plant in St. Louis is the sheer size and loneliness of it all. Some two dozen acres of milling machines noisily grind grooves, slots, and intricate patterns in airframe parts to a tolerance of 0.0025 inch. The machines for the most part, work alone—watchdogged by only a few men who glance occasionally at a control panel or sweep the cuttings.

Nor are these men in charge here. The machine tools are directed by numerical controllers, which in turn are directed by a whole hierarchy of computers presided over by a master computer. This 750,000 sq. ft. aircraft parts plant is among the most advanced computer aided manufacturing factories in the world. But it is far from unusual. Highly automated plants elsewhere in the U.S., Japan, and Europe turn out automobiles, engines, earth movers, oilwell equipment, elevators, electrical products, and machine tools. These plants—especially in Japan—are well on their way to evolving into what had been a dream for two decades: the automated factory.

The space contribution

"Unmanned manufacturing" may be a logical contradiction since "manufacturing" literally means "man-made," but it is a perfect description of the goal of many companies throughout the world. The concept had its beginnings some 25 years ago when numerical control tapes and computer graphics using light pens first entered the manufacturing process. These rudimentary automatons were given a powerful stimulus throughout the sixties as we entered the space age full force.

The sudden acceleration in the reliability and sophistication of all kinds of machines, especially computers and adaptive controllers, was a direct offshoot of NASA's zero-defects philosophy required by manned space flight. The forcing function of stringent space requirements imposed computers on American industry, and in the process they increased not just reliability of machines but efficiency and economy as well. As one measure of their success, computers today are growing at the rate of 40% a year (70% a year in industrial control). Soon, by 1980, we will have a million of them installed in industrial control alone. U.S. computer exports increased 1,400% in the first decade of the space age, and virtually every major

Overall view of McDonnell Douglas' heavily automated St. Louis plant.

computer in the world is American made.

All that was just the beginning of the transfer of space technology to the automated factory. Since then the space agency has been deliberately applying its technology to industrial processes. A group within NASA called the Technology Utilization Branch is charged with carrying out part of the Congressional mandate imposed when the agency was established, namely to transfer space technology to industry. In that way, the government attempts to derive double benefit from tax-paid R&D money.

The emergence of computers was a response to our need to derive complex systems for space travel and at the same time was a result of technical information transferred. Take it a step further and you can see how the elaborate advances in computers now have magnified productivity throughout the world in all industries that use computers—and that means just about all industries.

Three breakthroughs
In the slow but inexorable evolution of the unmanned factory, the first segment of the manufacturing process to be-come computer-aided was the fabrication machines that mill, drill, tap, and otherwise form intricate parts from castings or forgings. The breakthrough responsible was direct numerical control, in which a general-purpose computer is connected directly to several numerically controlled machine tools. At Mc-Donnell Douglas, about 100 machine tools are under direct control or soon will be. These machines range from very large multi-spindle, multi-axis profilers to point-to-point drills.

Soon thereafter came computer-assisted design engineering. Both CRT light pens and sophisticated flexible computer programs adaptable to a variety of design problems made it possible. Engineers now could draw their modifications directly on the tube. And programs such as NASRAN (NASA Structural Analysis—which is designed to analyze the behavior of dynamic or static structures of any size, shape, or purpose—began to save millions of engineering design dollars each year.

The third entrant to computer-aided manufacturing was the adaptive control system. Here both the speed and feed of a cutting tool are adjusted automatically from the environmental cutting conditions such as deflection, torque, and heat generated. In other words, environmental conditions feed back to the controller to determine what action is to be taken.

Planning the process
With these breakthroughs you now could design by computer and produce parts by computer. The large step in between—process planning—was next to undergo the rigorous definitions and thought disciplines inherent in computerization.

"Companies make or lose money on the effectiveness of their process planning," according to Louis N. Mogavero, chief of NASA's Technology Utilization Branch. Mogavero should know. Prior to coming to the space agency he was in charge of process planning at Vertol Corp. (a Boeing subsidiary) in Morton, PA. An entire floor of engineers and technicians he directed now have had their jobs upgraded as computers have largely taken over the process planning function.

In order to help push the state of the art and help transfer space-derived computer technology to industry, Mogavero's office last year supported a

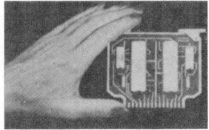

Computers in this extensive system range from 0-8k, $500-$3,500 micros to 6,000k, $4,7 million IBM 370s.

Drawing part changes directly on the CRT speeds their implementation in the manufacturing area.

project at McDonnell Douglas Automation Co. in St. Louis. NASA invested funds and expertise that were matched by a unique organization called Computer Aided Manufacturing International. CAMI is a nonprofit R&D association based in Arlington, TX, with 106 company and university members throughout the world concerned with applying computers to manufacturing.

Success stories involving computerized manufacturing have oversimplified the difficulties in achieving such successes. Thus CAMI both creates and disseminates information in an attempt to solve many fundamental problems in automating the various plants of its members. For instance the NASA-CAMI-funded project at McDonnell Douglas sought to automate the process planning phase in such a way that it could serve as a model for other manufacturers across diverse industries.

Today, as a result of that and similar projects, the entire spectrum of planning and producing a manufactured part are automated at McDonnell, both for greater economy and higher reliability. In fact, the Department of Defense credits computer-aided design and manufacturing here as being mostly responsible for the air superiority of the F-15 Eagle.

The automation of process planning is considerably easier in plants that produce parts in great volume, such as for automobiles. However, through the ingenuity of computer experts this technology also now can be used in small-volume plants. The complex fighter planes that cost $10 million or more each require relatively low-volume production, for instance. In fact, 75% of all parts made in the U.S. are made in quantities of 50 or less. The emphasis thus has had to be on flexible methods of planning batch manufacturing. One approach is to program machine tools to carry out different operations on a variety of parts with minimum human supervision.

Another is to redesign the part so it will fit existing machines. When engineers in an aircraft or other plant design a new machine, they invariably call for a host of entirely new parts. Then the process planners (who used to be called production engineers) redesign the part so it can be made faster or more simply, perhaps on available machine tools, or in combination with other parts. They establish a plan by which the part is made. The "process plan", for instance, specifies whether the part is to be made of titanium rather than aluminum, how it will be milled, which fixtures and jigs will accept it, how it is to be heat-treated and how, where, and when it will be sent for assembly.

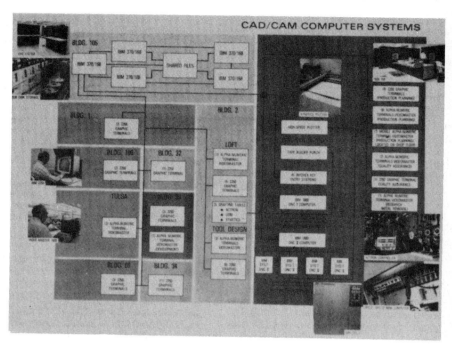

Block diagram of McDonnell Douglas' CAD/CAM computer systems shows 58 points of access to the system via CRT.

While some of the computer equipment has to be operated in environmentally safe rooms, such as the IBM 1800 (above) much of the control system must operate in a manufacturing floor environment.

Bulkhead for twin-jet fighter is one of the parts whose design and manufacture is heavily computer-controlled.

Finding common denominators

To automate that process, planners seek the common denominator among different parts. "You would be surprised," says Mogavero, "at the tremendous similarity among parts, even from one complex modern aircraft to another." Mogavero, who helped develop the idea of reproducibility in the early 1950s, simply extended the mass production premise that "you have to make a lot of the same part to make money."

Today, where process planning is automated, all parts that have been made for any product are defined and stored in the computer. The size, function, and other parameters of any part can be recalled and modified if necessary to fit the new requirement.

Yet reproducibility is only one ingredient in commercializing a product. Even if you can reproduce machined parts like a biological organism, by the millions, you still need to examine the market, the capital investment required, and other economic factors. "Engineers are notorious for tunnel vision," according to Mogavero, who himself is an engineer. "We normally think about *how* you can make something—not how you can make it *profitably*."

Process planning is the key to intricate manufacturing procedures. An example of how process planning integrates various manufacturing operations is offered by J. H. Schulz, director of industrial engineering at the McDonnell St. Louis plant.

McDonnell Douglas' system

Here parts fabrication is housed in a 750,000 sq ft building. Major and final assembly buildings containing another million sq ft each are nearby. In recent years the plant has turned out about 5,000 F-4 Phantom airplanes, lesser numbers of F-3H Banshees and F-101 Voodoos in the 50s and 60s and, currently, F-15 Eagles.

Schulz explains that computer-aided manufacturing has resulted in greater design freedom, better management control, shorter lead time, greater operating flexibility, improved reliability, reduced maintenance, reduced scrap and rework, and—as a result—increased productivity.

Design freedom: It doesn't do much good to design a complex part if it cannot be made efficiently. Graphic numerical control, in which the mathematical representation is stored in the computer's memory, allows process planners to produce the part.

The parts programmer accesses this same data to design the required fixturing, and then uses graphics to create the part programs to fabricate the tool-

ing. Finally, the quality assurace programmer, also using a CRT terminal, accesses the data to create a program for inspecting the part. Thus, computer graphics not only allows more complex parts design, but also reduces costs and time.

Adaptive control provides better part tolerances and guarantees that a given accuracy will be met, thus reducing rejects. Since the human machinist cannot override the feed rate, adaptive control also improves part run time. Another system, fondly called "IRS" for "Improved Reliability System," assures that part tolerances are not violated. These systems result in 20% more production.

Shorter lead times: Two factors shorten lead times: the design and programming of the part, and actual time required to fabricate the product. Time to produce a good parts program is substantially shortened through both the graphic numerical control and a remote processing system called "RAPID." RAPID is a tortured acronym containing an acronym: "Remote APT (Automatically Programmed Tools) Processing via Interactive Devices." Parts programs are created with coding manuscripts and the jobs are submitted to the computer in batch mode.

The parts program is stored in an online data base for retrieval through a CRT display. The parts program is viewed, modified, and processed. Its output is reviewed and placed in a retrieval queue, all interactively from the display. When the programmer is satisfied with his program, he transmits it to the large computer for plotting. These systems facilitate the incorporation of engineering changes to existing parts, eliminating the confusion and the sometimes panic of pre-automated times.

Greater operating flexibility is achieved by having the computer in the loop. A job can be transferred from one machine to another in minutes using direct numerical control. Changes can be made in programs and machining cycle restarted in minutes. The tedious task of bookkeeping parts programs is handled automatically by the computer assuring that only the properly updated command information is delivered to the shop floor.

Improved reliability is effected through several programs, of which the conversion to direct numerical control is the most significant. A recent analysis revealed a 55% improvement in scrap rate on those machines converted to direct numerical control. It is the mission of the direct numerical controller and the improved reliability system to insure that the programmed data reliably cuts the part once the information arrives at the machine tool.

Redundant data checks are built into the master computer (IBM 370), through the process-control computer (IBM 1800), down to the controller on the floor, thus increasing reliability. An information-management system upgrades the reliability of the initial data used to produce the part. This system assures that a valid parts program, with no unexpected changes, is being sent to the machine tool.

Reduced maintenance is the result of many factors. Direct numerical control entirely eliminates the high-maintenance tape reader of a conventional numerically controlled machine. Integrated circuits in the controllers have fewer malfunctions. And since most of the logic functions are accomplished in the minicomputer, less hardware is employed in the controller.

Less scrap: A machine tool run by a direct numerical controller and integrated into the improved reliability system virtually eliminates all scrap and rework. During the first month of operating a profiler watchdogged by the improved reliability system, two events took place that would have scrapped three F-15 titanium bulkheads and two DC-10 flap hinge fittings if the system had not shut down the machine. Value of the parts was $80,000. Cost of installing the improved reliability system was $20,000 per machine.

Higher productivity: The pressure to deliver reliable, highly sophisticated fighting-flying machines mandates objectives of increased productivity. Of course, in a broad sense, increased productivity is the goal of all manufacturing efforts.

At McDonnell Douglas, it is attained with adaptive control because the machines can cut metal faster and more efficiently. And parts programs are optimized even further using the RAPID system.

But another way of increasing productivity is to reduce "dead time:" the time a machine is not working caused by controllable factors such as lack of cutters, fixtures, or materials. Dead time at McDonnell was 7% before a management data reporting system was automated. Devices for manually entering information were provided on the direct numerical controller console and provisions made to sense certain machine conditions automatically. The result is a series of management reports indicating production bottlenecks—which still occur now but considerably less frequently than before.

Progress by the centimeter

The McDonnell Douglas progression toward the automated factory is fairly typical, although more advanced, than

Down on the shop floor, the operator rides herd on one of the big direct numerically controlled machines. The panel (above) keeps him informed of DNC and tool status.

at the average airplane, auto parts. or machinery producers. Such manufacturers as Otis Engineering, Caterpillar Tractor, Ingersoll-Rand, Sundstrand and Allis-Chalmers have automated their batch manufacturing processes quite ingeniously. Computers select parts from a transfer line and feed them to the cutting machines that mill, bore, turn, tap, and drill—all automatically.

Yet, all of these operations are experienced-based. They must be programmed for a specific task and so can't be transferred directly to other situations without modifications. While these factories are relatively lonely places, they are not unmanned.

You get the feeling that a dramatic breakthrough is required, a fundamental change. If the machines were alive, you would say they need a dose of intelligence, a mutation into a higher being. Intelligent machines that sense, recognize, remember, learn by experience, and respond like a rudimentary human brain, the robots of tomorrow, are theoretically feasible. Self-organizing systems that learn from their environment and their experience have been demonstrated repeatedly for two decades in research laboratories. But there they remain curiosities, unapplied to automated manufacturing.

The fact is that the United States—despite its enviable technological lead and despite a necessity mothered of high labor costs—is not pushing the unmanned factory any faster than other countries. The concensus at CAMI seems to be that Europe and the U.S. are on a par, and that Japan is forging somewhat ahead.

The Japanese edge
Japan's fast-growing industrial capacity not only supplies an enlarged domestic market but makes it possible to compete in most other countries. Perhaps the incentive to boost productivity is greater in this single-minded island

nation. Japan Inc. truly is an alliance of manufacturers and government, as opposed to the often-antagonistic government-industry relationship in the more-diversified United States.

Whatever the reason, unmanned manufacturing plants seem closer to achievement in Japan than in the rest of the world, according to several CAMI members. The Japanese Ministry of International Trade & Industry announced last year that the basic methodology for the unmanned factory has been completed. The statement implies utilization of a universal principal, which is to be demonstrated by 1980, with the first factories operational by 1990.

The unmanned plant the Japanese are considering need employ only one per cent of a conventional plant's labor force. Twenty people would operate a factory that employed 2,000 workers in pre-automation days. Not only will such a plant automate the design, process planning, and fabrication functions, but it also will bring the entire assembly operation under computer control.

Already at several factories operated by the $6-billion a year Hitachi Ltd. and by the Honda Motor Co., subassemblies are brought together on a conveyor line and held to each other by clamps. When the parts—electric machines or auto body panels, for instance—reach a welding machine, hundreds of welding heats are aligned automatically and the parts are welded. Other conveyors and staging areas converge to put together many of the subassemblies. Direct numerical controlled machines are more commonplace than in the U.S. or Europe. The whole country seems to be moving together toward a national goal of complete automation. First the tooling machines themselves are automated, then a group of machines, and finally the whole plant.

In the United States and Western Europe, a few sophisticated industries

such as aircraft, auto engines, farm equipment, electrical equipment, or machine tools have highly automated plants. But other companies that make ships, homes, steel, textiles, or scientific instruments seem to employ almost as many people as they did in the days of Charles Dickens.

Inexorable trendline
Despite that possibly exaggerated commentary, the automated factory continues its inexorable evolution. The trend is set. It simply may take longer in the United States and Europe. Some have predicted the first completely automated factories in the U.S. by the mid-1990s, soon after the Japanese forecast.

Factors contributing to the trend toward unmanned manufacturing are everywhere evident:

■ Economic forces such as inflation and higher labor rates, along with increased governmental regulation per employee.

■ New generations of faster computers and more flexible software.

■ The spread of automation from industry to industry, such as the recent entry of computer-aided manufacturing in the chemical processing industry.

■ Closer supervision of process through the use of improved man/process interfaces.

■ Upgrading of numerically controlled machines to direct numerical controls.

■ The influx of microprocessors and integrated circuit "chip technology."

■ A greater emphasis on the transfer of money-saving, often advanced, space technologies to a variety of industrial processes.

That these trendlines are converging toward unmanned manufacturing—the most dramatic breakthrough since Henry Ford first harnesses a conveyor belt—is unmistakable. Only the timetable is in dispute.   □

A robot army lines up for inspection

One of the fastest developing technologies must be robotics. And companies well-known in other fields – such as car manufacturing – are now contributing to the growing army of industrial robots. Brian Rooks, who monitors robot developments for Birmingham University, sends us this report from the recent robots exhibition in Stuttgart.

This Oglaend Move-O-Matic Mini-Mater has a load capacity of 6 kg and control is by electronic plugboard.

The exhibition which accompanied the Stuttgart conference demonstrated the extensive choice of industrial robots now commercially available. Most of the familiar names were there, including Unimation, ASEA, Trallfa, Siemens (selling Fanuc), Acheson (selling Prab), Bosch (selling Electrolux) and Olivetti. Unimation exhibited its large 4000 machine as well as the fast, highly manoeuvrable, computer controlled Vikarm. ASEA demonstrated the versatility of its units with arc welding and grinding operations. Trallfa had an arc welding application as well as its popular paint spraying robot, and Olivetti showed their Sigma robot which has little competition so far in assembly work.

However, despite these highly attractive demonstrations, probably the most striking feature of the exhibition was the number and quality of the less well-known robot suppliers now appearing on the scene. Many of these companies are well-known names in other areas of technology, but now it seems, they intend to make their presence felt in the industrial robot field. The most familiar among them was Volkswagen, which has been 'toying' with robots for five or more years. Judging from the effort put into its presentation, Volkswagen is now obviously a serious contender in the market. As a result of developments over the years, VW is now selling four robot devices, which it classes as its second generation. Three of them were exhibited at Stuttgart, a K15, an L15 and an R50. The K15 is of the articulated arm type with five axes of movement, a load ca-

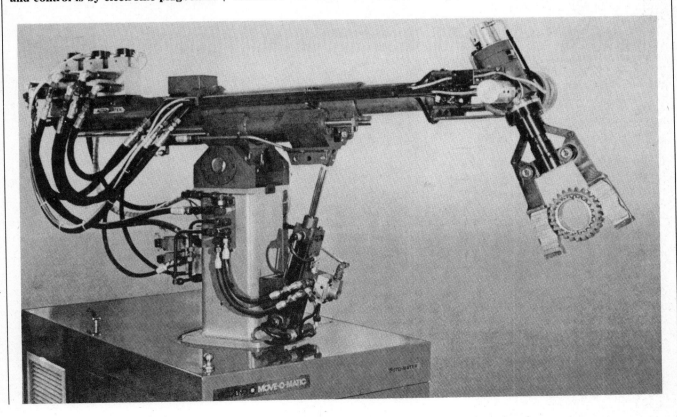

pacity of 15 kg, and was shown in an arc welding application. Both the L15 and the R50 are of the spherical co-ordinate type. The L15 is particularly suited to press loading/unloading, where its long (1800-mm) and fast (1·2-m/s) horizontal reach are very valuable. The R30 can handle loads of up to 30 kg with a positioning accuracy of ±1 mm, and is available in modular form with up to six axes of movement. The VW robot not exhibited – the R100 – can handle up to 100 kg, has a horizontal reach of 2000 mm, lateral traverse of 1000 mm, and is intended for spot welding.

Minicomputer control

All the VW robots have dc motor drives, absolute encoder feedback and operate under minicomputer control. Programming is by means of the now-familiar push-button 'teach-in' method. The normal method of control is point-to-point, but the K15 can also be used in a continuous mode. At present, VW has 100 of its robots in its own factories and 15 with other users. But with a current production rate of 3/week these figures can be expected to change soon. To assist in expansion of sales, three firms of international repute have been appointed agents for VW robots.

Zahnradfabrik Friedrichshafen is not as internationally well known as Volkswagen. The company is a volume producer of gears, which now also makes and supplies robots. The company produces and markets under licence the Oglaend Move-O-Matic range, which includes the Mini-Mater and Auto-Mater robots. The Mini-Mater is an air-driven 3-axis cylinder co-ordinate unit, with two adjustable positions per axis and a load capacity of 6 kg. Control of the Mini-Mater is by an electronic plugboard system. The larger Auto-Mater robot is of the spherical co-ordinate type, with a normal load capacity of 35 kg, which can be increased to 60 kg at reduced operating speeds.

This device uses a hydraulic servo drive with positioning accuracies of ±0·5 to ±1·5 mm on the three main axes. The normal horizontal extension is 500 mm but a reach of 1000 mm is also available. Operating speeds of 1 m/s can be achieved.

On show at the exhibition was a large cylindrical co-ordinate machine which has a load capacity of 35 kg, a horizontal traverse of either 1000 or 1200 mm, and a vertical movement of 600 mm. Both this latter unit and the Auto-Mater are available with a choice of control systems, namely plugboard, programmable controller or minicomputer (with a 'teach-in' programming facility). A fourth robot in Zahnradfabrik's range features modular construction with up to three main axes (cylindrical co-ordinates), each of which is fitted with two or more fixed stops providing positioning accuracies of ±0·1 to ±0·5 mm. The normal load capacity of this device is 20 kg, increasing to 40 kg at 50 per cent of the rated speed (1 m/s for the linear axes). Control of this robot is by either plugboard or programmable controller.

Modular units are also the basis of systems by two other manufacturers exhibiting at Stuttgart. The Swiss company Robitron offers a range of linear and rotary units – driven either by hydraulic rams or by stepper motors – which can be built up into various configurations of robots. One such robot on demonstration comprised three linear axes under continuous path control, and a rotary 'wrist' motion to which a spray gun was fitted. The control system uses a microprocessor and is capable of handling up to 99 different programs.

Fibro-Manta markets a range of modular units similar in concept and appearance to the Robitron range. Modules consist of four long-stroke linear units (up to 1250 mm), four short-stroke linear units (up to 150 mm), five rotational units, and four types of two-fingered grippers. All are hydraulically operated. In addition, several constructional elements are available, including a base unit (into which the hydraulic power pack can be built), box columns, gantries and C-frame units. The programmable controller system operates in a point-to-point mode with up to seven axes and 32 steps.

IWKA is a well-known supplier of

welding equipment to the car and construction industries. The firm also supplies industrial robots for a wide range of applications in addition to welding. The range includes the Aida Autohand, the PPI PM12, and the Kuka and Kuka-Nachi models. The latter probably represents the widest range of industrial robots available from a single supplier. On show was the Kuka-Nachi 5000, a 6-axis device of the articulated arm type primarily designed for paint spraying. It operates under continuous path control with a magnetic disc memory. Programming is in real time, by the normal 'teach in' method.

Other Kuka-Nachi models in the range are the cylindrical co-ordinate type 1000 for press, machine tool loading and so on; the spherical co-ordinate type 2000 for applications in hot environments; and the cartesian co-ordinate type 4000 for arc welding. The 4000 has a special control system which enables teaching to be carried out in a point-to-point manner but for playback to be under continuous-path

Two Volkswagen L15 robots working together to load and unload press components.

control, using linear interpolation between the programmed points. Program storage is on magnetic disc with a maximum capacity of 3200 points.

IWKA also markets Kuka robots, which are primarily designed for spot welding applications. The Kuka 6/60 is a 6-axis DC motor-driven device with a load capacity of 60 kg, or 100 kg at reduced speed, and is, therefore, capable of handling heavy weld guns or of being used in other heavy-duty applications. Control of the 6/60 is by a CNC system which in its standard version allows up to 600 program steps per axis, although this figure can be increased for much larger programs. For the really heavy-duty operations there is the Kuka 4/150, with a normal load capacity of 150 kg. This 4-axis cylindrical co-ordinate robot also has DC motor drives, and uses the same control system as the 6/60 robot.

The smaller end of the robot scale was represented at the exhibition by Fichtel & Sachs, which sells the modular Star-O-Mat pick and place unit, and by Felss, which offers the Felsomatt range of pick and place robots. The Felsomatt FE range is modular and can have up to six degrees of freedom. There are two base units which provide either a 180° rotary motion (FE29), or a 180° rotary motion plus a 75-mm lift motion (FE30). To this base unit various single, double or multi arms can be added. They are capable of handling loads of 5 kg at cycle rates of 30/min. Three control systems are available with the units – fixed sequence relay, fixed sequence electronic and programmable controller.

Expanding grippers

One exhibitor at Stuttgart was solely concerned with the sale of standard gripper devices. Carl Freudenberg sells a standard range of internal and external expanding grippers. Of particular interest are flexible fingers which under pressurisation, curl and thereby grip a component. These fingers are available as single units so that quite complex grippers can be built up, or in pairs mounted together on a cross member. Internal grippers operate on the expanding 'air bag' principle, and were demonstrated lifting a cylinder block by gripping its cylinder bores. These grippers are capable of withstanding lifting forces of up to 450 N.

The lasting impression gained from the exhibition was that West Germany now has a significant robot industry. Only five years ago there were no robot manufacturers at all in the country while now there are some 12 companies making or selling such equipment. This rapid advance indicates the impact industrial robot technology is having on the West German industry. It also suggests that the industrial vigour and dominance of that country as a manufacturing force is going to continue for many more years. □

AUTOMATION

MIX THE MODELS WHEN ROBOTS DO THE WELDING

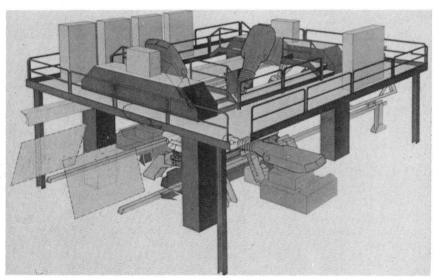

The Robogate welding line at Fiat enables it to switch models precisely to demand and change body design at low tooling costs. By John Hartley

By any standards Fiat's Robogate welding line is a highly automated and productive method of welding car bodies. But it also overcomes a number of problems inherent in the motor industry.

The line allows output of cars by model mix to match demand precisely; it enables body design to be changed at very low tooling costs; and in theory makes it possible for any model to be built in any factory.

Fiat has installed two Robogate lines, one at the Rivalta factory in Turin and the other at Cassino in southern Italy, to produce the new Ritmo in three- and five-door form. The plant at Rivalta, three months ahead of that at Cassino, is building 350 cars a day, compared with a production target of 800 a day.

Robogate is a method of welding the main assemblies of the body together — the framing operations — entirely by robots, so that the need for hard automation is almost eliminated. Fiat is also installing Robogates to weld up side assemblies, and these should be operational by September.

Instead of passing the body between rows of robots on a shuttle mechanism, Fiat takes the body by trolley from Robogate to Robogate. Each Robogate is a four-post structure with a pair of transverse gantries and overhead walkways carrying control cabinets.

So the Robogate itself is a standard unit with each gantry designed to carry a robot, while there are normally a pair of floor-mounted robots as well. The equipment is made by Comau, Fiat's machine tool subsidiary.

Trolleys. The Robogates are mounted parallel with one another, the body being carried from station to station on a Digitron trolley — Fiat calls it the Robocarrier — guided by cables under the floor.

The advantage of the Robocarrier over a shuttle mechanism is flexibility in that any model can be passed through the system with minimal changes. There is potential for by-passing a station, or for buffering or queuing between Robogates.

But accurate jig location is just as important with the trolleys as it is with a shuttle. Special pallets carried on the trolleys are located to the body at four precise points, while there are also two clamps.

When the Robocarrier arrives at a

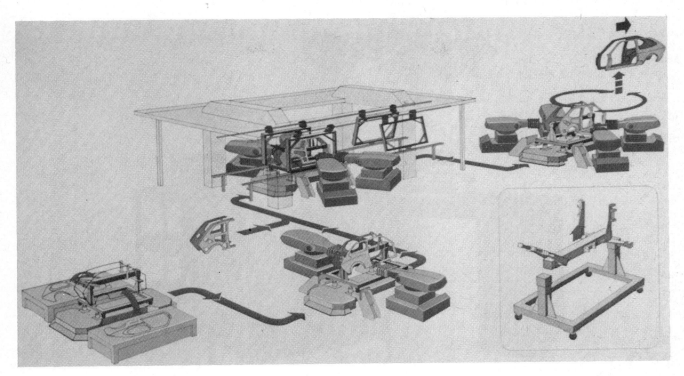

Above: The Robogate concept for body sides, which should be operative by September this year. Above left: Comau robots are used at only one station. Left: The Basic Robogate unit consists of a four post structure, four robots and the control system. Right: At the first station of the Robogate system, the body is located from its fixture and also by the side frames which are incorporated in the Robogate itself. Below: Equipment painted yellow only is peculiar to the Ritmo car

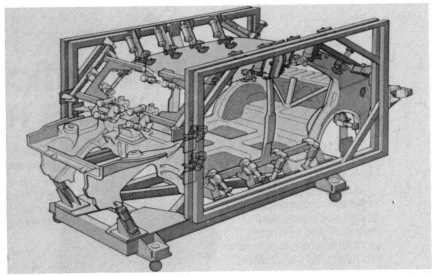

Robogate the pallet is located in the fixture. The pallet is dropped in position, a ball of approximately 120mm seating in a conical seat providing one positive location and a V-block the other. There are also a pair of flat pads.

At Rivalta the Robogates are installed in an area fenced off from the rest of the shop. Since plenty of space is needed on each side of the row of Robogates for the trolleys to manoeuvre the installation appears bright and spacious.

In all, there are eight Robogates with six stations; two Robogates are needed at the first and second stations owing to the number of operations carried out there.

At the first three stations each Robogate has four robots, two mounted overhead — these are all Unimate 2000s — and two on the floor. There are three robots at the fourth station, and two floor-mounted robots at the remaining positions.

Teething troubles. At one of the second station Robogates, two Comau Polar robots are used, the remainder being Unimate 4000s. So far Comau has built few robots, and I was told this is why only two have been instal-led. But plant director Augusto Riggi said these robots have 'not been a good experience', as numerous teething troubles have been encountered. In all there are 27 robots in the installation, with another 24 being installed for the assembly of the sides.

Fiat intends to continue to weld underfloors and similar assemblies by transfer press welders, the technique used on the Ritmo. At the end of the lines the assemblies are taken to a fixture where they are fitted together manually. Tabs locate the assemblies together — 12 in all, some simple tongue and slots, others folded over —

and then the body is transferred by overhead conveyor to the Robogate area.

Here Fiat has had problems and found it necessary to add a pair of operators to ensure that assemblies are located correctly before they proceed to the first Robogate. As the body is carried on the conveyor the sides tend to sway relative to the underbody.

At the Robogate area the body is lowered on to a pallet on a trolley. The men check the locations and add a filler panel, and then the trolley enters the first Robogate.

Installed at this station only are the side frames that locate the assemblies together, and reassert the basic dimensions. These side frames, which incorporate locations for both three- and five-door models, are suspended from rails in the Robogate and can move longitudinally. Their lower faces lock into position in clamps.

With the assemblies correctly located some 80 spots are welded to tack the body together. Since some of the positions where welds must be made are inaccessible, this operation is scheduled to take 1 min 58 s. When welding is complete the body is released and raised up by the trolley, which then reverses out of the Robogate and moves to the second station.

Here some 170 welds are made by the four robots in the same long cycle time. At subsequent stations 30-50 welds are made so the cycle time is nominally 59 s. Thus the robots weld at 10-22 spots/min, which is relatively slow.

Computer control. The robots, trolleys, side frames, and fixtures are all controlled by a PDP 1170 computer. A similar computer is kept as a back up; in event of failure it is possible to switch from one computer to the other in about 15 min since a special board changeover system has been adopted.

In making the Robogate system operational the main problems have been synchronisation of all units controlled by computer. Since each has to be controlled independently a lot of development was needed — and from what I saw there are still problems.

With a cycle of 59 s the plant has a nominal two-shift capacity of about 960/day. Fiat quotes a capacity of 840/day whereas a realistic rate is probably 750/day.

The limiting factor seems to be that the Ritmo body was not designed h Robogate in mind; many essential ʈackwelds involve the robots in long traverses. Presumably on the next body to be fed through Robogate — the 127 replacement expected in a couple of years — the design will be arranged so that tackwelding is faster.

Eight Robogates are installed in parallel at Rivalta, the bodies being moved between them on Digitron trolleys

The body is mounted on the special fixture when it arrives in the Robogate area; common fixture locations — the four posts — are used here and at the Robogates

At the moment 350 cars are being built daily. Although the system is set to the nominal cycle time there are still engineers and specialists around to keep things operating.

One feature of the project has been the large number of people involved from different countries. There have been Americans, Britons, Swiss, and others from firms outside Fiat in Italy. Yet despite that in four months a completely new concept has been

taken from nothing to almost 50% capacity — quite an achievement.

The costs. But how does the costing work out? Fiat claims that the Robogate line involving a total investment at Rivalta of £13 million costs 30% more than a conventional line. This includes some manual welding, and some presswelding, and the line occupies twice the area.

Against that the 125 people needed

on the traditional line are replaced by 25 on the new line. There are eight men on the line, two operators loading components, two computer programmers, two electronic and two mechanical maintenance men. The others are back-up maintenance staff.

Reduced manning levels clearly create the opportunity to cut labour costs by £500 000 a year. But what was the attitude of the unions?

'Positive', said plan director Riggi, because there was no reduction in the total workforce at Rivalta and because unions recognise that working in a framing section is unpleasant. Introduction of the Ritmo has led to an increase in the Rivalta workforce of some 300 people, so Fiat has not really had to face the problem of loss of jobs.

In the short term Robogate gives Fiat the chance to match the demand for three- or five-door cars precisely. Usually, the balance is not correct, with the result that one line is under-used and the other one is under continual pressure. The men welding the bodies manually feel the balance results in them working too hard — and that can lead to industrial unrest.

When the new 127 comes on stream Fiat will be able to pass two models through the same Robogate lines. One set of side frames will be stationed at each end of the Robogate, one for Ritmo, and the other for 'No. 1' as the 127 replacement is known. Therefore the Ritmo bodies would always move in and out on one side of the line and the No. 1s on the other side.

Economic. When Robogate is used in that way the economics will look much better. Cost of the extra pallets and side frames will be small and the system will occupy no more space. With traditional assembly, two lines would be needed for the Ritmo and No. 1. Then, when the Ritmo body is eventually restyled the tooling costs will be low — only the pallets, side frames, and computer program will need changing.

But perhaps the least obvious advantage is the effect of a failure. As systems become more complex, and the level of automation is increased repairing faults takes longer.

With a completely integrated line a small failure can completely stop production for an hour up to a complete shift.

The Robogate offers flexibility in that one line would be bypassed and the body would automatically be identified as being in need of some manual welding. The amount of manual welding needed would be small, since more than one Robogate is

A car body moves into a Robogate; the line at Rivalta cost £13 million, 30% more than a conventional line

The Robogate is designed so that four robots can weld simultaneously; 25 staff work on the line, against 125 on a traditional line

unlikely to be out of action at once.

In practice, although eight different models could be put through Robogate, the need for different side frames for each model limits the system to two different bodies. So long as the same side frames can be used many

variations can be incorporated.

Will Robogate become the body welding method for Europe? Many manufacturers are interested, particularly VW, and in the future many will need the flexibility a Robogate type of system gives.

The application of micro-processors to materials handling

by Mike Hessey

The author graduated in Mechanical Engineering from Birmingham University in 1967, at which time he joined the Lucas Research Centre. Since 1977 he has been Principal Systems Engineer at the Logic Systems Division of Lucas Industries Limited.

• What is a Microprocessor?

The most frequently encountered definition of a micro-processor is a 'computer on a chip'. While this is, very broadly speaking, true it is also very often a misleading simplification. What is usually on the microprocessor chip (by 'chip' we mean an integrated circuit) is only a central processing unit (CPU), which is only a small part of what is usually thought of as a computer.

A useable computer will also require memory, power, timing and capability to communicate with the outside world. Therefore in addition to the CPU chip — the microprocessor — it is usually necessary to provide a significant number of other chips to perform these functions. We shall now consider the significance of these various functions.

Firstly it is necessary to explain the function of the central processing unit (CPU) itself. This is the nerve centre of any digital computer system, since it controls and co-ordinates the activities of all the other units and performs all the arithmetic and logical operations. The arithmetical and logical functions to be performed by the CPU in any particular application must first have been defined by someone. Although the CPU is extremely powerful in its ability to perform these operations extremely rapidly, it is only capable of performing the operations it has been told previously to perform. The list of operations which are to be carried out sequentially by the computer are known as a program and are prepared by the programmer. This list of instructions must be stored so that the computer may access them, and this is done in the computer's program memory.

The program instructions in the program memory of the microprocessor do not require to be changed when the unit is in use for a particular application. The microprocessor only requires to read these instructions in order to perform them, and any inadvertent alteration of these program memory locations might be disastrous, since it would alter the operations carried out by the microprocessor.

For this reason the program memory of a microprocessor consists of some form of Read Only Memory (ROM). There are several variations in type of ROM. The term ROM itself is normally applied where the program instructions are designed into the memory, and are fixed at manufacture time. This type of ROM is the cheapest, but is only justified where quite large quantities (500 +) are to be produced. It also has the disadvantage that it is impossible to alter the instructions if an error is found or a change to the operations is required. The second type is known as Programmable Read Only Memory (PROM). In this the program is loaded by the user himself into the memory using special equipment. This is done on a one-off basis. Again, once the program is inserted in the memory it cannot be changed. The final form of commonly encountered program memory is Erasable Programmable Read Only Memory (EPROM). As its name suggests this is similar to the PROM except that it may be erased and re-used. The erasure is performed by a special unit generating high intensity ultraviolet light. Normal sunlight will not cause erasure, particularly as the unit will normally be inside a cabinet. During the development of programs, and in small-volume applications, the EPROM is the device most commonly used, whereas for the production version of a large volume product ROM would be used.

In addition to storing its list of instructions the micro-processor must also be able to store data received from the outside world and the values determined in its calculations. This requires memory which may be written as well as read. This type of memory is known as Random Access Memory (RAM). This memory takes the form of a further chip. Since it can be written as well as read it is necessary to take some care that this does not happen accidentally. In particular most memories of this type suffer from the disadvantage that this memory is cleared if the power fails. This can be disastrous in some applications, and micro-processor systems are commonly fitted with battery back-up purely to maintain this memory in the event of power failure.

In order for the microprocessor to be able to perform a useful task it is necessary that it should be able to receive information from the outside world (input data) and send out the results of its operations to the outside world (output data). These input/output operations are usually concerned with two basic categories of activity — input/output associated with conventional computer equipment such as teleprinters, paper tape, magnetic tape and magnetic disc devices, and direct measurement and/or control of process and production conditions. The latter category is of more interest to the production engineer and the control engineer, and is the one with which we are dealing primarily in this paper. The monitoring and control of processes and production is characterised by the need of the microprocessor to respond in real time — that is the microprocessor must receive data, process it and produce signals to control the external operation as it is in progress. These input output signals may again be divided into two categories — digital and analog. The former refers to signals with specific discrete levels — such as on/off switches or a digital thumbwheel switch. The analog signal varies continuously and is typified by signals from thermocouples, pressure transducers, voltages etc. The microprocessor is a digital device — that is it carries out operations internally in a digital form. It can therefore handle digital input/output more or less directly. Analog input signals will first be required to be converted to a digital form by an analog to digital converter, and analog outputs will be produced by the use of a digital to analog converter applied to digital outputs from the microprocessor.

As explained the microprocessor CPU chip usually requires to be used with other components such as memories and input/output chips in order to form a useable system. This useable system would commonly be built on a single, or perhaps multiple, printed circuit board. The definition of what constitutes a microprocessor and what constitutes a microcomputer is subject to different interpretations but the one that will be used here is that the microprocessor is the single CPU chip while the microcomputer represents the CPU (microprocessor) and the other chips required to make a useable system assembled on a board. The board and the precise configuration of additional components which it contains is usually associated with the performance of tasks specific to a particular application.

Having distinguished between a microprocessor and a microcomputer it remains to attempt to distinguish between these and a minicomputer. This is once again something which is subject to many different interpretations. The primary distinction made by the author is that the minicomputer is bought as a package, consisting of the computer in a cabinet complete with power supplies and often a control panel.

Perhaps one of the most significant differences between minicomputers and microprocessors/microcomputers lies in the fact that the former are usually supplied with high level (ie simple) programming languages and operating systems. This statement necessitates some understanding of how the program of instructions to be performed by the CPU are worked out in the first instance and stored in the microprocessor's program memory. The microprocessor itself is only capable of processing data represented by on/off signals — a 1 or a 0, that is binary data. The sequence of program instructions must also be represented in a binary form, where each binary number relates to a specific, fixed operation of the microprocessor known as an operation code. To memorise the binary values of the operation codes for a particular microprocessor and to write a program in this form (which is known as machine code) is virtually impossible. To overcome this problem all microprocessors have what is known as an assembly language, in which an easily remembered set of letters is used to correspond to an operation code — eg LDA, load accumulator. The instructions stored by the microprocessor must still be binary, and therefore it is necessary to translate (or assemble) these codes from the easily remembered mnemonics. This is normally done using a special-purpose microcomputer development system. Unfortunately these development systems often cost of the order of £10 000 — a far cry from the £5 for the microprocessor! Although the assembly language is easier to use than the machine code it is still related to the microprocessor operation codes and is un-natural and awkward to use.

Consider, for example, the expression
$$x = y + z + w$$
In assembly language this would probably be represented as:

LDA Y
ADA Z
ADA W
STA X

To simplify programming and reduce errors high level

The basis of most Lucas Logic micro control systems is this control processor board incorporating an 8085 microprocessor. The complete board was designed by Lucas Logic.

languages have been developed so that the above example could be represented as

$$x = y + z + w$$

There are no high level languages available for some microprocessors, while by contrast they are standard with virtually all minicomputers. This, together with the fact that the minicomputer comes packaged ready to use and is its own development system, means that for many one-off or small volume applications the minicomputer will be cheaper than the microprocessor, since the initially higher price more than outweighs the development costs. Naturally once the initial outlay on the microprocessor development system has been made, the necessary design expertise achieved and a sufficient number of systems built, the microprocessor can, however, become more competitive again.

The above discussion has given a very simple — indeed any expert reading this would say distortedly simple — overview of what a microprocessor is. Some of the problems presented in the final paragraphs regarding programming would naturally lead to questions as to why a microprocessor should be used at all. This is the subject of the next section of this paper.

● Why use a Microprocessor

This paper is concerned with applications of microprocessors in real time industrial control systems. The alternative to using a microprocessor is therefore usually to use hard wired electronic controls. Such controls are designed to meet a particular application, while the microprocessor is essentially a general purpose device in which the function which it is to perform is governed by the program stored in its memory. This program may be changed to alter the performance.

The primary advantages are:

1 Greater flexibility — since the program may be modified quite easily to alter the control function at almost any time.

2 More power. The microprocessor even in its most basic form has the capability to carry out an enormous number of arithmetic and logic operations on large quantities of data in a very sophisticated way if necessary.

3 Part of an integrated system. Individual microprocessors controlling particular functions may be linked together to provide a far more sophisticated control system. They can also be linked to a further centralised microprocessor or minicomputer to provide an integrated control system for a wide variety of production functions. Such a system can be of enormous advantage in production control and monitoring of work in progress.

4 Lower cost. Because of the improved process and production control capability provided by microprocessors it should be possible to effect savings in production which will more than outweigh any initially higher price.

The disadvantage of introducing microprocessor control systems lies primarily in the initially higher price in some instances, and the need to gain additional experience and microprocessor development aids at the time of starting to use microprocessors. These latter two points only apply of course where the users are to develop their own microprocessor control system. In many cases the potential user will buy the control system from a specialist with microprocessor experience and development aids, thus overcoming these disadvantages.

● How to use a Microprocessor

This section of the paper deals very briefly with the selection of a microprocessor for an application, the methods open to carry out development and shows schematically a typical microprocessor system design.

It is necessary first to distinguish between two basic types of microprocessor application — in a product and in a process

used in production. The obvious difference is that usually a product will be made in volume, so that the cost of components becomes increasingly important and the cost of developments somewhat less so. In this case, since development cost is less important and the user is likely to wish to retain the design expertise it is likely that development would be done in-house. In the case of control of a process or production it is probable that only a very small number of the systems will be built and development costs are very important. It is therefore well worth considering buying in the equipment from a systems specialist to avoid the need to obtain expert knowledge and experience in house, and to purchase a microprocessor development system. The possible advantage of a minicomputer bought in a useable form with high level languages, as discussed above, should also be considered.

Although for the process and production control applications with which this paper is concerned it is quite possible that a system specialist would be approached, some further details of the use of microprocessors will be given in this section. At the very least this will serve to give an appreciation of the work involved in doing it oneself.

Usually the first problem encountered is which microprocessor to use. Some of the manufacturers currently offering microprocessors are Intel, Motorola, Texas Instruments, Zilog, National, Semiconductors, RCA and General Instruments. Each of these offers several different microprocessors, and there are several other organisations in the market. It is impossible to deal with all these devices in this paper, but a few guidelines in studying what is available will be given.

The microprocessors available may first be categorised as 4, 8 or 16 bit microprocessors. The number of bits determines their internal accuracy and their power. Few 4 bit devices are now available and are normally restricted to very simple applications, often products produced in volume for the consumer market. The majority of microprocessors are at present 8 bit machines, and these suffice for the great majority of applications. The 16 bit microprocessors are few in number.

They have greater accuracy and power, although this is not needed for many applications, and their greater cost and complexity is probably a disadvantage unless this accuracy and power is really needed. They come closer to minicomputers in capability, but are not packaged as minicomputers. (Note, however, that some minicomputers are 'unpackaged' and sold as a computer on a board under the banner of a microcomputer).

In choosing the correct microprocessor it is necessary to choose a device with the right performance, as outlined above. Equally important, if not more so, is the availability and degree of support available from the manufacturer in this country. The list of manufacturers given above was placed in approximately the order of size in the UK microprocessor market.

At the beginning of this paper it was stated that it was usually necessary to provide additional memory input output, power supply etc in addition to the microprocessor chip itself. A number of microprocessors are now on the market, however, which include in the one integrated circuit package the microprocessor, some program and data memory and some input/output lines — the Intel 8048 is the best known example. These devices are extremely useful, but should not be thought of as superseding the separate components. Where the package contains the right amount of memory and input/output it is ideal, particularly in final product applications. However, for many applications, particularly in process and production control, it will be found that additional memory and input/output are required. In these cases it is often better to revert to the separate component approach since this normally offers more and easier expansion and flexibility.

A typical example of a current 8 bit microprocessor system

is shown below. This is based on the popular Intel 8085 microprocessor – an improved version of the well known 8080. (One of the greatest advantages over the 8080 is the need for only a 5 volt power supply). This system provides 2000 words of program memory (the 8755 EPROM) and 256 words of data storages (the 8155 RAM). 38 bits of input/output are also available through the memory chips.

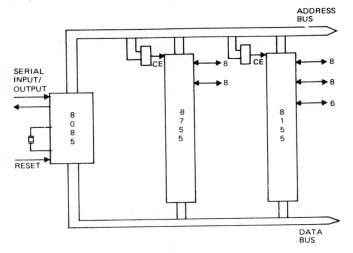

After deciding on the microprocessor to be used it will be necessary to embark upon the design of the total microprocessor system. It must not be forgotten that in addition to the microprocessor and memory, such as shown above, it will be necessary to provide interfaces between these and the signals from the outside world in order to provide the correct signal levels. Instrumentation to receive the signals, or for their output, must also be provided. These peripheral items, together with such equipment as power supplies, can easily equal or exceed the cost of the basic microprocessor and memories.

In addition to the design of the microprocessor electronics hardware it is necessary to develop the programs, which, as described previously, will usually require a development system. Because of the cost involved and the learning process involved it is common to make use of specialist suppliers for microprocessor control systems. Such organisations have the advantage of already having experience, microprocessor development aids and, often, standard microprocessor modules which may easily be assembled to meet the particular application. In selecting such an organisation, however, it is important to bear in mind the need for the system designers to fully understand the application. The practice of obtaining a microcomputer hardware from one source, programs from another and installation/interfacing/instrumentation from a third is also to be discouraged, since it will almost always result in problems at commissioning time.

When a microprocessor control system is required it is very important, whether it is to be provided in-house or by system specialists, that the specification for it is prepared carefully and fully agreed by all those who may be involved in its use. This stage is vital if the final system is to perform satisfactorily. In particular this should reduce the danger of the well known cry, just before installation, of 'wouldn't it be nice if it could also. . . 'All possible future expansion of the system should be considered at this initial stage, so that the system can cater for all future needs.

Following from the initial specification will be the process of system design. This can usually be divided into three parts – the instrumentation, transmission of data from the instruments to the processor, and the microcomputer system itself. The first of these subjects is one too large to expand upon in this paper, and the last has already been covered. It is worth, therefore, stressing the importance of the problems

in transmitting signals from the instruments to the processor. In particular this can involve enormous amounts of wiring and problems of signal corruption due to the presence of electrical noise. Careful design can help to overcome the latter, but it still requires a brave, or foolish, designer to enter the commissioning stage of a system without some fears regarding electrical noise. It is, of course, also an inconsistent and unpredictable phenomenon. The quantity of wiring may often be reduced where a number of signals require to be transmitted from a number of sensors to the processor by the use of a 'bus' rather than parallel wiring. This means all the sensors are connected to something akin to a ring main, rather than being individually wired back to the processor. Some additional circuitry would be required to identify signals on the bus. Alternatively a number of sensors in one particular area may be connected individually to a special remote data collection unit, which is then connected, as one device, to the processor.

This collection unit, or concentrator, may well in such cases contain a microprocessor itself.

On completion of the system two very important subjects must not be forgotten – the testing of the system and how it will be supported and maintained. The latter can present problems since it must be accepted that faults in microprocessor equipment cannot be rectified by personnel with limited skills and test equipment as easily as can relay logic. The solution to this is to arrange that individual circuit boards (or even complete control systems) can quickly be replaced to start the equipment operating, while the faulty unit is returned to the specialist for repair. In our organisation we operate just such a service, where a replacement would be returned as soon as a faulty unit is received. This procedure is simplified by the fact that only a relatively small number of standard circuit boards are used throughout a wide range of applications. Standard boards exist for:

1 Processor
2 Extension program memory
3 Extension data memory
4 Extension digital input
5 Extension digital output
6 Analog input
7 Analog input multiplexing
8 Analog output
9 Serial communication with teletype etc.

The above should have served to provide an introduction to the subject of deciding how to use a microprocessor – what is available, whether to do-it-yourself or go to a specialist, and the stages of a project using microprocessors. We will now turn our attention to where a microprocessor might be used – that is, some potential applications.

● Where to use a Microprocessor

As has been described previously the areas of application of microprocessors can be broadly divided into two categories – as a part of a product, and in a manufacturing control function. For the purposes of this paper the emphasis will be placed on the latter applications. Such applications are almost unlimited. Rather than produce a list of all the possible cases where microprocessors might be used in this way with benefit six applications with which I have been concerned will be described, followed by a summary of a few other applications which are currently popular. It is hoped that in this way the readers will be prompted to see possible applications in their own organisation.

Plastic Injection Moulding

Lucas Logic is marketing an electronic monitor/control unit for improved operation of injection moulding machines. This controls the transition from injection to hold pressure, and monitors all the more critical parts of the process – the tool temperatures, melt temperature pressures, cycle and hold times. The standard unit is a hardwired electronic unit. A more sophisticated system installed in one Lucas Factory has a number of these instruments linked to a central minicomputer . Any fault conditions on the machines are indicated centrally by the minicomputer as well as at the individual machines. Additional facilities are provided for counting machine cycles and for allocating non-production time to the appropriate cause. From this data the computer can produce printed reports to show machine utilisation, output and perform analysis over a period of time.

The equipment currently installed is very effective, but has a number of shortcomings — notably in the number of machines which can be connected to the minicomputer. This is overcome in a new system which has been developed where the instrument on each machine contains a micro-processor. This eases expansion of stand-alone units to the computer-based system and greatly increases the number of machines which can be linked to the computer. The central computer may also be smaller, and enhanced control cap-abilities, such as tool temperature control, are immediately available. The repercussions of breakdown of any part of the system are also greatly reduced. Equally important the facilities offered for controlling other aspects of the machine operation may easily be expanded in the future by modifying the micro-processor program. This is far more feasible than re-designing electronics which would have been necessary to provide additional facilities on the original system.

Heat Treatment

A minicomputer-based system has been in operation in one Lucas factory for over twelve months for controlling a gas carburising furnace. This is used to control the furnace atmos-phere and temperature, all mechanical operations (loading via external and internal conveyors, doors etc), safety checks and batch processing condition reporting by means of a teletype printer. To obtain satisfactory atmosphere control it is important that a fast, accurate means of measuring the atmos-phere should be available, and for that reason an oxygen probe is used.

The system is extremely effective in practice — control of operating conditions and throughput is greatly improved over conventional controls.

An important gain is the elimination of operator error as all operating conditions are punched on a plastic badge which is loaded into the controller at the start of each process. And which specifies all control functions. The principal problems lie in the high initial cost and the fact that control of mech-anical operations is inseparable from temperature and atmosphere control. The latter point is a disadvantage since some users only require automatic control of the process conditions, and mechanical operation differs greatly between different types of furnace.

A microprocessor-based control system has now been developed which provides the control of temperature, atmos-phere and timing, together with badge input at a much lower price than the original system. The mechanical handling and production reporting facilities are still available, but are now options and use separate microprocessors. In the case of the reporting function this may be shared between several furnaces. The microprocessor system has led to a far more flexible system, with lower prices for the individual modules and for the total system than was possible originally.

Machine Tools

A simple microprocessor control unit has been built for the control of a special-purpose 3-axis numerically controlled machine tool. The machine is used for rapid production of models of components involving styled three dimensional surfaces in a soft polyurethane foam. The controller consists simply of a tape reader, microprocessor and drives for the stepper motors on the three axis. The function of the micro-

processor is to perform straight-line interpolation between end points specified in three-dimensional space in a compact form on the paper tape. The paper tape is generated direct from a computer aided design system. Through the use of a microprocessor the option has been retained for adding further control functions at a later date — for example circular interpolation.

Plating

A sophisticated control system has been developed for plating plant. This handles all sequencing and timing of loads through some 25 baths, and controls all operations of several transporters and hoists. Autodosing of solutions, temperature and current control are also performed and print-out is avail-able giving details of the treatment given to batches of components. Extensive diagnostics are included for detecting failure of plant functions or safety conditions. This complete system requires a 32K minicomputer, and is hence rather larger than would be appropriate for a microprocessor. How-ever, less sophisticated controllers for smaller plating plants could well make use of microprocessors in the control system.

The above photographs show a conveyor system installed in a Lucas factory controlled by a microprocessor supplied by Lucas Logic. (The microprocessor is the small silver fronted cabinet beside the elevator).

Production Control and Data Collection

A system has been developed which used a microcomputer to count cycles on a variety of production machines, and (optionally) to record non-productive time. This system uses a printer or visual display unit (VDU) to produce utilisation reports, costing data etc.

Conveyor Control

A system is being developed, and has already run on a trial basis, for controlling a variety of operations on a drive and free conveyor system. A variety of different parts can pass along the conveyor, these being held in boxes, each containing a fixed number of parts. Boxes may be coded to show part type. Converge, diverge and lift operations are all controlled by microprocessors, each microprocessor controlling up to three such functions. The microprocessor offers a cost-effective means of performing these functions, but much greater benefits are anticipated when the microprocessors are linked back to a central minicomputer which will then be capable of monitoring work in progress, shortages, bottlenecks etc.

Other Applications

A major benefit of the introduction of microprocessors will be as described immediately above, where they are part of a distributed control and monitoring system within a factory. Individual microprocessors can provide enormous power in controlling individual control functions, but when linked to form part of a total factory system their scope is greatly increased. The move to integrated systems based upon microprocessors for controlling and monitoring manufacturing operations is likely to be one of the most important trends in the future.

Some other individual control functions with which microprocessors can be associated are:

a   Point of Sale data collection at time of sale.
b   Automatic Warehouses
c   Pallet movement and control
d   Industrial (or other) robots with greater control flexibility
e   Welding
f   Pick and place device controllers.

● Conclusion

This paper has sought to give a somewhat simplified indication of what a microprocessor is, why it should be used, how to use it and where it can be used. The ultimate objective was to show how readers might use it in their own application. It is probably fair to say that the range of applications for microprocessors is almost unlimited. However, care should be taken in its use in order to avoid costly mistakes and to obtain the best results.

Control Systems

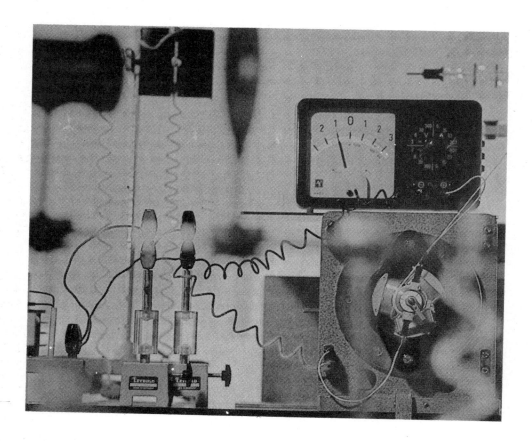

By RO LUTZ-NAGEY

As one sage of production engineering put it, "Keeping up with the latest in controls is a hassle. . .but it's not that bad, when you consider the alternative."

Years ago, there was no problem keeping up with controls. There was only the relay and its various derivatives. It did its job and it did it well.

But as industrial processes became more sophisticated and complex, limitations to relay control became obvious. One alternative was obviously the computer. Un-

fortunately, computers of the 1960's were, for the most part, either too expensive or too frail to be used on the shop floor.

Then, in 1969, as a promise of things to come, the programmable controller was introduced. Production engineers got the alternative they were looking for. The flood gates have been open ever since.

THE BASICS

In its earliest days, the programmable controller was a good alternative, but not a great alternative. Its applications were for the more complex relay systems or the simpler computer systems.

Since then, it has become small enough and cheap enough to tackle applications that might only require five relays. It has also grown large enough to take on the process computer in some applications.

Climbing the ladder logic

Probably one of the greatest reasons for the programmable controller's success was the PC's ability to emulate relay logic control systems. Ladder diagrams have been used for years as wiring charts for relay panels. Most PCs are programmed using the same diagrams. This contrasted sharply

Reprinted with permission from *Production Engineering*.

Relay replacement isn't the only reason for making the switch to programmable control. As relay systems are altered over time (above), they can get to look like abused birds' nests. One user decided to make

maintenance happy—and increase machine speed 50%, double reliability, and cut troubleshooting from 2 or 3 days to under an hour. His original system used only 11 relays. Source: Texas Instruments.

with other computers available at the time since they required programming in a special language. With the PC, however, few new skills were needed.

Further, with relays, the ladder diagram was but the beginning. The electrician had to spend hours making all the connections and debugging the system. With PCs, the program was entered directly into the controller—*it* made all the wiring connections. And since all of this wiring was "softwired", changes could also be made directly by revising the ladder diagram. . .versus the electrician crawling about, tracing wires. Today, part of the controller responsible for doing all this wiring and rewiring is, in many cases, a microprocessor. Where one manufacturer once asked an editor of this publication not to mention that their controller did, indeed, use a microprocessor, today the race is on among manufacturers as to who has the best. Originally the microprocessor used 4-bit words, today 8 is common and 16 is seen lurking close by. Larger word length adds to the speed of the controller—a very important consideration for large batch or process systems.

The microprocessor scans each line of the ladder diagram, checking each rung for the condition of

Electrically alterably read only memory (EAROM) is just now being introduced into programmable controllers, such as this one. The advantage? EAROM can be programmed and reprogrammed just as easily as RAM, but it does not require a separate battery supply for program retention like RAM does. Source: Square D.

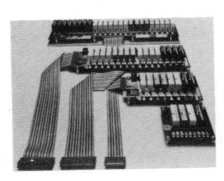

Retrofitting CNC and DNC to existing NC controllers? This tape reader reads and transfers parts program data at speeds up to 300 cps into solid-state storage. The reader and solid-state memory functionally replaces tapes and tape readers on most NC machine tools. Source: Alden Self-Transit Systems Corp.

Using microcomputers for control is made easier with the recent introduction of stand-alone I/O systems. Performance of the modules, when used with inductive loads, is enhanced through snubber filters. Transients, RFI, etc. are guarded against through the use of photo-isolators that provide 2500-v RMS protection. The system shown is compatible with a variety of logic systems and voltage levels. Source: Opto 22.

Special cards and functions can be added to most systems. A trend memory card (above) stores historical data, which can be called up on a CRT or printed on a terminal. Uninterrupted automatic control comes from a reserve controller director (below) that automatically detects the malfunction of up to eight controllers and signals a reserve controller to take over the functions of the failed controller. Source: Honeywell.

each relay present. Based on the conditions it finds, it performs the required output function. Obviously, the microprocessor can do much more—witness the capabilities of a handheld calculator. Many systems available offer internal latches, counters, and timers. Also offered are the common math functions available—add, subtract, multiply, and divide.

Since the controller uses solid-state logic, special care had to be used when putting it in an industrial environment. Noise-immunity was an earlier problem largely solved through better technology and user education. Either a high-noise immune circuit technology was used, such as C/MOS, or the voltage level for the "ON" state was particularly high, such as 12 v. Users have been taught equipment placement as well, to avoid having transient high voltage spikes occur near the controller.

On either side of the controller box are arrayed the input and output modules, which have a variety of capabilities, including analog-to-digital (A/D) conversions. Offered on some input/output (I/O) modules are separate fuses and LED indicator lights. Thus, in the simplest diagnostic testing, a user can slowly step the PC through the ladder diagram and observe the status of the I/O lights, checking to see if the program is actually doing what it intended to.

Programming methods vary. At the low end, a simple hand-held programmer will suffice. Typically, it displays a rung of the ladder at a time and special function keys (such as "NORMALLY OPEN" or "TIMER") permit quick key-in of the ladder diagram. On the other side, intelligent terminals permit a more complex approach. These terminals usually have a display screen capable of showing extended portions of the ladder diagram. While the PC can be programmed directly from the terminal, many offer a cassette storage facility. The program, when developed, is put on the cassette tape and the tape is played into the controller on the shopfloor through an intermediate device.

One advantage of this approach is that it provides a permanent record of the program and it can be shipped to a plant across country that has the same control application.

Undedicated control

While microcomputers and minicomputers utilize many of the same features as the programmable controller, they offer different advantages.

The microcomputer is the close cousin of the programmable controller. It uses much of the same hardware, but it is less restricted in the software. In short, the microcomputer is an undedicated programmable controller. You can choose the language, the logic, and the dedication. Depending on the language chosen, the micro can work its way through the program faster than the PC.

Most micros contain extra card slots in the control box which can be filled with optional or custom cards capable of performing special functions. In some cases, this modularity can lead to cost or space savings.

Minicomputers offer the greatest speeds and capabilities. Very sophisticated programs can be run in real time without losing control. The faster speeds of the minicomputer allow the use of higher level languages such as BASIC or FORTRAN in their programming without greatly sacrificing its speed advantages over the less powerful control computers.

THE UPDATE

Until recently, determining which type of control system—programmable controller, microcomputer or minicomputer—was a relatively easy task. Each had major differences. But in the last five years, the advent of industrial large scale integrated (LSI) devices have blurred the distinctions the different devices once had.

For example, programmable controllers were once viewed as only relay-replacement systems

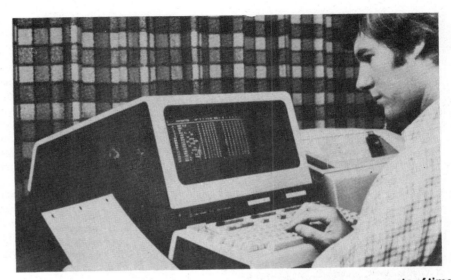

If you're building your own microcomputer, you'll save macro amounts of time by using a development system. These systems emulate the microprocessor you're using, but have additional software to make programming and debugging simpler and faster. It enables users to find, examine, and alter any selected portion of the program. Source: Hewlett-Packard.

Industrial strength microcomputers offer such features as a NEMA 12 enclosure, oil-tight data entry keyboard, and a compressed-air cooling system for operation under high ambient temperatures. This unit features a Z-80 CPU, four counter/timers, 2 serial I/O ports, 4 8-bit parallel ports, DMA, 4-8K PROM and 4K static RAM. Source: Heurikon Corp.

1985 controls in 1978

A 1977 Delphi-type survey of anticipated changes in manufacturing conducted by SME pegged 1985 as the year for the introduction of a three-tiered control system that includes real-time function monitoring. They were off by 7 years.

Rohr Industries, a major aerospace subcontractor in Chula Vista, Calif., has commenced a long-term manufacturing improvement program that is advancing the state-of-the-art in computer numerical control. According to Sam Schneider, manager of Equipment Engineering and NC Maintenance, the long-range plan calls for development and construction in-house of a new generation of CNC machine tools.

The on-line control system includes three computers, all made by Computer Automation. One continuously monitors 80 machine functions, another serves each tool as a Machine Control Unit, (MCU) and the third serves as a supervisory computer. The control system is supported by IBM 360/370 mainframes which store the entire library of parts programs, numbering in the thousands. As needed, parts programs are transferred from the mainframes to the supervisory minicomputer. The mainframe will become a fourth tier of control, but at present its primary functions are program development and mass storage.

Rohr describes the advanced control system as beginning the third evolutionary stage in numerical control. The first two stages of direct numerical control are generally characterized by a paper tape input and time-sharing of a central processing unit by several machines.

There are two major innovations to third-stage controls. The MCU is now a stand-alone 16-bit minicomputer, with 8K memory, housed within the

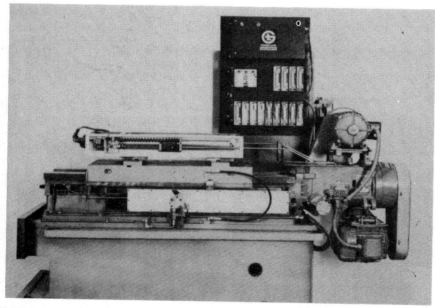

Better accuracies and faster speeds allow programmable controllers to be where an application requires precise, repeatable locations. This PC has full servo capability as an option which uses closed loop feedback with a precision resolver. Programming resolution is to 0.001 in. with a maximum of 99.999 in. The slide drive may be hydraulic or electric servo, stepping motor or a geared electromechanical drive. Source: Giddings & Lewis Electronics.

. . .if you were replacing more than 300 relays. Today, some companies are claiming that their PCs become cost-effective if you only replace 5 relays.

But that's only a small part of the picture. Production engineers are well aware of the PC's power in this area. What may not be generally known are the greatly enhanced math functions that are available. Now, instead of talking about replacing relays, some manufacturers are talking about replacing data loggers, micro, and minicomputers.

Among some of the new functions available is proportional-integral-derivative (PID) control, which is used to maintain some process characteristic (like temperature, flow, or pressure) at some given value. The process can deviate from this desired set point as a result of changing material, load requirements, or interaction with other processes. Programmable controllers offering the PID option are fast enough to do the repetitive summing required to do the integral and derivative portions of the PID equation while maintaining real-time control.

This is only one example of how PCs have begun to enter the process-control world. While the microprocessors used in PCs always had the capability to perform

machine tool. Input is via a data line interface from the supervisory computer, eliminating paper tape.

The second innovation is the incorporation of a dedicated "millicomputer", also housed within the machine tool, for real-time monitoring of machine functions. It's used to prevent major machine failures and to eliminate discrepancies in machining due to machine malfunctions.

"The minicomputer can determine in many instances if a failure is about to occur and, depending on the severity, will alert the MCU to shut down immediately or finish the block of data in process and then shut down," Schneider said. "Because the computer identifies and displays the problem, downtime is minimized. The capability of the computer monitor opens up a ripe area of investigation into adaptive control in which the computer makes more substantive decisions when a real or potential problem is detected."

The machines, which might cost as much as $800,000-$900,000 each on the open market, are designed, engineered, constructed, and maintained by Rohr personnel at considerable savings, he added.

these functions, they had to wait for improvements in the I/O devices that let them communicate with the shop floor. These improvements have occurred over the last two years as analog signal handling and conditioning devices let PCs handle information coming in from thermocouples, pressure sensors, and others.

I/O advances have also improved the PC's ability to act as an annunciator and data-logger. Data can be inputted through binary-coded-decimal (BCD) devices and outputted through seven-segment displays, flashing lights and alarms. Line printers and floppy discs can also be used with PCs in data logging applications. Operators of machines or processes are also able to do their job better thanks to the improved graphics handling capabilities of the controllers—factors like trends, deviations, and speeds can all be displayed on a CRT in a variety of formats.

Programming has improved greatly. Nearly every unit offered accepts the ladder diagram format of program entry. Many units, especially those with advanced math functions, can also use advanced English-oriented languages. In some applications like machine control, programmable controllers have to use more than

Programmable controllers can be justified as relay replacers in certain cases—but there are loads which are too heavy for solid-state switching. In those cases, PCs and electromechanical relays have to be used together. Source: Struthers-Dunn.

The physical similarity between microcomputers and PCs is obvious—the difference in their capabilities perhaps not so. Add optional I/O modules (ac, dc, A/D, D/A, bidirectional counters and pulse accumulators) to a microcomputer and it can function in much the same way as a PC. On the other hand, you can take advantage of the CPU's power—134 instruction set, including multiply and divide, 250 nanosecond clock-cycle time, and a 7-level vectored interrupt. Source: Warner & Swasey.

Programming panels are changing to meet the changing capabilities of PCs. This one offers square root, conditional equalities, and diagnostics along with the traditional functions. Source: Square D.

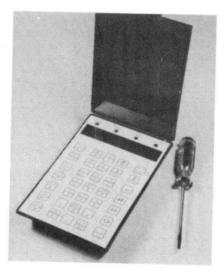

one program. In these cases, entering the program through a programming panel or terminal is too time-consuming. There are two alternatives. One is to get enough memory so the programs can be stored in the PC, where they can be used on demand. The other is to tie the PC into a minicomputer. The minicomputer can call on the desired program (stored, for example, in a floppy disc memory) and send it over to the PC on request.

The early attraction of PCs was due in part to the ladder diagram type of program entry—electricians and maintenance personnel were not required to learn computer technology to use computer control. This was a tremendous plus in getting PCs up and running. However, when the programmable controller malfunctioned, maintenance was no longer faced with a friendly relay-replacer. Suddenly, it became instead a rather menacing pile of solid-state junk.

This situation has improved considerably. Manufacturers routinely burn-in the solid-state components and perform vibration and heat testing, decreasing early failure. More importantly, diagnostics have been greatly improved. On the I/O side, the individual modules use LEDs as diagnostic tools. One LED blinks on and off to show that the module is shuttling current. Another LED is sometimes used as a blown fuse indicator.

Internal diagnostics have undergone major improvements as well. It's now possible for a controller to have a diagnostic program stored in its executive memory. While the controller goes about its normal functions, it can also be checking itself. Depending on the nature of the error it detects, it will either simply display that an error exists or, in the worst case, shut the controller down.

If an error is detected, PCs can now help maintenance locate the source of the problem—often to the point of telling which board is bad. In that case, the maintenance technician simply pulls the guilty printed-circuit board and plugs in a new one. In one case, it's even possible to perform remote diagnostics—where the programmable controller is diagnosed by the manufacturer's computer over the telephone.

Build your own

Due to increased in-house experience and technical improvements, more production engineers are building their own control systems using microcomputers. They come in a variety of sizes—one

If I knew then, what I know now

Especially for this article, PRODUCTION ENGINEERING conducted a survey of 1000 readers in an attempt to measure user reaction and satisfaction with PCs.

Approximately 44% of those responding currently use programmable controllers. Of the 56% currently not using PCs, over 44% said that they planned an application for PCs in the near future. Among the non-users' comments:

- "What is a programmable controller?"
- "The majority of our testing and production is hand-controlled."
- "Equipment set-up situation is relatively static with high volume."
- "We conducted a feasibility study and found it not applicable and in some cases not economical."
- "Until recently, I was not satisfied with the ability, reliability and cost of the units. I will use one in the next applicable situation."

Among the current users of PCs, about thirty different PC manufacturers were mentioned. Several control systems cost $85,000 (hardware only) . . . the cheapest a paltry $100 (for a programmable cam sequencer). Those that gave a dollar value for their system averaged out to about $22,000 per system. However, 45% of those giving this data spent less than $5,000. The average is boosted by a small number spending comparatively large sums for very sophisticated controls.

Users were asked, "Did the programmable controller create any *new* problems for you? What kind?". 45% said no. While the other 55% said yes, their answers indicated the problems weren't all PC oriented. 25% of those saying yes blamed maintenance and training as their source of problems.

- "No, nothing that teaching didn't cure."
- "Yes, caused some solenoid valves to chatter."
- "Need better electronic test equipment to troubleshoot."
- "Training programmers, teaching operators to trust controller."
- "Inventories became more important."
- "Lack of replacement parts."
- The most interesting response came from a manufacturer of electronic assemblies who claimed that, "It pointed out to us some low-quality component vendors that had *previously* sold us low-quality material."

Users were asked, "Were maintenance people easily taught how to service the programmable controller?" A whopping 84% said that maintenance people were easily taught.

Users were asked, "Now that you have experience with PCs, what would you have liked to know in advance of making the purchase decision?" Answers were too diverse here to make any statistical statement. Among the most common opinions voiced were:

- "More data of a hard engineering nature from vendors and more information from more manufacturers."
- "Shopfloor performance and maintenance characteristics."
- "More software."

The last question asked users was, "What simple advice would you pass on to other production engineers who are just now making their purchase decisions on PCs?" Again, the answers ran the gamut. Representative responses are:

- "Isolate! Isolate! Isolate from electrical noise (especially lightning). Make duplicate copies of tapes."
- "Take *full* advantage of PC manufacturers' schools and information."
- "Thoroughly understand what you need and what you are getting for your money."
- "Look for troubleshooting aids."
- "Try to visit installations and talk with the operating people."
- "Don't be afraid of PCs—they work and they're simple."
- "Leave room for expansion."
- "Is it easy to get spare parts and from where?"

Finally, users were asked a series of attitudinal questions. They were given a statement then asked to mark the degree to which they agreed to the statement. The range ran from an answer of "1" which meant strongly agree all the way to "5" which meant strongly disagree. "3" meant neutral. The statements are given below, and the full responses are given in the graphs.

"The programmable controller I bought was everything I thought it would be." 75% either agreed or strongly agreed.

29%	46%	19%	4%	2%
1	2	3	4	5

Strongly Agree — Neutral — Strongly Disagree

"My programmable controller did everything the salesman said it would." 74% agreed or strongly agreed.

26%	49%	15%	6%	4%
1	2	3	4	5

Strongly Agree — Neutral — Strongly Disagree

"Training material and/or courses were put together well and were very helpful." 54% agreed or strongly agreed.

21%	33%	25%	15%	6%
1	2	3	4	5

Strongly Agree — Neutral — Strongly Disagree

"I am very satisfied with the way the dealer followed-up on problems I encountered after the purchase." 53% agreed or strongly agreed.

18%	36%	27%	11%	9%
1	2	3	4	5

Strongly Agree — Neutral — Strongly Disagree

"Overall, I am very happy with my programmable controller." 77% agreed or strongly agreed.

33%	44%	21%	2%	0%
1	2	3	4	5

Strongly Agree — Neutral — Strongly Disagree

Try one at home first . . .

In case you've got the sneaky suspicion that PCs are everywhere, you're right. Since March of this year, Energy Technology Inc., Las Cruces, N.M., has been offering the Coby 1, one of the first home programmable controllers. Targeted for those who want energy conservation, convenience or security, the control unit can direct up to 100 remotes through carrier current signals sent over home wiring lines. Each remote can be turned on or off at any time or date and can be operated in a given period in cycles as short as two seconds and as long as 100 hours.

It uses an Intel 8085 microprocessor, 2K RAM, and 2K ROM. Its power supply retains the memory and continues to drive the clock during power outages up to several hours long. It communicates with

appliances through various devices—a wall plug adapter for 115-v, 18-a outlets, a unit that replaces a wall switch, an in-line 220-v remote unit for control of large appliances, and (in the near future)

remotes designed to switch 24-v control circuits rather than actual service current. The price depends on the number of remotes ordered, but a minimal system should easily come in for under $1,000.

manufacturer sells a one-bit microprocessor chip and gives you circuit diagrams to convert it into a programmable controller. More often, the microcomputer is sold either with additional components—either as a single board or a boxed system.

Microcomputer peripherals are increasing as well. Several companies are now offering input/output modules and systems designed to let you tie your controls into the micro. Retrofitting machine tools with microcomputer control is also increasing and companies are now offering solid-state memory boxes which will store the control programs and eliminate punched paper tape.

The microcomputer control industry seems to be settling on two standards for interfacing—the IEEE-488 and CAMAC. As these standards become more accepted, it will be easier to add instruments and controls to a microcomputer system. . .until now, production engineers pretty much had to figure out how to get an instrument to talk with the computer.

Program languages have improved. In some cases, the language offered for a micro is even simpler than ladder diagram languages. Manufacturers are also offering more canned software applicable to the shopfloor.

The real excitement is focused on the battle between microcomputers and minicomputers. 16-bit microcomputers are just now being offered and are blurring the differences between the two systems. In the meantime, some manufacturers are putting more than one microprocessor on a board. For example, in a 3-axis contouring system, there might be one microprocessor per axis: or one microprocessor might be used for communication, another for servo updates, and a third to handle I/O.

An important growth area for minicomputers is in microcomputer and programmable controller control. Minicomputers stand at the top of the shopfloor hierarchy. Production engineers are finding that, just as they obtained increased productivity by putting a machine or machines under programmable control, they are now getting an increased measure of productivity by putting the programmable controllers under minicomputer control. Not only can minicomputers supervise the other computers, they can also do complex number-crunching that is

either too difficult or time-consuming for the smaller systems.

ACKNOWLEDGEMENT

Material from the following companies was used in the preparation of this article: Alden Self-Transit Systems Corp., Natick, Mass.; Allen-Bradley Co., Systems Div., Cleveland; Applied Systems Corp., St. Clair Shores, Mich.; ATO, Interstate Electronics Corp., Anaheim, Calif,; Automatic Timing And Controls Co., King of Prussia, Pa.; Beckman Instruments Inc., Process Instruments Div., Fullerton, Calif.; Bendix, Industrial Controls Div., Detroit; Computer Automation, Irvine, Calif.; Data General, Westboro, Mass.; Dynage Inc., Bloomfield, Conn.; Emerson Electric, Doric Scientific Div., San Diego; Energy Technology Inc., Las Cruces, N. M.; Fisher Controls Co., Marshalltown, Iowa; General Electric, General Purpose Control Dept., Bloomington, Ill.; General Instrument Corp., C. P. Clare & Co., Chicago; Giddings & Lewis Electronics Co., Fond du Lac, Wis.; Gould Inc., Modicon Div., Andover, Mass.; Gulf + Western, Eagle Signal Div., Davenport, Iowa; Heurikon Corp., Madison, Wis.; Hewlett Packard, Palo Alto, Calif.; Honeywell Process Control Div., Fort Washington, Pa.; Industrial Solid State Controls Inc., York, Pa.; Kinetic Systems Corp., Lockport, Ill.; Modular Computer Systems Inc., Fort Lauderdale, Fla.; Motorola Semiconductor Products Inc., Phoenix; NCR Corp., Dayton, Ohio; Opto 22, Huntington Beach, Calif.; PolyMorphic Systems, Santa Barbara, Calif.; Process Computer Systems Inc., Saline, Mich.; Rath & Strong Inc.; Lexington, Mass.; Rockwell International, Electronic Devices Div., Anaheim, Calif.; Square D Co., Milwaukee; Struthers-Dunn Inc., Systems Div., Pitman, N. J.; Stynetic Systems Inc., St. James, N. Y.; Sybron Corp., Taylor Instrument Co., Rochester, N. Y.; Texas Instruments Inc., Control Products Div., Attleboro, Mass.; Warner & Swasey Co., Computer Div., Minneapolis; Westinghouse Electric Corp., Industry Systems Div., Pittsburgh.

How microprocessors simplify and extend future of NC machines

Preparing NC control tapes has changed little but now the microprocessor will help improve matters. By Professor John Davies

NUMERICAL CONTROL of machine tools has been an accepted method of component manufacture, particularly in metal cutting batch manufacture, for two decades. During that time, performance and reliability of systems have improved markedly and data processing has become easier.

Except for a relatively few installations, however, the general concept of preparing a control tape through a geometric description of the part with tool path instructions to control the function of a single machine has not changed very much. This has been due mainly to the limitation of complexity and cost of data processing.

Reductions in cost and size of data processing have been continuous during this whole period under the pressure of the enormous military space and commercial data processing market, which dwarfs the NC requirement. The stage has now been reached when a micro-computer can be produced on a few large scale integrated circuits the size of large postage stamps, in quantity and for several tens of pounds. The time is near when micro-computers will be low enough in cost to include in motor cars and domestic equipment.

Quite apart from cost considerations, this development has an important bearing on the way NC systems are developing. Up to and including the mini-computer stage, NC data processing has been done serially with the computer dealing with a range of operations such as data input, feed drives, interpolation and ancillary equipment control on a serial priority basis. This has made the software complex and imposed some constraints on the speed of operation of the systems as well as the scope of functions and data controlled by the NC systems.

Multiple. Because of the low cost of micro-processors, it is now economic to design multiple micro-processor systems in which individual tasks such as data input, interpolation, motor drive and production data reporting can be allocated to separate micro-computers. Means of communicating between micro-computers, micro-processors and stores have been developed to do this.

This multiple micro-processor approach has a number of advantages. The most important one is that NC systems can be modular in both hardware and software.

Software can be written for particular functions, without concern for other functions. This simplifies initial software writing and development and also greatly simplifies extensions to the system. This approach is likely to be the dominant one for NC systems of the future. Some systems are already based on these principles.

Of even greater importance is the ability of distributed data processing on the shop floor to form both hierarchial and network data processing systems. Traditionally NC equipment has been inward looking, but NC systems have integrated the machine and the control system very well.

Adaptation. To some extent the machine operator and the part programmer have been incorporated into the system design, but men in these functions have to adapt to the system rather than the system adapt to the worker.

Relatively little progress has been made with the incorporation of work transfer, tool and fixture transfer, machine loading and batch status reporting into the design of NC systems. This has been principally due to the cost of data processing hardware and software.

Distributed data processing now makes this economically practical. Much can be achieved in overall system performance without increasing the cost of the mechanical hardware.

Because of the investment climate in the UK, it is doubtful if the special integrated machine and work transfer hardware, and control hardware and software found, for example, in flexible manufacturing systems in the US, East Germany and Japan, will be acceptable in the UK.

This concept of broadening NC to the control of the operation and loading of a group of men/machine sub-systems in a network or hierarchy broadens the definition of NC. However, this can be considered justified because so much of the under-utilisation of present NC installations arises from poor overall manufacturing system design, rather than inherent defects in the machine and controller sub-system.

Interactive. Another important concept in the development of the manufacturing NC system is interactive operation.

Methods of operator/computer operation have been developed in which a dialogue is conducted between the operator and computer, usually through a visual display unit. This dialogue can be structured in such a way that either the computer or the operation is dominant.

It can be arranged for example, that routine operations can be carried out by the computer, whereas non-routine operations calling for the judgement of a skilled man can be left to the operator.

Important benefits to NC manufacturing systems arise from this concept.

For example, shop floor acceptability should be improved because computers will assist rather than dominate the operators. The operator will be relieved of routine and tedious tasks, which can well be done mechanically or by computer, and left with computer aid for the more interesting judgements which he as a skilled man on the spot can make on cutting technology and job priorities.

So much of the detailed unpredictability occurs on the shop floor due to men, machines, material and information that provided the right incentives can be given, the best place to make non-routine decisions is at the lowest point in the system in which the necessary information and aids can be given.

Distributed computing systems should be able to provide, on-call, the information required, and have the local computing power to compute and display the effect of alternative decisions, so that a reasonable on-the-spot choice can be made.

Such decisions may relate to feeds and speeds in which the computer gives advice on preferred conditions and will predict change in tool life, if conditions are changed. They may also relate to which of several jobs is the best to tackle next, taking account of priorities.
Reduction. A further most important feature of interactive working is that, despite the somewhat greater complexity of programming in an interactive mode, it greatly reduces the overall software development time.

The great problem with NC manufacturing system software is predicting the exceptional cases and devising ways of dealing with them. This can greatly extend software writing, and extend even longer software development as unexpected exceptions arise to cause system failure.

An interactive system can be written and debugged far more quickly because only the normal cases need be dealt with. The skilled men can be left in the system to deal with the exceptional cases preferably with computer assistance. It is quite feasible now to provide local computer and data storage facilities on each machine which can communicate with data processing and storage in other parts of the system.
Higher level. Computer-assisted part programming has been developed in a period in which no general-purpose computing power was available on the shop floor. Input format is therefore orientated to the minimum shop floor data processing.

Data processing for NC usually has been carried out in main frame computers in a processor/post processor mode. The input language is commonly APT-like in batch mode.

Distributed interactive computing permits a rethink of the form of data input to NC machines. Desk top mini-systems are now available such as supplied by ESP which allows interactive part programming through a VDU and

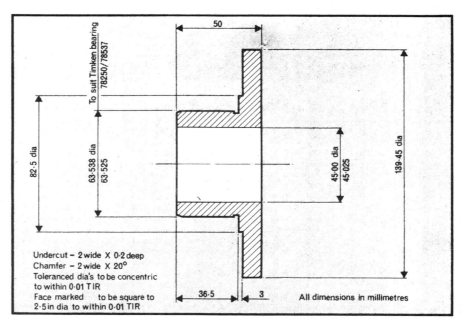

Undercut – 2 wide X 0·2 deep
Chamfer – 2 wide X 20°
Toleranced dia's to be concentric to within 0·01 TIR
Face marked   to be square to 2·5 in dia to within 0·01 TIR

All dimensions in millimetres

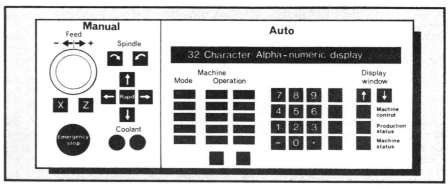

Above: Operator's control station for a lathe. Below: Wadkin TCD 2235 with six drilling spindles and a milling head. Bottom: Wadkin TCH with z-axis slideways

on/line tape checking, with a plotter.

Interactive geometric modelling systems are being developed, for example, by I. Braid — the BUILD 3D Modelling System — of the Computer Laboratory of the University of Cambridge, and by the University of Leeds, PADL, in association with the University of Rochester, and by G. Spur of the University of Berlin.

These allow geometric features such as lines, surfaces and volumes to be shifted, rotated and added and subtracted to define a turned or non-rotational part in a way more natural to an operator or planner than the APT language.

NC tapes can be generated automatically from the description of the component generated by the computer though this process, and conventional drawings can be produced also. Thus, the design process can be integrated into the manufacturing process.

For some time, the design of special components such as turbine blades, aircraft aerofoil surfaces, broaches, and rolls for steel sections have been integrated with NC tape preparation.
Orientated. Dr S. Hinduja of UMIST

```
PART NAME:TEST     PART NO:856632   DRG.NO:80220   ASSY.NO:89020
MATERIAL :EN 9     MACHINE:T.LATHE  BATCH :30      SET-UP :30 MIN
MAT.FORM :BAR      MAX.CUT:2 MM     DATE :MAR.78   PLANNER:MILANY

        PLANNING SHEET FOR TURNING OPERATIONS

---------------------------------------------------------------
OP  NC  OPER'N DEPTH  CN  DIAMTR  LENGTH  FEED  SPD  RPM   H.T.  M.T.
---------------------------------------------------------------
 1   0  CHUCK    0     0    0        0       0    0    0    0.35   0
 2   1  R.FACE  2.2    1   145      75     0.6   61  134    0.2   0.93
        FACETL
 3   2  R.TURN  2.5    1   140      55     0.6   61  139    0.2   0.66
        SRTOOL
 4   3  R.TURN  29    15    83      45     0.6   61  234    0.2   4.81
        SRTOOL
 5   4  R.TURN  9.5    5    64      40     0.6   61  304    0.2   1.1
        SRTOOL
 6   1  C.DRIL  2      1     3       3     0.26  14 1486    0.4   0.01
        CDRILL
 7   6  DRIL-G  20     1    40      55     0.26  40  318    0.45  0.67
        GUN-DR
 8   6  R.BORE  2.4    1   44.8     55     0.2   97  690    0.3   0.4
        RETOOL
 9   6  REAM    0.1    1    45      55     0.3   38  269    0.45  0.68
        REAMER
10   4  F.TURN  0.25   1   63.5     38     0.2  108  542    0.2   0.35
        SRTOOL
11   3  F.TURN  0.25   1   82.5      5     0.2  108  417    0.2   0.06
        SRTOOL
12   1  F.FACE  0.3    1   63.5     15     0.2  105  527    0.2   0.14
        FACETL
13   5  F.TURN  0.2    1   63.1      1     0.2  111  560    0.2   0.01
        SRTOOL
14  14  CHAMFR  2      1   63.5      2     0.2   80  401    0.2   0.02
        FACETL
15   0  RECHUK  0      0    0        0       0    0    0    0.35   0
16   2  F.TURN  0.28   1  139.4     15     0.2  106  242    0.2   0.31
        SRTOOL
17  10  R.FACE  2.2    1  139.4     55     0.6   61  139    0.2   0.66
        FACETL
18  10  F.FACE  0.3    1  139.4     55     0.2  105  240    0.2   1.15
        FACETL
19   0  DEBURR  0      0    0        0       0    0    0    0.3    0
20   0  UNLOAD  0      0    0        0       0    0    0    0.3    0
21   0  INSPCT  0      0    0        0       0    0    0    0.4    0
---------------------------------------------------------------
TOTAL TIME/PART, IN MIN.= 17.66
```

is working on a process orientated language as a direct input to a machine controller, incorporating multiple micro-processors. For example, the input to a lathe is in the form of push button controlling parameterised macros such as Turn, Face, Bore, Groove, Thread and so on. Such macros are independent of the machine tool and are easily understood.

This approach has several advantages:

☐ The 'post processor' phase of computer aided part programming is effectively eliminated.

☐ The volume of data required to specify the machining process is drastically reduced.

☐ The operator may program parts himself, quite simply using interactive prompting to specify the operations. This allows NC to be introduced into small companies without the need for the organisational back up for data processing which is currently required.

In companies with adequate data processing it also allows small batches to be machined without need for programming. A preliminary version of the

Top left: Typical turned part with planning sheet shown above

Below: Wadkin TCM2 trepanning 185 mm hole in Jones Cranes 355 body

operator's control for a lathe is shown.

Advice to the operator on cutting technology will be incorporated in the system which will be developed to provide, receive and supply batch status information to a central production control file. A Gildermeister lathe type incorporating a FANUC micro-processor based control system already provides a first step towards operator/machine communication in an operator orientated language.

Sequence planning. T. T. El-Midany and B. J. Davies at UMIST have developed a simple experimental version of an interactive operation sequence planning for turned parts using a PDP-8 mini-computer with a 256 k byte disc store, suitable for small shops.

Much of the work of operation sequence planning is tedious, involving reference to tool files and cutting data and routine calculations. The object of the operation sequence planning programs are to speed up the production of planning sheets and to make them more consistent.

Turning operations and tool files are generated interactively to cover the requirements of machining the features of a master part. To produce the planning sheet, the planner identifies the sequence of operations required and the length and depth to be removed.

The program selects the appropriate tools, feeds and speeds, cutting times and handling times and produces a complete planning sheet and total process time. An example of a typical turned part and the planning sheet produced is illustrated. Cost and time reduction by a factor of five to ten has been obtained.

The system is being further developed to include computer assisted operation sequence selection, and a start has been made on a similar system for non-rotational parts. Somewhat similar systems are under development by Spur at the University of Berlin, by G. Jakobsson at the Royal Institute of Technology, Stockholm, and by M. Sandell at ASEA (PRAUTO).

Job shop control. Interactive mini-computer based job shop control systems are being developed. In many ways they are better suited and more acceptable to the shop floor than the batch mode main frame systems, because of the complexity and uncertainty of the activity, as well as shop floor attitudes.

Systems of this type have already been installed for example, by the EBS 11 System, running on a PRIME 300 mini-computer. Systems of this type have also been developed by O. Bjorke of NTH Trondheim and are being developed by H. Jagdev and B. J. Davies at UMIST on a PDP-8 mini-computer with a disc pack.

Ⓔ

All you have to do is answer back

MARTIN ATKEY

An operator at the control unit of the M1 CNC machining centre.

It's only in the past couple of years that microprocessors have really come on to the manufacturing scene. But even in this relatively short time they have already made an impact on the process and machine-tool control side of production engineering. And almost just as important is the speed with which NC machine-tool builders are latching on to microprocessor developments.

One of the very latest microprocessor-controlled machine tools to hit the UK market is the TCL/Hurco M1 CNC machining centre. And in addition to being one of the newest, it's also one of the most interesting as it shows just what microprocessor technology is all about. The machining centre features an advanced method of programming which is both simple and quick to master, yet provides a highly productive solution to the demands of both small- and medium-batch production. All you basically have to do is answer some simple programming questions.

The M1 machine has been introduced by Toolmasters Controls Ltd (TCL) of Reading in association with Hurco Manufacturing Co Inc of Indianapolis. This transatlantic tie-up follows investigations made by the British firm into microprocessor developments in the United States. TCL was already marketing NC systems and was actively looking for a suitable CNC package.

A meeting between TCL chairman Edward Hallewell and the Hurco president Gerry Roch at an exhibition in Detroit, a year ago last May, revealed that the American company was, in fact, looking for a suitable European outlet for its CNC system. At that stage, the three-axis system which caught Edward Hallewell's eye was being demonstrated on a Bridgeport turret type mill. And it had obviously caught other people's attention too as in the first year, since its introduction in 1976, over 100 systems had been sold in the States.

In addition to Hurco's interest in

the European market, the American company was also persuing the idea of developing a total machining centre package. Instead of fitting its CNC system to machines like the Bridgeport, it decided to build its own vertical mill, specifically designed for the control system. This was something of a departure for Hurco which had never before been involved in straight machine-tool design and manufacture. Until then the company was probably best known in the UK for its automatic back gauge system for guillotines and the like – which is still a sizeable chunk of its business and started it off on the microprocessor trail.

The results of all this design, manufacturing and development effort is the introduction of the M1 CNC machining centre both in this country and the United States. As far as the UK market goes, TCL will be manufacturing the CNC system and receiving the machine itself directly from

Reprinted with permission from *Machinery & Production Engineering.* 2nd August 1978. © Machpress Ltd 1978.

the States. It will also be handling all marketing and servicing in Britain plus last line servicing in other European countries.

While the control side of the M1 will almost certainly grab most of the limelight, the vertical bed type mill itself warrants some attention as it has some interesting features too. Design of the machine includes a computer-controlled AC spindle drive motor giving steplessly variable speeds, a traversing head (as opposed to a quill) and replaceable element slide guiding units which feature pre-loaded re-circulating ball screws held in a Gothic arch-type set up.

Brief specification of the machine, which has DC motors driving re-circulating ball leadscrews, includes traverses of 26 in (x axis), 13 in (y axis) and 14in (z axis), a table size of 12 by 52in, and a 3 hp AC spindle drive providing steplessly variable speeds from 150 to 3500 rev/min.

Despite the machine's design, it is the control side of the package where most of the goodies are to be found. The control system is seen as a big step forward in programming. All the operator has to do is respond to a logical sequence of questions by feeding in answers simply read off the component drawing.

Programming is carried out in a direct question and answer routine, usually performed by the operator at the machine's console, and in plain English (no programming codes are used whatsoever). A CRT display makes precise enquiries of the operator as to what type of operation he wants to do and the basic positional dimensions necessary to produce the desired shape. So the control actually guides the operator through the programming steps in a logical sequence, and all he has to do is insert a minimum of data by way of an MDI unit.

Say, for example, the operator wants to machine a rectangular pocket. Following the sequence of questions on the CRT display, he just feeds in the pocket's overall size, its positional co-ordinates, the cutter diameter he is using and its length calibration, the depth of cut required and the necessary feeds and speeds. All this information is retained by the control memory as the enquiries proceed. Sub-routines, held in the execu-

A general view (right) of the Hurco machine recently launched on the UK market by TCL. The control unit (below) will accept a mini-cassette which can hold 32 part programs.

tive program, are automatically called upon as and when required to complete the program build up.

If, after this operation has been programmed, the operator wants to machine another profile on the part he just calls up a new data block – so long programs are built up on a data block-by-block basis. And as each new data block appears on the CRT, the information previously programmed is automatically carried forward, requiring the operator to enter only modifications and changes. Before any programming data are fed into the control the zero data block is called up and displayed to enable tool reference points, table or fixture zero and cutting tool diameters to be fed in. As previously mentioned, the cutter diameter can also be fed in during any other data block.

When a part is programmed, the operator quickly reviews the data on the CRT and edits any mistakes or takes in any alterations. After a part has been correctly run (and there is a special dry run sequence used for program try-out) the program can be transferred on to a mini-cassette for future use. Each mini-cassette holds up to 32 part programs and although it records the memory data it is not used to control the machine on playback. All it is used for is feeding the data back into the memory at some future point in time when the job may have to be repeated.

On the programming side incremental or absolute dimensions can be used in any combination and full cutter compensation allows true part edge programming. The cutter length calibration operation, mentioned earlier, eliminates the time-consuming task of accurately presetting tools in their

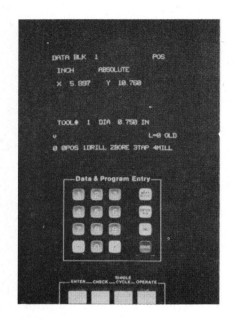

Close up (left) of the CRT showing a typical data block of information and the MDI unit. Programming for the test piece (below) was carried out in under 10 min.

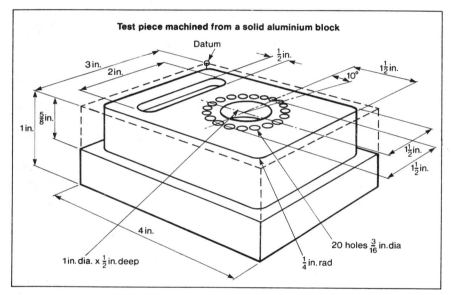

Test piece machined from a solid aluminium block

holders. Once a tool has been loaded into the spindle for a certain operation it is manually jogged down to just kiss any reference point on the surface of the workpiece. At this point the tool calibration button is pressed so that the position of the tool relative to the workpiece is recorded in the memory. From then on, z axis movements are called up in either + or − values depending whether the cutter movement required is up or down.

Up to 100 data blocks may be programmed for any part. This one-step machining cycle allows the operator to interact with control and machine. Master programs for the control logic are changed by entry through the tape cassette, allowing continuous upgrading of the entire system as different master programs or diagnostic programs are developed.

While the system's memory has a total capacity of 24 k, only about 6 k is available to receive operational instructions. But this offers ample storage capacity for the user due to the powerful and comprehensive capability of the executive program. Included in the executive program are a number of sub-routines which allow the operator to program many machining cycles in only one or two data blocks. Sub-routines available include loop/repeat, copy, frame mill, circle mill, pocket mill, peck mill/drill, arc mill, bolt circle diameter and cutter right/left.

One of the main advantages of the M1 machining centre is the high degree of productivity it offers by being able to build up a program simply, quickly and logically at the machine by just following a component drawing. However, for production

engineers who have strong views on the subject of shop floor programming and editing, the system can also be provided with a remote desk top programmer. This would allow planning office staff to prepare programs and record them on mini-cassettes well away from the shop floor.

To introduce the machine to Britain and to assess just how quick and easy programming is, TCL and Hurco staged a demonstration recently at the United States trade centre. Just working with a plain aluminium rectangular block measuring 4 by 3 in, the test piece shown in our diagram was built up and programmed by information given by visitors. So the type of machining operations, the dimensions and the position of the main features to be machined were decided right off the cuff.

Gerry Roch and one of his colleagues carried out the demonstration, one programming the machine and the other explaining just what was being done. Programming, which consisted of building up 10 blocks of information for this particular part, was done inside 10 min. But Gerry Roch reckoned that without all the time wasted to explain what was going on, the complete programming operation could have been completed in about 5 min. Just to prove the program and show the machine in action a couple of the parts were produced.

The M1 CNC machining centre is seen by both TCL and Hurco as opening up new possibilities for increasing productivity in short to medium batch production, and that is what it is designed for. However, there is no reason why the machine could not be used on long production runs too. And another plus for the machining centre is its price, most attractive, £23 000, by today's standards.

Both Gerry Roch and Edward Hallewell are excited about the future of the M1 machine in the UK and enquiries to date are certainly most encouraging. But it doesn't end there. Already there is a bigger brother for the M1, known as the M2. This model will feature a 16-station tool changer and it will sell for around £47 000. □

Section 4

Other Microprocessor Applications

Microprocessors are already being used in an amazing variety of ways — one 'chip' manufacturer has identified some 25,000 possible applications. This section provides examples of their use, ranging from cars and medicine to video games.

µP and µC-based control systems cut engine pollution, up mileage

JIM McDERMOTT

Facing the need to satisfy contrary government requirements—extremely low exhaust-gas pollution and high gas mileage—in a relatively short time, the auto industry has turned to microprocessor and microcomputer-based engine-control systems in a big way. The low pollution and high gas-mileage levels set in the government's timetable (see Table 1) simply cannot be attained by mechanical and electromechanical engine-control systems. Electronic engine controls must be combined with catalytic converters to get results.

Meanwhile, the auto industry also seeks to attract car buyers with a range of electronic niceties including µP-tuned radios, and µP-controlled instrument panel displays and information systems. One example is the Cadillac Seville Trip Computer, which not only tells the driver where he's going, or if he has enough gas to make it, but also informs him when he's arrived.

All this microprocessor-oriented auto design is creating several system trends. For one thing, the idea of having one large central computer control all engine, sensing, display entertainment, and body functions—popular as late as last fall—is giving way to distributed processing systems throughout the car: one for engine control, another for electronic dashboard and display control, and others for electronic radio tuning, transmission control and engine diagnostics.

Separation pays

There are a number of reasons for this. First, separate systems mean improved reliability. If one breaks down, the others aren't affected. In addition, as the cost of electronic packages comes down, it's getting easier to distribute modules around the car.

Simulating real-world conditions on a test car helps prevent electromagnetic interference, which can stem from AM and FM transmitters, radar, mobile radios, medical equipment and other sources, from disrupting critical automotive electronic controls. Anechoic chambers like this one at the General Motors Technical Center in Warren, MI, help by subjecting cars running on a dynamometer to radiation from the kHz to the GHz regions.

A third reason is that many of the proposed µP control systems are options that can be sold separately. An example is the Cadillac Seville Trip Computer, which provides a driver with data that are displayed upon driver command, ranging from average and instantaneous fuel economy to estimated arrival time at a preset destination.

Meanwhile, the emergence of multiple families of single-chip microcomputers has tilted auto designers towards using one of these standard µCs together with a custom LSI I/O and interface, rather than putting time and money into developing all-custom chip sets.

µPs control spark advance

Engine control begins with the spark. The first microprocessor applied for spark control, a Rockwell 10-bit serial PMOS device, is designed into GM's Microprocessed Sensing and Automatic Regulation (MISAR) system,

which found a home in the 1977/78 Oldsmobile Toronado. Engine speed, manifold pressure and crankshaft position are among the key inputs.

The instruction set is tailored for interpolation between data points contained in look-up tables. The program cycle, asynchronous with engine operation, requires about 335 program instructions and makes a new computation for spark advance and dwell time every 12 ms.

A microprocessor will soon find its way into Chrysler cars. Chrysler's analog Electronic Lean Burn system, which also controls ignition timing, will be superseded in 1979 by a digital system whose µP is a four-chip RCA 1802.

But probably the most sophisticated µP-controlled system to be offered on production cars will be the second generation of Ford's Electronic Engine Control, the EEC-II (see Fig. 1). Slated to be introduced on 1979 Model 351 CID (5.8-liter) V-8 engines, the system will come the closest so far to meeting the emissions-control and fuel-economy standards set for the 1980s.

The EEC-II system, which incorporates a 12-bit μP supplied by both Toshiba of Japan and Texas Instruments (Dallas), succeeds the EEC-I, which was introduced on Model 305 CID (5-liter) V-8 engines in the 1978 Lincoln Versailles. Whereas the EEC-I controls only spark advance and exhaust-gas recirculation (EGR) back into the intake manifold, EEC-II adds control of air-to-fuel ratio by incorporating an electronically controlled Feedback Carburetor as well as a three-way catalyst system. Pioneered this year by Ford in the U.S., the catalyst system is part of the 140 CID (2.3-liter) engines that were put into Ford Pintos and Mercury Bobcats sold in California.

The EEC-II is smaller and lighter than the EEC-I. Its package has been reduced 40%, the number of microcomputer parts 36% and the weight nearly 55%. The result is a more reliable system that performs more functions for less money.

Inputs to the EEC-II system, which calculates and controls spark timing and exhaust-gas recirculation rate, include barometric pressure, manifold absolute pressure (MAP), throttle position, inlet-air temperature, engine-coolant temperature, crankshaft position, and exhaust-gas oxygen content. Three basic look-up tables are stored in the EEC-II μC: air-to-fuel ratio, spark advance and exhaust-gas recirculation rate. The computer, looking at such fundamental parameters as manifold pressure and rpm, selects the best control point for the spark, the air-fuel ratio and EGR from the tables. The outputs go to a set of modulator/drivers that change these variables through actuators. For example, the Feedback Carburetor is controlled by a stepper motor that adjusts fuel-metering rods.

Sensor inputs are fed to the computer through a chip containing the input multiplexers and a/d converters. The a/d receives input-channel commands under software control from the CPU, and the selected input channel is routed to the a/d converter by the input multiplexer. When data conversion is completed, the a/d circuit notifies the CPU that data are available to be read. Total conversion cycle time ranges from 1.5 to 3.5 ms.

Filter networks aren't needed on any of the input channels because noise filtering is inherent in the a/d subsystem—a ratiometric, self-calibrat-ing, dual-slope integrator that provides eight data bits. Each a/d conversion includes two calibration cycles and a single measurement.

The spark-advance, EGR and fuel-control subsystems are located on a single chip. The spark-advance function requires a crankshaft position signal and a spark-advance command from the μP. These inputs are then processed to generate a spark firing command. The EGR subsystem converts a digital command from the CPU to a precise pulse width for the EGR-valve control.

Maintaining efficiency

Precise electronic control of air and fuel at the stoichiometric ratio—at which all of the hydrocarbons are theoretically consumed by the oxygen in the air—is necessary because the three-way catalyst system drastically drops in efficiency when it deviates from that ratio by even a small fractional percentage (Fig. 2). With the proper fuel-to-air ratio, the catalyst system keeps exhaust emissions of hydrocarbons, carbon monoxide and nitrogen oxides to very low levels by oxidizing the hydrocarbons and carbon monoxide and converting the nitrogen oxides to nitrogen and water.

The stoichiometric ratio is precisely controlled with an input from a titanium oxygen sensor in the exhaust manifold that detects very small variations and sends a signal to the processor to make necessary change in the carburetor setting. At the same time, the system controls the thermactor, a pump that adds air to the exhaust system, and diverts air to either the catalyst system or to the exhaust manifold to maintain maximum catalyst efficiency.

ROM calibrates EEC-II

The microprocessor control system for the EEC-II, located inside the passenger compartment, is wired to engine-compartment elements

Table 1. Federally mandated production-weighted fuel economy and allowable exhaust emissions

Year	Fuel economy, mpg	Exhaust emissions, grams/mi.		
		HC	CO	NO$_x$
1978	18	1.5	15.0	2.0
1979	19	1.5	15.0	2.0
1980	20	0.41	7.0	2.0
1981	22		3.4	1.0
1982	24			
1983	26			
1984	27			
1985	27.5	0.41	3.4	1.0

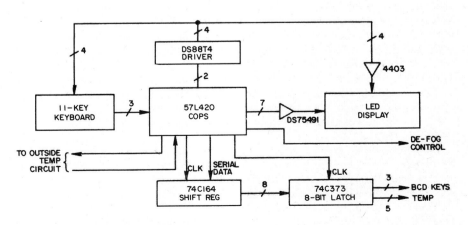

Passenger-compartment climate control is a typical application of National Semiconductor's new COP400 series, which is tailored for auto use.

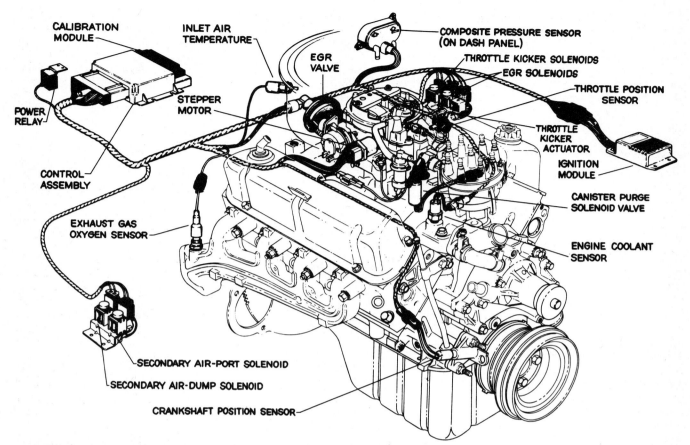

1. The most sophisticated engine-control system yet to be announced by the auto industry, Ford's second-generation Electronic Engine Control, the EEC-II, reduces exhaust pollution to new low levels, yet maintains fuel economy. Ignition timing, exhaust-gas recirculation, flow rate and carburetor air-to-fuel ratio are controlled by the EEC-II using the outputs from seven sensors: crank-shaft position, throttle position, coolant temperature, exhaust-gas mixture, manifold vacuum, barometric pressure, and exhaust-gas-recirculation valve position. The signals are fed to a 12-bit custom μP with dedicated I/O peripheral interface chips.

through the fire wall. A calibration module (Fig. 1) permits the basic microcomputer and I/O circuitry to be used with various models of autos whose differing characteristics affect EEC operation.

For example, each car model has a unique power-train combination, engine size, weight, and gear ratio, which means that the μC system must be tailored to that model.

The calibration module holds a 2-k ROM containing the basic μP operating program, which is the same for all cars. The module also contains a 0.5-k ROM as well as a set of resistors, which can be clipped out to match the system to the characteristics of the particular car model.

Since these ROMs aren't inventoried by dealers, they have been required to pass stringent reliability tests. They will be available only through central distribution points throughout the country. Normally, these ROMs remain with a car throughout its life. Because the more complex processor

assembly, which contains the μP, peripheral circuits, and power supply, is expected to have higher failure rates, it will be inventoried by dealers.

Protective interface circuits cost

Much of the cost of applying μCs to engines is actually tied up in the interface circuits that protect the μP and other LSI chips from the harsh electrical and physical environment. According to a study of the EEC-I and EEC-II systems conducted by G. Cilibraise, principal engineer at Ford's Electrical and Electronics Div. (Taylor, MI), only 29% of the electronic module cost stemmed from the microprocessor (see Table 2). Of the remaining 76%, about 41% was required to perform support functions such as power-supply regulation and data-form conversion. Some 30% of the cost went to protecting the unit from the vehicle environment.

Looking at it from another angle, 46% of component complexity is needed

for environmental protection while 12% is required for the general computations in the strategy program; 42% is allocated to the support functions.

Moreover, in the EEC-type μC systems, single-chip μPs can't do the whole job, Cilibraise points out. A special interface and I/O systems need to be developed. However Cilibraise does concede that for a single, stand-alone control function, a single-chip device can be effective.

Brian Knowles, automotive microcomponents marketing manager at Intel (Santa Clara), agrees.

"A single function like carburetor control can be comfortably handled by available single-chip microcomputers," he notes. "In that kind of an application we're offering the 8048 and also its interchangeable EPROM part, the 8748."

The 8748 has significant advantages over ROMs, Knowles insists. "The automotive industry is used to making small modifications in its production on relatively short notice. With the mechanical systems, changing a spring or a weight in a distributor to correct an ignition timing problem was easy to do.

"But now," Knowles goes on, "if the Environmental Protection Agency rejects an audit of a new car's system because something has drifted out of tolerance, it's a crisis situation."

Knowles notes that ROMs can't be changed quickly. "But the EPROM can quickly fill the gap between the original ROM code and a new ROM code with the fix in it."

As a matter of fact, Chrysler is using a small, fusible-link PROM in its new microprocessor-based equivalent of the analog Lean Burn Spark Control Computer. With this PROM, 4, 6, or 8-cylinder engines can use the digital system without requiring a new ROM. The primary control algorithm can be modified easily. As a result, engine designers can change the operating characteristics without having a new ROM mask made. Control constants in the PROM are loaded at Chrysler's Huntsville, AL, assembly plant.

Because extensive test equipment for the analog version is already located at Chrysler dealerships, the new digital Spark Control Computer mounts all components on a single PC board that's no bigger than a custom analog module. The μP system is designed to match the functional and operating characteristics of the analog spark-control unit, which means that from a black-box point of view the digital system is compatible not only with the engine systems but also with the diagnostic test equipment.

The PC board contains five other ICs besides the fusible-link PROM: an RCA 1802 microprocessor, a quad comparator, a custom I/O chip and a 32-byte ROM. It's spec'd to operate at 4-V for cold-weather cranking, and in an over-all range of −40 to 125 C.

Single-chip μP has a/d

Nevertheless single-chip systems are being geared to low-cost automotive uses. One being evaluated now by auto companies is the 8022, a single-chip μP that includes a two-input, 8-bit a/d converter. This is seen as a low-cost system having one or two possible options, such as monitoring fuel flow and giving miles-per-gallon consumption.

A member of the 8048 family, the 8022 has an MSC-48 CPU architecture, 2 k of ROM, and 64 bytes of RAM, in

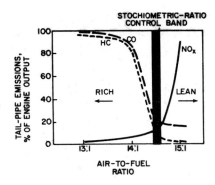

2. For maximum reduction of exhaust pollutants, the input to a three-way catalyst system must be maintained within critical stoichiometric limits.

addition to the two a/d inputs. In a year or two, Intel expects to capitalize further on the 8022 technology by adding more a/d functions for engine-control systems.

For low-cost, simple control functions such as dashboard displays and automatically tuned radios, TI's single-chip PMOS TMS-1000 is being designed

in for now. But soon there'll be a low-power, low-cost CMOS version.

Mostek's single-chip entry, the NMOS MK 3870, is a single-chip F-8 with 2 k of memory and a 5-V supply. Its architecture is control, rather than arithmetic oriented. Two other control-oriented single-chip NMOS μPs are the COP420 and 421 from National Semiconductor (Santa Clara). Suitable for automotive applications such as climate control and multiplexed vacuum-fluorescent displays in electronically tuned radios, they are TTL/CMOS-compatible in and out. LEDs can be directly driven from them.

One major advantage of both NMOS and CMOS is that, unlike PMOS systems, they can operate at well below 5 V. This feature is important because cranking an engine at −40 F can reduce battery terminal voltage to close to 4 V. CMOS can also operate reliably at high temperatures.

Mostek's 3870 has been designed into Chrysler's trip and mileage computer, which will be competitive with the

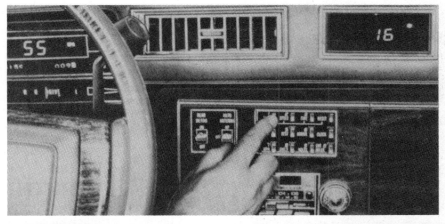

Microprocessors are appearing in automobile systems like those for trip computing, which keep track of mileage, time, fuel left and other related items. The Cadillac Trip Computer (top) comes with the 1978 Cadillac Sevilles. The on-board computer by Prince (bottom) can be installed in any type of car or truck.

The display problem

With massive amounts of data being received and processed by multiple engine-control and passenger-compartment microcomputers, dashboard displays are becoming an important interface between these systems and drivers. The displays not only keep them informed of normal operational conditions but also provide alert or warning signals for malfunctions or catastrophic failures. But producing a display acceptable to the automobile producers is tough.

As one automotive display expert put it: "We'd like to see a display that will never fail, is very bright or has high-contrast ratio, is pleasing to look at, uses low power, can be multiplexed and interfaced directly with microprocessors—and costs next to nothing."

Reliability is at the top of every car maker's requirements. The reason? The reputation of these new, complex electronic systems in the eyes of the consumer depends heavily on how well these displays perform. And a bright display in eye-pleasing color will also hasten customer acceptance.

Chasing this lucrative market is a variety of producers, offering LEDs, plasma-gas discharge panels, planar vacuum-fluorescent devices, electroluminescent panels and liquid crystal displays, among others.

But at this point, not one of the various, display types can satisfy all the auto makers' requirements. In fact, some types have more than one bad mark. For example, red LEDs are undesirable because they wash out in sunlight, and because red is associated with warning signals. Yellow or green LEDs are more acceptable but they cost too much. Liquid-crystal displays have limited viewing angles and, so far, inadequate lifetimes. Without heaters, they can't function across the temperature range required of car electronics. And their ability to be multiplexed is uncertain.

A review of all available types has led car manufacturers to select the vacuum-fluorescent display as the optimum choice. It is eye-pleasing, operates off of the battery, and can be multiplexed and microprocessor driven. Rapidly gaining favor, the vacuum-fluorescent display promises to dominate the field until the early 1980s. By that time, the problems plaguing liquid-crystal and electro-chromic displays today, notably temperature and lifetime, are expected to be solved.

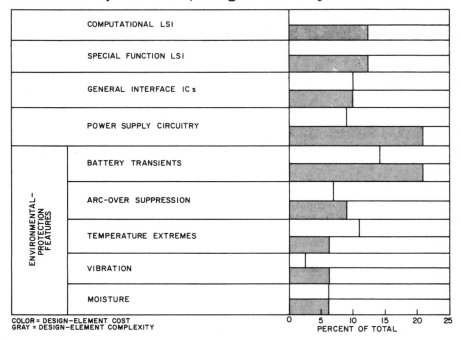

Table 2. Comparison of the relative cost and complexity of design elements of representative μP engine-control systems

COLOR = DESIGN-ELEMENT COST
GRAY = DESIGN-ELEMENT COMPLEXITY

Cadillac Seville's $875 Trip Computer and is expected to show up in 100,000 of Chrysler's 1979 trucks.

For car owners who would like to retrofit their vehicles with such a device, an On-Board Computer from Prince Corp. (Holland, MI) provides data on 24 different functions. The $400 system uses a custom 4-bit μP by National Semiconductor with 12 kbits of memory. Twin yellow-LED displays provide digital readouts, while a fiber-optic lighting system provides panel illumination.

Motorola's 6801 is an upgraded version of the 6800, including an on-chip clock generator and scratchpad RAM. And Mostek has doubled the ROM and RAM capacity of the 3870 in its new MK 3872, the second member of its single-chip family. The 3872 includes 4032 × 8 bytes of mask-programmable ROM, 64 bytes of scratchpad RAM and an extra 64 bytes of executable RAM.

Engine controls are multichip

But high-performance fuel and ignition controls for engines are still multichip applications. While TI is providing custom designs like the EEC-II μC for these applications, other car manufacturers are using standard TMS-9900 16-bit family products. With these designs, the lowest-cost approach is to do the basic processing with a standard CPU while designing interface and I/O circuitry to handle particular peripheral requirements.

For engine controllers, Intel is marketing the 8048/8049 and 8085 systems.

"The 8049 is capable, with its 11-MHz clock, of handling table look-up and interpolate routines at the speeds necessary in a spark control or fuel-injection system," says Intel's Knowles, adding "and at reasonably low cost."

A Motorola MC 6800 has been chosen by Bendix for a digital version of its Electronic Fuel Injection System.

At this point, applying microcomputer systems to automobile control systems is still in the infancy stage—but growing fast. Of some 26 electronic systems or products in the 1978 model year cars, only four have them. The rest are analog systems. And problems still exist. For example, the lack of accurate, low-cost sensors of all kinds is restricting the use of μCs. But experts predict that by 1985 the percentage of μC systems to that of analog type systems will be essentially reversed.

But there will always be some applications where the use of μPs and μCs simply won't be cost effective, like Monroe Auto Equipment's analog vehicle-leveling system, which uses a simple LED-photocell arrangement to keep shock absorbers pressurized to a certain height.

Single-chip microcomputer as a petrol pump controller

It has been estimated that 80% of all single-chip micro-computer applications will be as some form of controller. The application described here shows how the Intel 8048 might be used as the control element in a petrol pump.

In this application the microcomputer is called upon to perform five separate functions:

(1) Measure the amount of petrol dispensed by the pump.
(2) Display the amount of petrol dispensed and compute and display the cost.
(3) Control valves and motors necessary for correct pump operation.
(4) Allow the fuel type to be selected and monitor pump status.
(5) On completion of the sale, transmit the details to a central point over a serial transmission line.

For this application 18 output and 7 input lines are required. The 8048, used in this application, has what is known as quasi bi-directional ports. This means that individual lines in a port can be either inputs or outputs on a bit-by-bit basis. It can be seen that port 2 in this application is used as both an input (for system reset) and an output (for motor control and serial communication with the central control point).

Port 4 is used to control the four valves internal to the pump. Here the individual bit set and reset capability using 'logic immediate' instructions of the 8048 enable any valve to be individually opened or closed. For example, if a binary 1 opened a valve and a binary 0 closed it and if each bit position in a 4-bit binary code correspond to one line of the port as follows:

VALVE 4   VALVE 1

0000

then the valves can be operated using AND and OR instructions:

AND immediate data at port with 0000
   Result 0000 — all valves closed
OR immediate data at port with 0100
   Result 0100 — valve 3 opened
OR immediate data at port with 0010
   Result 0110 — valves 2 and 3 open
AND immediate data at port with 0010
   Result 0010 — valve 3 closes valve 2 remains open

In the above example one instruction was used for each valve operation. There is no reason, however, why one instruction could not be used to change the state of all four valves simultaneously.

The serial communications link with the central point is quite interesting. Normally, serial communication is not implemented at maximum processor speed since this would require special, and expensive, high-frequency transmission lines. There has to be a delay, therefore, between each bit transmitted. This could be achieved by inserting a software delay in the form of a timing loop in the section of the program dealing with communication; this, however, is not recommended by Intel because it is extremely wasteful in processing time. They say a better approach is to use the non-chip programmable timer on the 8048 to interrupt the processor each time a bit is due to be sent. In this way the processor can carry out other tasks at the same time as it is implementing serial communication. In this technique the programmable timer is set to provide a delay equal to the

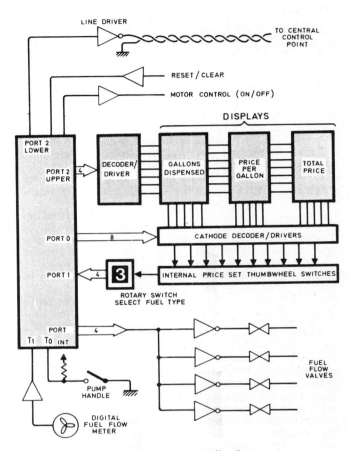

Schematic of petrol pump control application

desired bit rate. At the receiving end another 8048 could receive the data in exactly the same way.

In the petrol pump the on-chip timer is also employed for another purpose. The amount of fuel being dispensed is measured by a digital flowmeter which provides a pulse for every known fraction of a gallon. This pulse is applied to input T1 of the 8048 and the timer is programmed to operate in a counting mode in which it counts the number of pulses output by the flowmeter. At the end of the dispensing operation the timer will hold a count proportional to the amount of fuel dispensed for use in cost calculation. Since serial communications and petrol dispensing take place at different times, there is no problem in using the timer for both tasks.

The fact that a customer requires petrol is signalled to the system when the pump handle is lifted. This action operates a pair of contacts in a solid-state switch connected to input T0 of the processor. The processor has the ability to test the status of T0 and to jump to a routine on a specified condition — this takes one instruction.

Practically all the computation required in the petrol pump application involves either gallons or money which can be conventionally handled in binary coded decimal form. It is therefore important that the single-chip microcomputer has a series of instructions capable of efficiently handling bcd quantities.

Reprinted with permission from *Measurement And Control,* Vol. 11, April 1978.

The sound of silence

The silencing of diesel exhausts by out-of-phase cancellation using a microprocessor has now been achieved. By Professor G B B Chaplin and R A Smith*

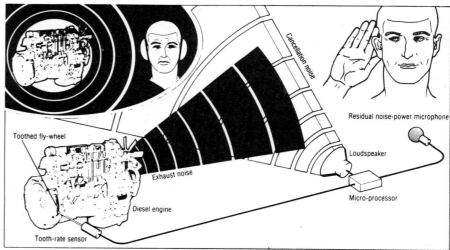

A revolutionary method for the silencing of low frequency, repetitive noise, such as that produced by internal combustion engines, compressors or pumps, has successfully completed preliminary trials at Essex University and the nearby firm of Sound Attenuators Ltd. The system dispenses with the conventional exhaust silencer, and cancels the noise by actually adding an 'anti-phase' noise at the exhaust outlet; this anti-phase noise is, to the human ear, indistinguishable from the original exhaust noise. However, when the two noises meet, they subtract and, if accurately balanced, the result is *silence*.

Fig. 1 represents the experimental rig in which a single-cylinder engine has an exhaust pipe but no conventional silencer. A loudspeaker is mounted in a box with an outlet adjacent to the exhaust outlet, and a microphone is placed nearby to detect any residual noise. The loudspeaker may be placed close to the exhaust outlet, as shown here, or at some distance from it, with the cancelling wave form transmitted to the exhaust outlet by a sound pipe. The anti-phase noise waveform is generated by a microprocessor which monitors the residual noise power from the microphone. The microprocessor does not require any information on the shape of the exhaust noise waveform, but simply generates the anti-phase waveform by attempting to minimise the residual noise power fed to it from the microphone.

Adaptation time

Fig. 2 shows the rate at which the exhaust noise is reduced when the engine is running on constant load. It can be seen that the system has adapted itself to an overall cancellation of 18 dB, which is subjectively quite impressive, in about 30 seconds. This

* Professor G B B Chaplin & Mr R A Smith are at the Department of Electrical Engineering Science, University of Essex, Colchester.

Reprinted with permission from *Engineering*.

adaptation time is perfectly adequate for constant-speed installations, such as standby power generators, but it is anticipated that the adaptation time can be reduced, by further development of the circuitry, to a fraction of a second which will be more than adequate for almost all variable-speed applications, such as medium and heavy vehicles. Note that there is a second input to the microprocessor which automatically synchronizes it to the speed of the engine. This forms a trigger for both the scan of the residual noise power and the subsequent initiation of the cancelling wave.

The cancelling waveform

Fig. 3 shows the exhaust noise waveforms (**a** and **c**), and the cancelling waveforms generated by the microprocessor (**b** and **d**), before and after cancellation. The original exhaust noise waveform shown at (**a**) is reduced to the residual waveform of (**c**) and this is accomplished by the cancelling waveform adapting from zero at (**b**) to its final shape at (**d**). Note that the final cancelling waveform (**d**) is not simply an anti-phase version of (**a**) but has automatically compensated for the loudspeaker characteristics and any reverberation.

Low frequencies

The most significant characteristic of this new silencing method is that it becomes more effective at the lower frequencies, whereas conventional silencers have the opposite characteristic of being more effective at the higher frequencies. The optimum cross-over point is a function of the actual system, but in general is around 250 Hz. Thus a silencing system optimised for maximum performance and minimum cost might have a small conventional 'straight-through' silencer to deal with frequencies above 250 Hz and an electronic

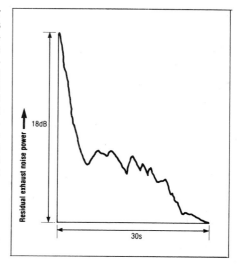

silencer to cancel frequencies from 250 Hz down to 30 Hz, or even into the infra-sound region. The infra-sound is significant because there is a considerable component of noise at the firing cycle frequency of many engines which, in the case of medium speed four-stroke diesels is between 5 and 15 Hz. Although intrinsically inaudible, infra-sound can produce audible sound by induced vibration, and can itself have unpleasant effects on people exposed to it – such as fatigue and sickness.

Bigger engines

Fig. 4 shows the exhaust noise pressure waveform of a 16-cylinder 1750 hp diesel engine driving a 1.5 MW generator. Note that the waveform is not much more complex than that of Fig. **3a** and so, on waveshape considerations, it should be possible to achieve the same degree of cancellation in the same adaptation time (i.e. 18 dB in 30 seconds). There is, however, a considerable difference in noise power

1 Experimental set-up

In a really spectacular demonstration of the system, a small engine driving a generator was used. A straight-through silencer in the exhaust pipe removed the high-frequency portion of the noise, leaving a deep 'thump' which reverberated in the laboratory causing some items to resonate. The loud speaker was mounted in a box close to the point where the exhaust pipe fed into a flexible duct that took the fumes to the exterior, with the microphone in a sealed box about 18 inch away.

On switching on the 'silencer', there was a rapid diminution of the noise until in around 20 seconds all that remained was the slight patter from the sound-insulated box containing the motor and generator. Measurements showed that the level had been cut by 20 dB in the 120 Hz frequency band and by around 16 to 18 dB at other frequencies. The silencing covered the whole of the room and those items, such as window panes, which previously had been resonating became still.

2 Typical plot of the reduction in residual exhaust noise power during the first 30 seconds of adaptive cancellation on the basic system

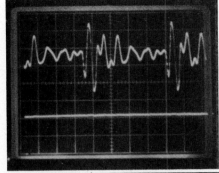

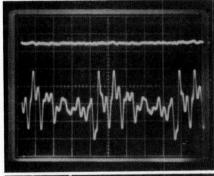

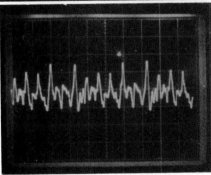

3 Oscillograms of exhaust noise before and after cancellation,

a Exhaust noise waveform before adaptation

b Cancelling waveform before adaptation

c Residual noise waveform after adaptation

d Cancelling waveform after adaptation

4 Exhaust power waveform of 16-cylinder 1750 hp diesel engine on quarter load at 750 rev/min. The waveform is clearly repetitive and not much more complex than that in Fig. 3a

produced by the two engines, the latter requiring a more powerful amplifier and loudspeaker. Extrapolation from the power required to silence the small engine indicates that a 500 to 1000 W public-address amplifier driving an array of 100 W loudspeakers should provide effective and raeltively compact silencing.

The back pressure produced by a conventional low-frequency silencer can have an adverse effect on the efficiency of the engine, especially if the exhaust system includes a turbo-compressor.

The relative importance of this effect will depend on a number of factors, but the absence of any back pressure from the electronic silencer can be a considerable advantage.

Vehicle cab noise

In the preceding example the noise was cancelled at source – i.e. at the outlet of the exhaust – resulting in cancellation at all points in space. However, there is another

class of noise problem, typified by the cab of a vehicle, in which the noise originates from more than one source, such as structure borne machinery noise, and airborne machinery and exhaust noise. In this case, cancellation over a large area is difficult, but cancellation over a limited region could be achieved simply by placing the loudspeaker and microphone in the cab. If the microphone is sited near to the driver's head, then a zone of comparative silence can be created. This zone is centred on the microphone, and extends to a radius of more than $1/12$th of a wavelength – which at 60 Hz results in a cancellation zone considerably more than 0.75 m (2.5 ft) in diameter. The siting of the loudspeaker is not critical, and an existing audio system in the cab could double-up for the noise cancellation function.

An intriguing feature of this system, which differs from the insulated quiet-cab approach, is that the driver would still be able to hear extraneous sounds, not synchronised to engine speed. He would there-

fore be able to hear traffic sounds and warning shouts, which could contribute significantly to safety.

The future

This new method of noise suppression is not just a direct replacement for some existing conventional silencers, but presents some unique properties. It follows that, although there are several fairly obvious applications, there are likely to be many more, as yet unknown, which will be made possible by its low-frequency capability, relatively small size, absence of back pressure and ability to discriminate between noises of different origin.

The pattern which emerges therefore is of a silencing system which should be more effective, more efficient, and less expensive overall, and which could well be a timely answer to the increasingly stringent noise legislation, both in the UK and in many export markets, such as Scandinavia.

Microprocessors in Aerospace Applications

by

Lance A. Leventhal
Engineering and Technology Department
Grossmont College
8800 Grossmont College Drive
El Cajon, California 92020

INTRODUCTION

The microprocessor has already found many applications in aerospace systems because of its low cost, small size, low power consumption, and high reliability. The most serious difficulties in using microprocessors are the lack of adequate software and hardware support from the manufacturers and the high cost of the development tools that do exist. Aerospace applications seldom generate enough volume to absorb the costs of developing systems. Therefore, users must stress methods which will reduce these costs rather than emphasize the savings of memory or hardware.

This article reviews the current state of the art in the microprocessor field and suggests some solutions to the special problems faced by aerospace designers. The use of microprocessors to make systems easier to operate and maintain is also briefly discussed. This approach to the use of microprocessors also applies to other low-volume applications in such areas as process control, industrial control, test equipment, and military systems.

TYPES OF MICROPROCESSORS

There are two distinct types of microprocessors that aerospace designers will find useful:

(1)   The single-chip MOS processors[1-5] which are essentially low-cost, low-speed CPUs. The most widely used devices are the Intel 8080, Motorola 6800, Zilog Z-80, and Fairchild F-8.

(2)   The bit-slice bipolar processors[6-9] which are intermediate in complexity between the single-chip CPUs and standard logic elements. The bit slices can be connected in parallel to form part of a standard CPU with any word length. The most widely used slices are the Advanced Micro Devices 2900 and the Intel 3000. Since these two types of microprocessors have distinct application areas and associated problems, we shall discuss only the MOS processors here. A later article will deal with bipolar devices.

SINGLE-CHIP MOS DEVICES

The widely used MOS microprocessors have the following general charcteristics:

- 8-bit data words and 16-bit addresses. (The longer addresses are necessary to access a reasonable amount of memory.)

- Instruction execution times of 1 to 10 microseconds depending on the type of instruction and the addressing method used.

- Minicomputer-like instruction sets with 50 to 80 separate instructions. Hardware multiplication, division, floating-point arithmetic, bit manipulation, text search, block input/output, and communications error-checking instructions are not usually available.

- Separate data and address buses. The data bus is bidirectional.

- Computer-like features such as interrupts, direct memory access (DMA), varied addressing methods, stack operations, multipurpose registers, and status words.

- Limited software support, seldom consisting of much more than a simple monitor, an assembler, a software simulator, a version of BASIC, and a high-level language based on PL/I. Most of this software can run only on special development systems with extra memory and peripherals or on larger computers. Real-time operating systems and other advanced software are just beginning to appear on the market.

- A family of compatible circuit elements including memories, buffers and drivers, parallel and serial interfaces, interrupt and DMA controllers, timers, and single-chip peripheral controllers for communications lines, printers, keyboards and displays, cassettes, floppy disks, and CRTs.[10]

- A chip cost of $10 to $50 in small quantities. Complete board-level computers cost $100 to $1,000, depending on features.

The cost of CPUs is negligible except in such limited-purpose, high-volume applications as controllers for electronic games, cash registers, appliances, and small instruments. There the repeated costs of hardware, however small they are per unit, soon overwhelm the fixed costs of software and development. Few aerospace applications are of that type. Rather, typical applications such as keyboard and display controllers, navigational aids, phase-locked loop controllers, low-speed data-acquisition systems, communications interfaces, data loggers, and instrument controllers seldom involve volumes of more than a few hundred units. Many applications, in fact, are one-of-a-kind prototypes. At such levels, software and engineering costs (even though they occur only once) greatly outweigh the cost of CPUs, memories, and other hardware.

Much of the literature on MOS microprocessors does not consider the low-volume aerospace user. The literature is often directed toward high-volume users with no computer experience; the emphasis is on low-level software and the minimization of memory usage and chip count. The aerospace user, on the other hand, typically is more concerned with the cost and time involved in hardware and software development. Most aerospace users, furthermore, either have computer experience or have ready access to such experience and to large computers.

The question for the aerospace user is how to handle software costs that are typically $5 to $25 per word of program.[11] Programming in machine or assembly language leads to lengthened schedules and higher costs which cannot be spread over a large number of production units. Furthermore, the cost of hardware and interface design[12] and of developmental hardware and software cannot easily be justified for a single application.

A STANDARD MODULE STRUCTURE

An obvious way to handle the high development costs is to divide them among many applications. Clearly, a set of standard modules, either purchased or developed in-house, is a useful approach.[13-18] The standard modules must include:

* Processors

* Random-access memory (RAM)

* Programmable read-only memory (PROM) for programs and tables

* Interfaces for such peripherals as teletypewriters, RS-232 devices, cassettes, cartridges, floppy disks, and IEEE-488 devices

* Interrupt and DMA control

* Parallel and serial I/O

* D/A and A/D conversion systems

* Relay boards

* Timers

* Real-time clock

* Keyboard and display controllers

* Full and half-duplex communications interface.

Users should try to avoid dependence on a single processor since none is suitable for every application and the market is by no means settled. However, since almost any of the processors will be satisfactory for most applications, no wide variety is necessary. In general, second-sourcing, the availability of supporting software and hardware, and the availability of parts that meet military and other specifications will be more important factors in choosing processors than will benchmarks or specific architectural features.

There is no real need to strive for full interchangeability of processors, memories, I/O interfaces, etc. These devices are all too new to be fully standardized, and internal buses that allow the use of any processors, memories, and other associated devices do not appear to offer clear advantages. Standard module structures should be left flexible enough to cope easily with continued technological change.

Programmable I/O interfaces, timers, and controllers are particularly convenient since the designer can configure them in software to perform a variety of functions. Most of these devices are only readily usable with the single processor for which they were intended but some can be configured for use with several different CPUs. These devices should be used whenever possible since they can greatly simplify interfacing problems and they can be shared among many applications.

A standard external busing structure is, of course, essential. The IEEE-488 bus is one possibility.[3] Others that are widely used include the Intel Intellec bus (or Multibus) and the Motorola Exorciser (or Micromodule) bus. The hobbyist S-100 bus[19] is still another possibility, since many peripherals and boards are available for that configuration. The MUBUS standard[17] is a recent European development.

Aerospace designers should try to limit special-purpose hardware development because of its high cost. Rather, they should emphasize the use of standard interfaces or, if these are not available, programmable interfaces or special microprocessor-compatible devices and systems. The microprocessor-compatible systems include A/D and D/A modules, complete data-acquisition systems, synchro-to-digital and digital-to-synchro converters, voltage-to-frequency converters, etc. Microprocessor compatibility typically means tri-state outputs (i.e., an open-circuit third state which does not affect the overall bus), byte-parallel I/O (i.e., 8 bits at a time), addressable registers, status and control signals which can serve as DEVICE READY, VALID DATA, or DATA ACCEPTED signals, TTL voltage levels, and adequate buffering and driving capability for interfacing to MOS devices.

Intel's new Universal Peripheral Interface (UPI-41) is a single-chip microcomputer that can be programmed (with on-chip ROM or ultraviolet erasable PROM) to be an intelligent peripheral controller. This device could handle many of the interfacing functions required by small printers, plotters, analog control units, keyboard and display systems, paper-tape readers, and other low-to-medium-speed peripherals. Once programmed, such devices could be used as plug-in units by designers. This would save on both hardware and software development costs without requiring a multiplicity of parts or custom chips.

A STANDARD SOFTWARE STRUCTURE

Software may also be shared among many projects by the use of library routines and PROM-based monitors, operating systems, editors, mathematical packages, loaders, interpreters, and other modules.[20] Standard documentation procedures are essential.

All the procedures that have increased programmer productivity in larger computing systems also apply to microcomputer software development. Important techniques include[21-26]:

- Modular programming

- Top-down design

- Structured programming

- Walkthroughs

- Structured testing

- Structured flowcharts.

The engineers who will most often use microprocessors will require a thorough introduction to these techniques since they are seldom part of engineering training.

As usual, programmer productivity will be highest if suitable high-level languages are employed. No entirely adequate language is yet available and some assembly-language programming is almost always necessary.[27] Criteria for a high-level language include:

(1) Suitability for control applications

(2) Compatibility with top-down design and structured programming

(3) Ability to describe the configuration and use of programmable interface chips, timers, and controllers

(4) Ability to handle distributed multiprocessor systems

(5) Efficient compilation so that memory use is not excessive

(6) Extensive compile-time error-checking. Compile-time testing, as described by Hamlet,[44] would also be helpful.

The languages based on PL/I are the most satisfactory at present, but more research in this area is necessary.

The emphasis in software design must be on limiting total software cost. Saving a few words of memory or a few chips will hardly ever be worthwhile. Designers should follow the rules of top-down design and structured programming as much as possible since these methods greatly reduce debugging and testing time. Compatible LSI devices that are available at reasonable cost should be used whenever possible; there is no need in low-volume applications to replace receiver/transmitter chips (UARTs and USRTs), converters, and encoders with software.

STANDARD DEVELOPMENT AND PROTOTYPING SYSTEMS

Not only must hardware and software be standardized but so also must development and prototyping systems. In fact, a standard prototyping board should be one of the family of modules. Such a board should have the following components:

- CPU

- Some on-board RAM, preferably around 1K

- A ROM-based monitor-debugger

- Serial teletypewriter and EIA RS-232 interface

- Space for on-board erasable PROM for nearly completed programs

- On-board parallel I/O

- Adequate buffering and decoding so that off-board expansion is simple

- On-board timer/event counter.

The addition of a hexadecimal keyboard for input, seven-segment displays for output, and an audio cassette interface for mass storage will make the prototyping board usable without a terminal and viable as a working system in many prototypes and extremely low-volume applications. For examples of such complete prototyping boards, see Reference 28. The use of programmable I/O devices and timers will make the board usable in a wide variety of applications without any additional hardware.

More advanced development tools than a simple monitor/debugger require more memory and peripherals than can be justified for each prototyping system. Several projects must therefore share a central set of development tools (or development system), which may be based on a microcomputer, a minicomputer, or a large in-house computer.

Any development system should have the following features:

(1) Ability to handle more than one type of processor so that the user is not tied to a single device which may be unsuitable for a particular application or which may become outmoded

(2) Adequate software including assembler, monitor, loader, editor, debugging packages, and compilers. The software should be user-oriented, interactive when possible, easy to understand, and well-documented.

(3) In-circuit emulation, i.e., the ability to attach a prototype of the computing system under development to the development system and test it

(4) Adequate I/O devices so that the entering of programs and listing of results do not use a major amount of time

(5) Mass storage (preferably random-access, e.g., floppy disk rather than tape) so that programs can be conveniently stored and retrieved

(6) Ability to interface with logic analyzers and other hardware development tools

(7) Statistical packages for the generation of random interrupts and other inputs and the analysis of test results

(8) Real-time operation and emulation so that timing problems can be handled in a realistic environment

(9) Extendibility to future generations of processors

(10) Transparent system software and hardware which does not limit designs by using part of the memory space or control system.

Various kinds of development systems exist. Stand-alone systems are relatively inexpensive to operate and easy to use but may represent a substantial initial investment and be limited in software and power.[29-31] Already available in-house large computers or minicomputers can be used[32-35]; they have adequate capabilities but may be expensive and difficult to operate and to interface to prototypes.

The cost of a microcomputer development system must be balanced against the potential savings in development cost and time. A development system that offers most of the mentioned features can easily cost $20,000. However, the added engineering and programming time required to design applications without such a system or to create and maintain a development facility based on an in-house computer may be still more expensive. The cost of software development is still regularly underestimated by project managers. Inadequate planning may result in large cost overruns, particularly when a partially completed project must be either abandoned or continued.

The requirement is for a complete software and hardware development system. Software simulation is ful to check program logic but cannot help with I/O and timing problems. Most microprocessor applications involve tightly coupled software and hardware. As with hardware modules, fully generalized software systems are available but do not appear to offer any real advantages over separate software for each processor.

One option which has not yet been fully explored is the use of very flexible microprogrammable computers or universal hosts. Such computers can emulate microcomputers in real time and may also be able to emulate programmable I/O devices and multiprocessor systems. Reference 36 discusses this subject more extensively and Reference 37 describes an emulation service available through the Arpanet. Emulation has the usual advantages of simulation since it allows software development prior to or concurrent with hardware development and even prior to the construction or design of a particular processor.[38,39]

It can also aid in benchmarking, performance evaluation, and feasibility studies.

DESIGNING FOR USABILITY AND MAINTAINABILITY

Microprocessors give the aerospace designer the opportunity to add important features to systems at relatively low cost. These features include:

● Error tolerance

● Operator interaction, including immediate feedback of entries

● Simpler input procedures and improved displays

● Remote error-checking

● Self-test[41]

● Fault diagnosis

● Self-calibration.

Such features not only produce more usable and maintainable systems, but they also make the systems easier to debug and test. Here, some additional software effort can result in large payoffs throughout the life cycle of the system.

One important new technique that designers should consider is the signature analysis procedure developed by Hewlett-Packard.[42,43] In this procedure, the service person simply attaches the Signature Analyzer to specified nodes in order and looks for the correct signatures (4 hexadecimal digits). The system documentation describes the order in which nodes should be examined and the signatures that should be obtained. The advantages of the technique are:

(1) Dependence on a single relatively inexpensive instrument, the Hewlett-Packard 5004A Signature Analyzer. The Analyzer is portable and easy to operate.

(2) Ability to find a large percentage of all types of errors. Signature analysis is based on the feedback shift registers which have been used so successfully in coding and communications error-checking.

(3) Support from a large and well-respected manufacturer of text equipment.

(4) Ability to pinpoint errors at the component level without requiring expensive equipment or highly trained personnel. The error-tracing procedures can be described simply and systematically.

(5) Use of software rather than extra hardware to provide stimuli and test patterns. The required software can be standardized.

The Signature Analyzer may also be used as an in-house test and repair instrument.

CONCLUSION

Aerospace users of microprocessors will find software and engineering costs to be the overwhelming problem. Few aerospace applications generate the volumes necessary to effectively amortize these costs. Aerospace users must therefore adopt methods designed to reduce the cost of development. Such methods include the use of standard modules (including prototyping boards), high-level languages, compatible hardware, structured programming, and top-down design. Languages and development systems must not only help reduce the total cost of development but also must provide a unified approach to interrelated software and hardware. The use of microprocessors can make the final products easier to operate and maintain if the designer includes the necessary features in software in a usable and systematic manner.

The microprocessor revolution hots-up

Control of fuel-fired furnaces using micro-processors can result in dramatic cost savings, even for the small furnace user. Brian Kellock takes a look at the equipment developed by the BNF Metals Technology Centre.

Fuel-fired furnaces can now be added to the growing list of equipment and processes which are benefiting from the micro-processor revolution, as the result of work carried out by the BNF Metals Technology Centre, Wantage. A fully-automatic control system based on a relatively inexpensive micro-processor serves very effectively to monitor and control all the main furnace variables.

At BNF, application of the micro-processor has also been taken a stage further with the construction of a diagnostic trolley. This unit is a simplified 'monitoring-only' form of the fully-automatic controller, and has been designed particularly for the benefit of fairly small users of furnaces and foundries operating a large number of furnaces. One trolley

is at present operating in an aluminium foundry, where it has simplified the setting up of crucible burners and permitted ready determination of the control valve adjustments needed to obtain optimum operating conditions.

Until two years ago, when the impact of micro-processors and micro-computers began to be felt, it was only the large and complex systems which lent themselves to computer control. The introduction of large-scale integrated devices changed all that by making it possible for single-board micro-computers to be built for as little as £500 – which is approximately one-twentieth the cost of a 'conventional' mini-computer. Thus it became feasible to apply computer control to smaller installations and to

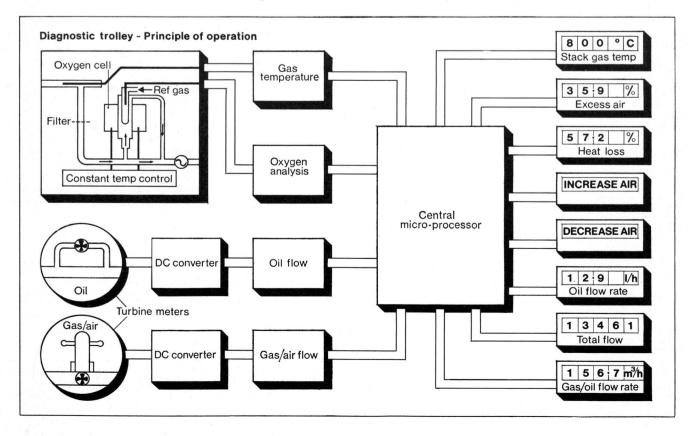

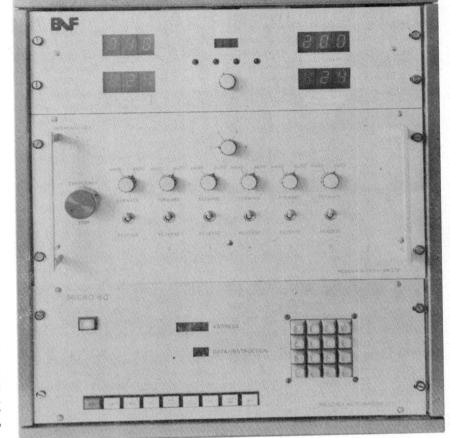

such individual items of plant as furnaces.

Several inter-related factors make the introduction of computer control to furnace operation worthwhile. These factors include the benefits of having complete control in an environment such that it is difficult to recruit and retain high-quality workers. However, the single most important benefit is the significant savings in fuel costs which are possible. In the days when fuel was a comparatively cheap commodity, and there was little national interest in energy conservation, the practicability of applying automatic controls to furnaces was not considered seriously.

However, present-day emphasis on energy conservation and concern at high fuel cost have resulted in conditions whereby the adoption of low-capital equipment such as the new breed of micro-processors has become practicable, to reduce fuel consumption considerably with correspondingly large savings in fuel costs. According to BNF, it is quite feasible for companies using conventional furnaces for melting and reheating metals to reduce their fuel bills by as much as 25 per cent with the introduction of more effective control.

To substantiate this contention, reference is made to a survey of the secondary aluminium industry in the UK, carried out by the Aluminium Federation. The survey showed that the average total energy consumption for production of 1 tonne of aluminium was 14 GJ (14×10^9 joules). Assuming that 50 per cent of this energy was actually employed in the melting operation, BNF consider it quite feasible for the resultant figure of 7 GJ to be reduced to 3 GJ. In money terms the saving is equivalent to £3 to £5/tonne at present-day prices.

The modern computer-based plant control system is required to receive and process information concerning a number of controllable variables

which affect performance. It may also be required to issue instructions for these variables to be modified. In the case of fuel-fired furnaces, the variables which affect thermal efficiency are the fuel/air ratio; the furnace pressure and the ingress of excess air; the fuel flow rate; and the quality of combustion.

The importance of air

It hardly needs to be stated that the burning of a fuel using either too much or too little air leads to wasteful use of energy. With too much cold air entering a furnace, flame temperature will drop so that the rate of heat transfer from the flame to the charge is reduced, to the detriment of melting performance. On the other hand, with too little air there is wastage as a result of incomplete combustion of the available fuel. Generally in practice, there is a tendency to err on the side of too much air. Indeed, it is not uncommon for furnaces to be operated with excess-air levels of 50 per cent or more, and this factor alone could account for a 25 per cent wastage of fuel.

With the aid of a computer it is possible to monitor the composition of

the stack gases discharged from a furnace and continuously to compare the figures obtained with similar data relating to the fuel and air being fed to the burners. In this way can be determined the actual amount of excess fuel or air entering the furnace. With the BNF equipment, such analysis is performed automatically by the micro-computer, which then initiates a sequence of events resulting in the optimum air/fuel balance being achieved.

During operation of a furnace, unwanted air can also be drawn in through cracks in the superstructure and other openings, particularly if there is a negative pressure in the furnace at or above hearth level. Resultant energy losses could be as high as 1·5 GJ/h or £2/h. The monitoring of pressure within the furnace, by means of pressure transducers, provides the processor with the information necessary to determine the extent to which the stack outlet should be throttled to increase the pressure in the furnace. Having made the calculation, the micro-processor can then issue instructions to provide for the necessary adjustments.

Excess air and negative furnace pressures are just two of the condi-

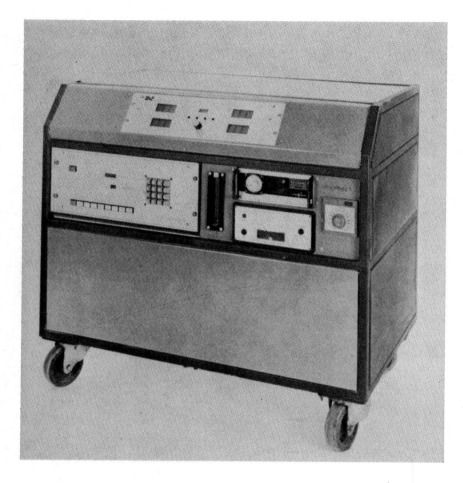

Close-up (far left) of the control panel for the micro-processor-based automatic control system. The BNF's portable diagnostic trolley (left) for monitoring fuel-fired furnace operating conditions.

tions which the BNF micro-processor system monitors and controls. Built into the control panel of the system are four digital displays, which can be switched between 16 different transducers to provide a direct visual indication of each of the selected values being monitored. The micro-processor is programmed to monitor output from fuel and air-flow meters; stack gas suction pyrometers; oxygen analysers; furnace pressure transducers; damper air flow detectors; and various refractory and body thermocouples.

In addition to monitoring, the system is designed to control six motorised butterfly valves for the fuel and air supply to the burners. As a safety precaution the computer will always monitor air supply before it monitors fuel supply and both are given priority over the main control programme. BNF estimates that the capital cost of installing this type of system for the control of a furnace with a melting capacity of 2500 tonnes/year would be recovered in one year.

The diagnostic trolley built by BNF also incorporates a micro-processor, but since the equipment serves merely to monitor furnace conditions it is less expensive than the control system discussed above. In operation with this trolley-mounted equipment, the user is provided with the information needed to adjust a furnace manually to achieve efficient performance. Using the trolley, the furnace operator can periodically check any number of furnaces to optimise combustion conditions. All the transducers required for monitoring form part of the trolley equipment thus obviating the need for them to be permanently mounted on each furnace.

Keeping watch

The micro-processor is pre-programmed with information concerning the type of fuel being used and the permissible oxygen levels. Oxygen content of the flue gases is determined using a gas sample extracted from the flue by means of a suction pyrometer. This pyrometer measures the temperature of the combustion product, after which the gas sample is passed through a constant-temperature solid-state zirconia/platinum oxygen probe which determines the oxygen content. The fuel flow rate is measured and recorded directly using a standard transducer in the fuel supply line and the air flow rate is recorded in a similar manner.

A digital display unit incorporated in the trolley provides an indication of the four main factors which form the basis of any decision taken to adjust the furnace controls. These factors are: the temperature of the gases passing through the stack; the oxygen content of the stack gases; the heat losses as indicated by the temperature of the stack gases; and an approximate indication of the furnace efficiency based on an arbitrary value of the overall heat losses from sources other than the stack.

A fifth display designated 'air control' provides the furnace operator with an indication as to what action must be taken to improve combustion conditions within the furnace. Predetermined air-supply excess figures are programmed into the processor. If these figures are exceeded, either because excessive or insufficient air is being supplied, the situation is indicated on the air control display. The operator is then able to reset the air/fuel ratio until the correct balance is obtained and indicated on the display. If the optimum air supply condition is obtained at the expense of heat-transfer rate within the furnace, this fact will be indicated on the stack-temperature display and appropriate compensation will need to be made.

The diagnostic trolley can also be used as a continuous logging and updating system, with the information obtained from all the furnaces being utilised for production control and maintenance purposes. Where the unit is used for this purpose the information needed can be obtained from the micro-computer by means of a printer. □

Micros get CNC costs under control

The portable RUSC Editor unit

The first major exhibition at which CNC appeared to any extent and in a practical form was the Chicago show in 1976 – where the 'new' systems dominated. In contrast, MACH 76 a few weeks later in the UK surprisingly had very little CNC – and that exhibition was the last major UK event of general type for the production engineer. There will, however, be plenty to see at PEP 78.

As far as the production engineer is concerned, the most obvious application for mini-computers and micro-processors is in machine-tool control systems. Advantages in this connection include the extended operating capabilities of NC, notably to include programme storage and editing facilities, and compactness. Microprocessor technology has advanced so rapidly that the mini-computer – only a few years ago the sole practical way to obtain these and other benefits but an approach thought by some to be like cracking a walnut with a sledgehammer – is fast being eclipsed for CNC systems. Im-

proved compactness and lower costs have resulted.

Systems particularly notable from a low-cost angle form an important part of the machine-tool control equipment currently available. Such systems are often intended particularly for retro-fitting to existing machines, and falling into this category are those in the American-developed Anilam range, to be displayed by Anilam Electronics – Europe Ltd (Stand 363/460). Latest addition to this range is the Commando system, available in two-axis form for De Vlieg machines and two- and three-axis forms for other machines.

A memory in the Commando system has capacity for 999 cycle-steps, and programming is undertaken manually – either by entering data direct by way of a keyboard or by setting the machine-tool slides to the required positions and then entering the position data indicated on display screens. Editing facilities are incorporated, and an output enables stored programme information to be 'dumped' on to a cassette tape.

Another Anilam control system is the established MDI-200 type, with which data are supplied by thumb-wheel switches to a memory with capacity for 64 or 96 cycle-steps. Editing can be undertaken. The system is provided as a complete retro-fit 'package' for knee-type milling machines.

The new Talisman NC system introduced by Toolmasters Controls Ltd (Stand 239) is intended for automating lathes, milling machines, drilling machines and other basic types. A feature of the modular system is that it is self-programming, in that when the first component in a batch is being produced, machining data including traversing movements and feed rates for instance, are entered by means of thumbwheel switches and other controls.

Such data are recorded on magnetic tape, and then transmitted to stepping motor drives which are used for traversing the slides on the machine. When subsequent parts in the same batch are to be produced, the tape is played back, and controls machine movements automatically.

Another stand that should be visited by those interested in low-cost, highly-compact, manually-programmed control systems is that of IPT Systems (Sales) Ltd (Stand 555) where an example of the American-developed Bandit range will be demonstrated on a small milling machine. This system is claimed to be of considerable versatility, and one feature is that in addition to use of a keyboard, control data can be supplied to the 250-step capacity memory from an external source – in memory format with the basic Bandit and in EIA or ASCII code with the Level I or Level II forms. Normal features include those for repeat cycles, inch/ metric working, and feed rate control. Tool offsets, programme changes, and backlash compensation are obtained with the Level I type, and in addition the most advanced form provides for absolute and incremental programming, and canned cycles.

Debut at Chicago

Another must, if you're interested in manually-programmed systems will be the stand of Mark Century Co (227) on which will be seen possibly the latest addition in this category. The Chicago machine-tool exhibition, which finished only a few days ago, saw the introduction of a type designated 1050HL, to extend the 1050 range of CNC systems developed by General Electric, USA. This system is of two-axis type, and is intended specifically for lathe.

For visitors seeking manually-programmed systems to control rather more complex machines, the Giddings & Lewis Sales Ltd stand (646) may provide the answer. The Numeriset with memory system will be shown hooked up to a simulator, to enable the features to be demonstrated as if it were applied to a G & L Fraser horizontal borer or machining centre. The system provides for three-axis working, with simultaneous positioning on two axes, and five different operating modes permit use in various ways, also the addition of information to a programme.

Control systems with the broader capabilities more conventionally as-

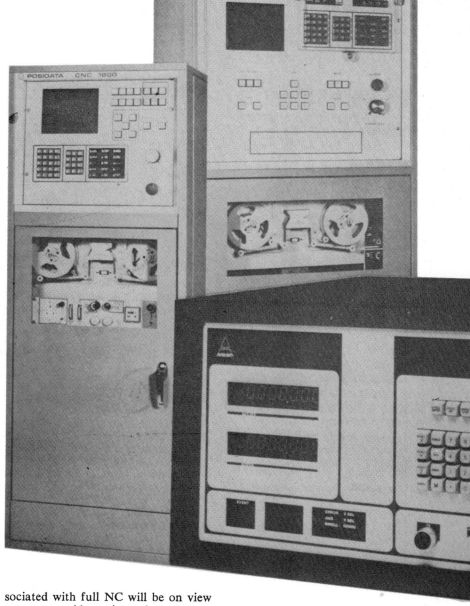

sociated with full NC will be on view to meet a wide variety of needs. For relatively simple requirements, the display by Siemens Ltd (Stand 351) might fit the bill as it includes examples of the Sinumerik System-5, of which different forms are available. System-5D, for drilling and milling machines, is of three-axis type for point-to-point working and line milling; straight-line and continuous-path operation in four axes is obtained for milling machines and machining centres with the System-5M; and System-5T provides continuous-path control for lathes. These systems are based on microprocessor technology, and the specifications for them have recently been extended to include

multiple repetitive machining cycles.

Among systems designed to meet particularly extensive needs will be the CNC 2800 type to be exhibited by Posidata Ltd (Stand 447). This system covers requirements for contour machining, and enables linear movements to be controlled on a maximum of six axes simultaneously. The Posidata CNC 1800 system is of simpler type, and provides for point-to-point positioning and linear interpolation only for drilling and milling operations. Facilities for circular interpolation are available as an option. Control is provided on a maximum of four axes, to cover operation of say, a rotary table set-up on a milling or drilling machine.

Systems of each type will be displayed with software packages to provide CRT displays in the English and German languages. Each can be supplied for lathe applications with tip radius compensation, screwcutting and other software options.

The Sinumerik System-7 (Siemens Ltd) is an advanced 4-axis system, and there are forms intended specifically for complex milling applications and machining centres, and for high-performance or large turning ma-

chines. Notable facilities include 24k-capacity character store, programmable sub-routines, circular interpolation, tool compensations, correction for traversing-screw errors, and eight-decade programming for high-accuracy resolution.

The Westinghouse W2560 CNC system (Westinghouse Electric SA. Stand 516) has the notable feature that it is based on a mini-computer, of 16-bit capacity. Modular design enables the controller to be readily obtained to suit a wide variety of machines, for numbers of axes from

two to six. An extensive range of facilities can be provided, including, a large CRT screen or a single-line alpha-numeric display; programme storage and editing arrangements which can be combined with those for tape punching; and various fixed cycles for different machines. Diagnostic software is among the normal facilities.

Three types of Acramatic NC systems by Cincinnati Milacron Ltd (Stand 247/249/350) cover a wide variety of machining requirements including 8-axis contouring at the top end of the range. At the lower end, there is the Acramatic 8-D system for point-to-point positioning on three axes and contouring on two axes, whereas Acramatic 10E firm-wired equipment occupies the middle position and provides facilities for programme storage and editing and automatic cutter radius compensation. It is available in forms for applications on lathes and machining centres. The top end of the range is occupied by three Acramatic CNC systems for machining centres, turning and profiling applications.

Digital read-out is another area to benefit from microprocessor technology. As a result, DRO systems are getting even smaller and include capabilities not possible with earlier forms.

Three DRO systems will be displayed on the Anilam stand, including

The German-made 5041 digital read-out system (above). On the left are two systems designed to meet extensive needs, the Posidata 1800 and 2800, while in front of them is the Anilam Commando microprocessor with capacity for 999 cycle steps.

the latest addition to this company's range – the MiniWizard. This advanced, yet low-cost DRO is microprocessor-based and is of two-axis type. Features include a keyboard for data entry, incremental and absolute preset, datum memory, a preset memory, and inch/mm and radius/diameter switching arrangements.

Also of microprocessor type, the Wizard DRO system is the most advanced in the Anilam range. It incorporates a fully-programmable memory to accept 12 or 99 steps of three-axis information. The design approach is to avoid the need for any recalculation by a machine operator, in connection with data entry, and editing can be undertaken. Among other notable features is an address facility for a correction factor to compensate for machine-tool error.

At the other end of the scale, Anilam offers a 'conventional' DRO system, said to be of particularly low cost. This system is available for numbers of axes up to three, and the facilities include preset and inch/mm switching arrangements.

Photo-electric measuring

Engineers considering DRO equipment should also visit the stand of Heidenhain (GB) Ltd (209), where the display will include the German-made type 5041 system. Forms of this system are available to suit machines of different types, and the sealed, photo-electric measuring units can be supplied for travels up to 1740 mm. The resolution is 10 μm, and the claimed accuracy, 10 or 5 μm. Control units may be of single- or two-axis form, and may incorporate facilities for presetting reference values, storing such data, and inch/mm conversion.

Sony digital readout, marketed by Stanmatic Precision Ltd (Stand 325), can be retrofitted to most types of machines for single- or multi-axis measurement of linear and angular movements. The measuring system is based on a magnetic scale on which a sine wave signal is recorded. This scale is read by a flux-responsive multi-gap magnetic head which transmits signals to the display unit by way of a detector for interpolation. The display provides a seven-digit readout, and resolution can be as good as 0·001 in/

0·002 mm   or   0·0005 in/0·01 mm.

Among exhibitors showing off NC tape-preparation techniques will be Manufacturing Data Systems International UK Ltd (Stand 456). The COMPACT II computer-aided programming system will be operational on this stand by way of a terminal linked to an international time-sharing network. It can also be implemented on in-house IBM 360/370 computers, and – in an alternative form – on a minicomputer. For time-sharing applications, a new terminal designated ST-I will be demonstrated, and is claimed to provide extensive capabilities for on-line and off-line editing and tape preparation.

GTL language

British Olivetti Ltd (Stand 628) will also seek to aid those with tape-preparation difficulties, by demonstrating the capabilities of the GTL programming language for solving continuous-path and point-to-point problems in connection with machining the new UDS-Ricoh RP40 'double and turning centres. The GTL system is implemented on the company's P6060 desk-top minicomputer.

For what is probably the latest in tape-preparation equipment, a visit should be made to the stand of Ultronic Data Systems Ltd (Stand 232), where the UDS 7000NC makes its debut. This unit is said to be capable of performing all the routine punching, reading, code-conversion, and editing of NC data in EIA and ISO codes. In addition, it incorporates the new UDS-Ricoh RP40 'daisy wheel' high-speed printer.

A new UK-developed N Coder machine for tape preparation to be shown by Computer & Data Machines Ltd (Stand 732) is based on microprocessor technology. It is of modular design and can be supplied with various options. Features include multiple code punching, automatic code conversion, tape duplication, block search, on-line CNC interface, a 30 or 50 cps tape punch, and a 30, 55 or 250 cps printer.

Various items of tape preparation equipment will be exhibited by Control Tape Services (Stand 226), including the new CTS 765 VDU/floppy disc editor. This equipment is designed for preparing and editing programme data on a large scale, and it includes a 14-line VDU, a 150 cps, reader, a 75 cps punch, and up to 28 k of working store. There are two storage discs, each of which has a capacity of 250 000 characters, and data can be transferred to either or both.

An entirely different approach to the problem of optimising the preparation of NC programmes is represented by the well-established RUSC Editor unit made by Plessey Controls Ltd (Stand 326), which will be demonstrated. This portable unit, it may be recalled, can be used independently to prepare a fresh programme or edit an existing type, and the data can then be recorded in various forms by means of separate equipment. Alternatively, it can be connected to an NC system, for editing and on-line prove-out duties.

Users of machine tools equipped with Mark Century 550 control systems – and who are interested in obtaining programme storage and editing facilities with this hard-wired equipment – should also consider the U Stor unit. Details will be available on the Mark Century stand.

Standard hardware

Equipment mainly of interest to machine-tool builders will be displayed by various exhibitors. In connection with the Plessey/Allen Bradley 7300 series of CNC systems, for example, Plessey Controls Ltd will draw particular attention to the built-in PAL (Programmable Application Logic) feature. Such programmable interface arrangements are increasingly being provided by control-system makers (as also with the Mark Century 1050HL and the Westinghouse type mentioned earlier) and they offer indirect benefits to users by permitting standardisation of the hardware involved in applying a system to different machine tools.

British-developed automation equipment to be displayed by ASR Servotron Ltd (Stand 125) will include Syndexer servo positioning and control systems, on show for the first time in the UK. Such a system is said to provide a low-cost method of positioning a motor shaft by digital control, and resolvers provide for closed-loop work-ing. Positioning movements are said to be obtained with considerably less vibration than with equivalent stepping-motor set-ups. Resolution is determined electronically, and may range from 18 to 15 000 steps/rev, and overall accuracy is claimed to be better than 9′ of arc, non-cumulative. The units have been designed for use in conjunction with the company's high-performance transistor Servodrivers and permanent-magnet dc servo motors, and examples of these items will also be exhibited.

Servo-drive controllers

Servo-drive controllers, of both transistor and thyristor type, will also be displayed by Contraves Industrial Products Ltd. They will include the NC 400 multi-axis type – the latest addition to the NC range supplied by Control Systems Research and on show for the first time. Modular construction is employed to obtain systems with ratings from 700 W to 5 kW. Also on view will be Varidyn Compact thyristor controllers. Different forms cover a wide variety of power needs, and additional printed-circuit units provide for a range of specialised applications.

In addition, the Contraves display will include such industrial positioning systems as the Dex-Syn and Op-Ex arrangements, together with programmable sequencers. These items will be intended to indicate the company's capabilities for controlling specialised machine tools with high accuracy and repeatability. □

Medical Applications of Microcomputers

Current Technology with a Look at the Future.

Dick Moberg, Department of Neurosurgery, Jefferson Medical College.

Computerized arms and legs . . . electronic speech synthesis . . . voice recognition . . . visual pattern recognition. Robots? No, humans! The introduction of microcomputers into the medical world has brought us a giant step closer to bionic people. Although at present the majority of medical applications of microcomputers are in making intelligent instruments (and smart they are!), in the near future we can expect to see microcomputers used in replacement parts for the body or to extend our present functions. In this article we will take a look at how microcomputers are being used in various health care areas today, and then we will briefly step into the future to see what we can expect.

THE BEGINNINGS

Biomedical engineers have long awaited the microcomputer to solve some of the problems in medicine. In medical instrumentation, safety and reliability are of utmost importance since, as in aviation and space electronics, lives depend on their correct function. So, when the microcomputers arrived and when engineers finally learned how to make them work, they were used immediately for data collection, signal processing and display, in addition to improving safety and reliability.

But even before the mass marketing of microprocessors, an engineer at Massachusetts General Hospital,

Ed Trautman, realized the benefits of a programmable instrument. He put together some memory, logic, and a calculator chip to construct an instrument that, with nearly identical hardware, carried out two entirely different functions by mere software changes. The two instruments were a cardiac output computer and a neuromuscular transmission analyzer.

Although the instrument was calculator-based, Trautman saw the advantages of microcomputers in bio-engineering research and in hospital instrumentation. He predicted that with microcomputers:

- cost savings, increasing the number of instruments available to hospitals, researchers, and clinicians, might be produced by the ability to change instrument function with software changes.
- modifications and adaptations could easily be implemented to keep pace with changing requirements.
- functions which are now prohibitively expensive to instrument could be very possible.
- monitoring, which is currently far too expensive to provide commonly, could be available for every patient who might require it.

Trautman's predictions have largely come true in the four years since his original paper. One exception is that some manufacturers seemed to have used the new "com-

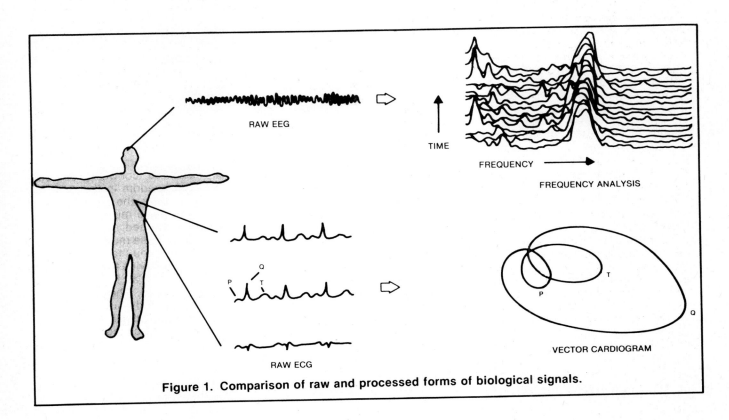

Figure 1. Comparison of raw and processed forms of biological signals.

Reprinted with permission from *Interface Age Magazine*, Vol. 3 Issue 7.

puterized" capabilities of their instruments as an excuse to increase their prices when, in fact, they have decreased their production costs.

MICROCOMPUTERS AND MEDICAL INSTRUMENTATION

Although microcomputer systems are being used widely in medicine, medical applications account for only 3% of all uses of microcomputers. This, of course, is due to their mass consumption in the automotive, appliance, military, and personal computer markets. personal computer markets.

By far the most prevalent use for microcomputers in medicine today is in making patient monitors "smart." These intelligent instruments process the raw signals from the patient, producing an output display which is clinically much more useful. This can be seen in Figure 1. The first example denotes how three different electrocardiogram (ECG) tracings can be electronically reduced to a single plot called a vectorcardiogram. The vectorcardiogram (VCG) is a spatial summation of the electrical activity of the heart and represents the net direction of heart muscle depolarization. Changes in the shape of the VCG can be used to diagnose a variety of heart conditions.

The second example shows how an electroencephalogram (EEG) can be processed to analyze its frequency content. An EEG, unlike an ECG from the heart, is a noncyclic and seemingly random signal. Thus, it is more difficult to extract usable information from the EEG by mere visual inspection. Using fast fourier transform techniques, smart monitors can provide the physician with a chart indicating how the frequency content of the brain waves is changing in time.

These examples indicate how microcomputer-based monitors can be used to extract the clinically useful parameters from the raw physiological data. Presently, the raw EEG and ECG are used clinically more than the processed forms. However, with the future availability of smart monitors, the trend will continue towards computer extraction of more useful parameters.

Now let's look at some microcomputer-based medical instruments that have been designed to date. When an instrument contains a microcomputer, it can process data and also do several unrelated functions largely by software changes and, to a lesser degree, hardware additions and changes. Engineers at the Microcomputer Engineering Lab at MIT have used this concept and have designed a box containing a microcomputer into which a number of different modules may be plugged (Photo 1). The modules consist of such things as analog-to-digital convertors; interfaces to Selectric typewriters, teletypes, and oscilloscopes for input and output; and interfaces to tape and disk systems for mass storage. Also included are modules which do signal processing such as spectral analyses and correlations.

By selecting the right combination of modules and programs, the following instruments may be realized:

- cardiac output monitor
- arrhythmia analysis monitor
- portable EKG computer
- vestibular function tester
- regional blood flow monitor
- pulmonary function tester
- microwave radiometer

Of course, countless other instruments may be made; the number is limited only by the user's imagination.

To aid the user in developing his own custom applications, the MIT engineers have developed a programming language called STOIC (for STack Oriented Interactive Compiler). The language allows one to create his own commands to use the instrument as he pleases and eliminates the need for a technician having to learn a computer language. Since the instrument design is done only once (and no redesign and manufacturing need be done for each instrument configured), the cost of the system is drastically reduced, eliminating one of the problems of medical instrumentation today.

Another example to demonstrate just how smart these instruments are is a microcomputer-based patient monitor developed in San Diego. Completely contained inside one plug-in module for a standard physiological recorder, the unit was designed so the user needs only to turn the instrument on and connect the patient. The computer does the rest. It is primarily used for monitoring bioelectric data but can measure and process just about any of the important physiological parameters. In addition to its signal processing tasks, the system can automatically do the following:

- continually check itself for correct operation
- verify incoming data by checking lead impedances
- adjust analog input gain to keep signals within range
- calibrate itself
- notify medical personnel in case of emergency
- communicate with the physician by various displays

The prototype unit was built at a cost of $3,000, but subsequent units could be manufactured for much less, making this computer-based instrument well within the budgets of most intensive care units.

What is commercially available today? Not a lot, but new products are appearing every week. There is a desk top pulmonary function computer which is pre-programmed with predictable normals for male or female, adult or child. The unit displays eleven different lung parameters calculated from a single breathing into a disposable sensor. The calculations take into considera-

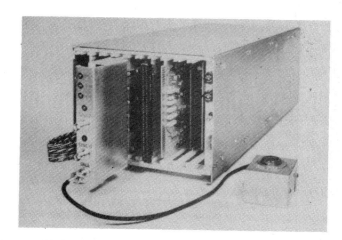

PHOTO 1 Medical Instrument Module Box

tion the age, sex, and weight of the patient, the values of which are entered prior to the test. The device is portable and requires minimal training to operate. Another device monitors the pulse rate of a person riding an exercise bicycle and calculates a "health factor" based on the rider's weight, age, sex, pulse rate, and the loading on the bicycle pedals.

In the previously mentioned devices, the microcomputers were used as "computers." In one of the new computer automated tomographic scanners (CAT scanners), they are used as "components" in a larger minicomputer-based instrument. The CAT scanner takes thousands of dot-sized X-ray pictures radially around a particular part of the body and reconstructs an image representing a "slice" through that part of the body. Four microcomputers are used to control the fast analog-to-digital converters that must be used to collect all the data in a reasonable amount of time.

Another widespread use at present is in automating

the clinical laboratory. The microcomputers are being used to automate radio-immuno assays, differential blood cell counts, toxocological studies, and a host of other procedures.

COMPUTERS FOR THE HANDICAPPED

Most of the applications already mentioned could have used minicomputers although awkwardly and costly. Rehabilitation medicine, however, offers some areas of applications unique to a miniaturized controller such as a microcomputer. In particular, prosthetics (artificial limbs) is where much of the work has been concentrated.

The major problem with prostheses to date has not been so much with their mechanical nature but rather with their control. Electrical signals from muscles (EMGs) have been successfully used to control prosthetic devices. The more degrees of freedom in the artificial arm, indeed the more functional it is, the more complex must be the control signal from the muscles. That is, EMGs from many muscles must be used.

Two problems with obtaining these muscular control signals are: (1) the more muscles you "tap" for control signals, the more awkward is the device to wear, and (2) every amputee's stump is different as to the location and fidelity of the signals available. These problems, however, can be rather nicely solved using microcomputers. Using a microcomputer-based function separation algorithm, finer detection of usable control signals is possible allowing a reduced number of electrodes. And since the control function processing is done in software, parameter changes can be made to tailor each device to the individual wearing it (see INTERFACE AGE, June 1977).

But what about the severely handicapped, such as quadriplegics? How can they communicate with the world? How can they be educated? Quite possibly this will be accomplished by the movement of their eyes. Bioelectric signals from the eye muscles are one of the last physiological systems to be degraded in many neurological impairments. Noting this, Mr. Ira Laefsky, a student in the Computer and Information Science Department of the University of Pennsylvania is designing a microcomputer-based educational and environmental control device for the severely handicapped using eye muscle movements or electro-oculograms (EOGs) as the means of communication with the student (Figure 2). Various words or symbols are displayed on the TV-typewriter display. As the student looks at one, his eye positions are digitized and sent to the microcomputer, and in this manner he can "tell" the machine answers to questions (for educational purposes). He can also tell it to turn on lights, dial phones, and, if connected to a speech synthesizer, to talk.

There are many projects of varying degrees of difficulty that would be potentially beneficial to the handicapped, such as a talking terminal for the blind using a speech synthesizer, a voice input telephone dialer for the severely arthritic, a cheap and reliable device for embossing the Braille character set, and a computer communication network for shut-ins. Unfortunately, there are problems with the commercial development of these devices in that the market is limited for a particular device. Therefore, the price must be high, and many of the handicapped can barely afford even the most basic items presently available to them today.

To this end a small group of interested people, under the leadership of Dr. Robert Suding (The Digital Group), met at Personal Computing '77 in Atlantic City last August to discuss some problems of the handicapped and how the computer might help. Efforts of the group have largely been carried on by Warren Dunning of the Franklin Institute in Philadelphia and myself. The group's main purpose is to let people know what problems need solutions and also what items have potential appli-

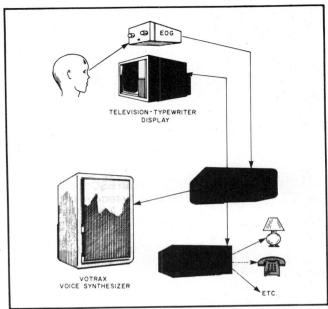

Figure 2. Educational and environment control device for the severely handicapped using electro-oculograms for person-computer communication.

cations towards helping the handicapped. We are doing this through articles in the computer publications, by having booths at the major computer shows, and by a newsletter soon to be published. For more information on this group, write to Computers for the Handicapped, c/o Warren Dunning, 5939 Woodbine Avenue, Philadelphia, Pennsylvania 19131.

MEDICAL OFFICE MANAGEMENT

Small systems aimed at managing small medical practices are beginning to be seen. Several are available and are in the $10-15,000 range. These usually include CPU, 32 to 64K memory, dual floppies, CRT, and printer. Software included covers patient information, treatment, accounts payable and receivable, insurance coverage, and payroll.

A new publication aimed at keeping the physician informed about office management systems as well as a host of other developments on microcomputers and medicine is now available. It is called Physicians Microcomputer Report and is edited and published by Dr. Gerald Orosz, Box 6483, Lawrenceville, NJ 08648.

THE FUTURE

Medical instrumentation will continue to shrink in size and double in capacity until the physician's black bag actually contains a tiny diagnostic computer system. Stethoscopes will connect to it for on-line recognition of abnormal heart sounds and opthalmoscopes will be connected for visual studies. But there will be more. Pop a few electrodes on the patient and the black bag will do ECGs, nerve conduction studies, evoked potential analyses, EEG spectral analysis, and EMGs. It will then process the data, tell the doctor if there are any abnormalities, and store the data in its memory until the day's results can be dumped into a central hospital computer.

Hopefully, fewer people will be in the hospital due to the personal computer revolution. When the day arrives when home computers are as common as television sets and when all of these computers are tied into central information networks, primary medical care might just as well be done electronically. A fairly comprehensive physical examination could be carried out by an average person guided by a computer graphics terminal and using only a minimum of readily available, inexpensive instruments (penlight, tongue depressor, stethoscope, reflex hammer, etc.).

Before self-diagnosis programs come about, there will be programs dealing with preventive medicine, and rightly so. Health risk analyses, to help you prevent diseases, are just now appearing on computer screens. The computer asks whether you smoke, drink, exercise, what you eat, your weight, height, sex, and age, and many other questions. It then reports back with a health appraisal in the form of how many years you can expect to live continuing the same life style. Most important, it can analyze your life style, diet, and social habits and make recommendations for living a healthier life.

Prosthetics research, however, with its bionic flavor, will certainly be the field to lead us into the "far out" future of microcomputer applications in medicine. Artificial appendages will increase in complexity until they approach their human analogs. They will be complete, from the optimum control and functions down to artificial skin itself. The real advance that will grow out of this field will be the development of a method of direct brain-computer communication. Once this has been achieved we will truly step into the Bionic Age and hope for a peaceful symbiosis of man and computer. □

An annotated bibliography of microcomputer applications in medicine is being prepared by the author. If you are interested in receiving a copy or in corresponding about the impact of microcomputers in medicine, write to: Dick Mobert, Department of Neurosurgery, Thomas Jefferson University, Philadelphia, PA 19107.

The Bedside Microcomputer in the Intensive Care Nursery

ROBERT C. A. GOFF M.D.

Fellow in Neonatology, Children's Hospital Medical Center of Northern California.

ABSTRACT

Software is being developed to enable pediatricians and neonatologists to maintain bedside microcomputers in the Intensive Care Nursery, providing instant processing of, and access to the voluminous laboratory data and event summaries generated by each infant. The data is stored in a problem-oriented format, and may be accessed with an inquiry to any particular problem. The program is being written in North Star extended disk BASIC (version 6, release 3, — which utilizes random disk file access) and is implemented on a SOL/20 Terminal Computer with 48K RAM, and North Star Microdisk drives.

INTRODUCTION

The use of computers in the Intensive Care Nursery is not a new idea, but I am unaware of previous attempts to use a microcomputer in such an application. This article will discuss the structure of the software, and the reasons for both the programming language used and the selection of the hardware configuration.

As a general background, one must realize first of all that infants in an Intensive Care Nursery (ICN) are usually highly unstable patients with multiple, complex medical problems, when compared to older patients in other hospital settings. Secondly, and as a result of this first consideration, infants in the ICN generate an overwhelming quantity of both data and narrative description of clinical events, conditions, and procedures. As an example, the daily progress note written in a typical patient's chart (in most areas of the hospital) will require perhaps 8 or 10 lines on one page of his chart, and will include all new laboratory results and procedures, as well as the patient's clinical condition for that day. In the ICN, however, it is not at all uncommon to find a progress note for one day requiring as many as 2 to 3 full pages of discussion and laboratory values. In addition to this voluminous daily documentation, there is at the bedside of each infant a flow chart of all the daily laboratory results and the daily computations of fluid intake, fluid intake per kilogram per day, calories per day, calories per kilogram per day, urine output per kilogram per hour, and so on.

While today, with no less than a Herculean effort, we are still capable of managing and reacting appropriately to the reams of information generated by our ICN patients (up to about 40 at full census), we are realizing that the current trend in Neonatology is toward more laboratory tests per infant and more documentation of the increasing number of procedures required by each infant. If this trend continues, then it will be virtually impossible to keep apace of this information deluge. Future trends aside, it is currently a major task, each time one of our infants is discharged from the hospital, to review his records (often consisting of three to eight volumes of hospital chart), understand his two to three month hospitalization, and then dictate a usefully concise and accurate summary. Our present practice is to dedicate one to three hours in preparing each summary, with our nursery requiring, on the average, two and a half summaries per day.

The solution to this problem is obvious — to utilize some form of computer processing and synthesis of both laboratory data and event description to maintain instant access to any past information, to accept daily input of data and, at the time of discharge, to abstract from the patient's file those pertinent items appropriate for inclusion in a discharge summary.

SOFTWARE

The program, written in North Star BASIC, is fairly simple in structure, but because of the multiplicity of types of data manipulations required and the extensive

> . . .infants in the ICN generate an overwhelming quantity of both data and narrative description of clinical events, conditions, and procedures.

text editing capability required of a narrative summary, the program length is projected to run to about 60K bytes, exclusive of the space needed for variable manipulation. As a result of its length, the program is structured in the form of disk files and BASIC sub-programs (stored on the disk), and is directed by an executive program which chains into RAM whichever sub-program is called. The program resides in one disk drive and stores all patient data on the other disk (a triple drive will enable the use of one microcomputer for every two infants). The organization of the sub-programs is a modified version of the Problem Oriented Format, now popular among physicians, and extensively used in Intensive Care Nurseries across the country. Rather than being oriented strictly to patient problems, the sub-programs are representative of body systems. This approach allows the formatting of virtually every type of clinical data or problem and will permit easy access, at a later date, to any particular information required by patient follow-up or retrospective data analysis.

Reprinted with permission from *Interface Age Magazine,* Vol 3 Issue 7.

It should be noted that, because of the relatively stereo-typed set of clinical problems common to premature and sick infants, an estimated 90 to 95% of all data and event summary information can be specifically encoded for later search and retrieval. The remaining 5 to 10% of the information would be accessible only by manually searching a category such as "OTHER", included under each body system. This situation is not the case with general medicine or, for that matter, general pediatrics, in which the multitude of commonly encountered clinical entities would require a much more complex structure of software in order to accomplish a comparable textual product with comparable data access capability.

Executive Routine

This is a short program which displays on the CRT a menu of the major sub-routines of the system. If the hardware consists of three disk drives for use on two different patients, then the patient is selected within the executive routine. At this point, the physician chooses the particular body system of interest and the executive chains in the sub-routine which has been called. With the sub-routine loaded, the physician is presented with a menu of routines included, such as:

1. Enter Data
2. Enter Events
3. Review Data and Events
4. Plot Data
5. Print Textual Summary
6. EXIT

On selecting, for example, HEMATOLOGY, the CRT displays a menu of events and laboratory tests related to that body system. When an event has been selected, the computer will then request the time and date of the event, and then compute the infant's age at the time of the event. This is now displayed for confirmation, and if approved, will be recorded in the appropriate file on the patient's disk. An opportunity is given to record additional events, then control is returned to the initial sub-program menu. On exiting the sub-program, the executive routine is chained into RAM, and it is then used to access further sub-programs.

Sub-routines

The major sub-routines serve to format the data and events into either random or serial disk files, whichever is most easily manipulated for the given type of information. The plotting functions are capable of producing graphs of data, plotted simultaneously with certain event markets, as well as standardized curves for reference. For example, the plot of the growth chart will, on a single page, plot three graphs: weight, length, and head circumference, each with appropriate standard percentile curves, and each in the format of the Babson growth chart. Because of the ease of generating these curves, and their usefulness to the physician who follows the infant after discharge from the ICN, they may be included in the final discharge summary and be available to the referring physician immediately. Additionally, attempts are being made to represent complex data, such as arterial blood gases and ventilator settings in easily interpretable graphic form.

Text

Most of the infant's admission history (primarily pre-natal and maternal history) is encoded, and at the time of review decoded by the History sub-routine, so that most of this textual material is confined to the program disk and does not require space on the patient's disk. However, uncommon items of history can be typed in as text and are stored as strings on the patient's disk. This is also the case with each of the other sub-routines. The finished discharge summary is in the form of a standard textual discharge summary and may optionally be formatted as a letter.

An additional feature of the output capability of the software is that it can print the forms (presently filled out by hand) which are required by the State of California for each infant who is transported from a referring hospital to an Intensive Care Nursery.

Diagnoses

Each sub-program possesses considerable diagnostic capability. Any diagnoses which can be made solely on the basis of laboratory data and encoded events or encoded history will automatically appear in the summary as discharge diagnoses. While the attending physician has the option of deleting any of these diagnoses, or adding other diagnoses to the list, it is anticipated that by far the majority of diagnoses will be accurately made by the diagnostic algorithms, and will maximize future access for statistical study of patient care information. An additional feature of the diagnostic algorithms is that any suggestive (but not conclusive) diagnoses can be pointed out to the physician as possibilities which may warrant further clinical or laboratory investigation. (Once again, the rather circumscribed nature of Neonatology allows this capability to be implemented on so small a system.)

Choice of Programming Language

The languages considered in setting about this project were 8080 Assembly Language, FORTRAN, and BASIC (those currently available on the 8080 microcomputer). Assembly languages would allow for a much more concise program structure, considerably less RAM, and more rapid program execution. FORTRAN was eliminated because of the complexity of its string manipulation techniques in an application which extensively utilizes text manipulation. BASIC was chosen instead, for several reasons. Most importantly, it would allow the program to be quickly modified to run on just about any hardware system, including time-shared systems and the large systems available at most university hospitals. A second advantage to BASIC is that it would allow other users to easily modify any of the graphic,

> **A network of microcomputers is certainly in the near future for most hospitals.) The one major criticism that I would level at the SOL's keyboard is a fault of the application rather than the machine itself.**

textual, or diagnostic routines to meet their exact needs or preferences.

North Star extended disk BASIC (version 6, release 3) was chosen in particular, for a number of reasons. First, it is an extremely powerful and easy to use BASIC. Second, it possesses the CHAIN function needed for non-stop use of the multiple sub-programs. It allows complex string manipulation. It offers several instructions for calling any assembly language sub-routines which might be needed for future development of real-time vital sign analysis. Finally, this was a natural choice to use with the North Star disk driver as discussed below.

HARDWARE

The hardware chosen consists of a SOL/20 Terminal Computer with 48K bytes of RAM, at least two North Star Microdisk drives, a Sanyo CRT monitor, and a Diablo 1610-3 receive-only "daisy wheel" printer. If the system is to be used for one patient, or several, and disks are changed for each patient, a dual disk drive will suffice.

The choice of the SOL/20 was based on two major factors. The first is size. The SOL will fit comfortably at the bedside in the ICN, whereas most other microcomputers are simply too bulky. The enormous backplane capacity of the larger units is not needed. If the 48K RAM is all on one high density memory board, and the North Star controller on another, then the SOL will have 3 empty slots for further hardware development. The second major factor in the choice of a SOL is its user-oriented keyboard and lack of a front panel. The optional numeric keypad is a tremendous advantage when entering large volumes of laboratory data. Perhaps a third consideration is the ease with which the SOL may be set in a "terminal mode" and networked to a laboratory minicomputer for direct data acquisition. (A network of microcomputers is certainly in the near future for most hospitals.) The one major criticism that I would level at the SOL's keyboard is a fault of the application rather than the machine itself. That is, an ideal keyboard for a direct patient care application would be a continuous-sheet neoprene keypad which would allow easy cleaning in an application which is directly involved in cleanliness and antisepsis. Hopefully, such a keypad will be made available for just such applications.

In considering the various disk drives available, again two factors were of greatest importance. First, once again, was size. The large disk drives simply require more room than is available presently at the bedsides of ICNs. The North Star drives can be tucked away just about anywhere. Second was flexibility in interchanging one patient's data at the time of his discharge, for that of another patient. A large disk would be wasted if it contained the information of only one patient, and flexibility would be lost if a large disk were used for more than one patient. The 90K byte capacity of the 5-inch disk seemed to be only a slight overkill and could easily justify the use of one disk per patient.

The software was developed using a DECwriter as the hard copy output, and all graphics have been implemented so that any serial printer would be capable of generating entirely adequate graphs. Selecting a Diablo "daisy wheel" type printer was prompted by not only the desire for more precise graphics, but also the preference of most physicians for reading a solid type font rather than dot-matrix. The printer, whatever the type, is not intended to be at the bedside in the ICN. It should ultimately be a part of an additional system located in some other area of the nursery or nursery offices and would be used solely for printing the discharge summaries. This additional system can easily be cost justified by using it the remainder of the time for inventory, scheduling, accounting, and numerous other tasks. Alternatively, the printer may be placed on a mobile cart, and rolled to the bedside unit for use at the time of discharge.

COSTS

The system described, including the Diablo printer, should cost approximately $8,500 with all necessary supplies and sales tax. Substituting a DECwriter for the Diablo 1610-3 will drop the cost by about $1,200. To this must be added the cost of two diskettes per patient bed (one for current use, and one for a backup).

Justifying such an expense should be in the light of the cost of typical monitoring electronics used in the ICN. As an example, the PSI infant monitor (which monitors heart rate, respiratory rate, blood pressure, heart rate trend, respiratory trend, and blood pressure trend, along with appropriate alarms) runs in the neighborhood of $10,000 per bed. Less expensive monitors are still in the $4,000 range. By using one triple disk drive SOL system for every two beds, the cost is about $2,200 per bed, plus the cost of one printer, spread over the entire nursery. These figures, of course, do not measure the improvement in patient care that would result from instant data access at the bedside, as well as increased physician time attending to matters other than a dictaphone. There is also a significant savings in medical transcription costs by eliminating the need to transcribe lengthy ICN discharge summaries. Perhaps the greatest cost justification for a large referral center, such as Children's Hospital in Oakland, is that by generating discharge summaries at the instant of discharge, the hospital will render better service to the referring physician, and certainly thereby improve community-hospital relations.

I should mention one final reservation that I have concerning this hardware configuration. For a small number of beds, such a system seems to be the most cost effective. However, as the number of beds increases, the investment in disk drives will far exceed the cost of hard disk memory and its development costs.

SUMMARY

A general description of a microcomputer implementation of a bedside computer for the Intensive Care Nursery is presented, with some of its basic features, and the author's justification for selecting North Star BASIC, and the SOL/20 North Star Disk combination. Costs and cost justifications are also discussed.

ACKNOWLEDGEMENTS

The author wishes to thank Dr. Barry Phillips of Children's Hospital, Oakland, Peter Hollenbeck of the Byte Shop of Berkeley, Dr. Adam Osborne of Osborne and Associates, Adam Grossman of the Black Pine Circle School, Berkeley, and Bruce Bargmeier, Berkeley, for their assistance, suggestions, and encouragement in this project.

A New Generation of Biomedical Instruments

John M. Brus

The development of four microprocessor-controlled medical devices at Biomedical Engineering Center for Clinical Instrumentation (BECCI), based at Cambridge, Mass., is pioneering the research trail to a new generation of these devices, according to the consensus opinion of the BECCI research engineers.

Jointly sponsored by the Harvard/MIT Program in Health Sciences and Technology but funded by a National Institutes of Health three-year contract, BECCI's aim is to build a technological resource offering an integrated and modularized set of hardware and software specifically designed for biomedical applications.

To this end, BECCI published last year an upper-level language called STOIC (authored by John Sacks) and developed an "on-line debugging" card, designed by electrical engineer Paul Schulter.

Staff engineer John Volvano explains that "Given the time and effort spent on the background hardware and the STOIC software base...future projects will have little of this work. Engineers need only design one or two hardware cards to interface their particular project and develop the software on STOIC"— considerably telescoping the time needed to transform an instrumentation idea into a prototype.

John Sacks, BECCI's software specialist, says STOIC gives the programmer complete control over the execution speed vs. ease-of-programming tradeoffs inherent between machine and higher-level languages. Additionally, the debugging card, designed for microprocessors using an Intel 8080, uses a "memory mapping" feature to conveniently "patch" programs as if they were read/write locations, avoiding frequent read-only memory reprogramming.

The purpose of the medical instruments under development is not only to monitor and analyze biological signals but also to present this information in a usable form to the physician. In another sense, however, the research engineers are confronting the question: "How do you program a physician's clinical judgement into a computer?" The best example illustrating some of these difficulties is BECCI's portable arrhythmia monitor, scheduled for limited field-testing this summer.

Monitoring Chaotic Heart Beats

There are almost 700,000 heart-attack victims each year in the United States. Heart attacks usually occur when blood flow to a portion of the heart is reduced or blocked, disturbing the natural rythmic wave of electrical impulses regulating the heart's beating. This leads to ventricular fibrillation— uncoordinated beating of the heart's chambers—and cardiac arrest. People with heart disease are prone to intermittent arrhythmias, and monitoring these patterns provides valuable medical information of the heart's physical situation and response to medication. Since the heart beats about 100,000 times in a 24-hour period, however, a 12 or 24-hour electrocardiogram (ECG) monitor generates mountains of data but only a few of the medically important arrhythmia periods.

BECCI is developing a portable, microprocessor-controlled ECG monitor that recognizes and stores only arrhythmia patterns. In theory, after strapping on the unit in the morning, a

The Portable Cardiac Arrhythmia Monitor contains an Intel 8080 processor, 256 8-bit words of read-only memory, 4096 8-bit words of read/write memory, ECG amplifier, 10-bit analog-to-digital converter, bit-serial transmitter-receiver, patient interaction interface, and a DC-to-DC power converter.

patient can go about all his daily activities. At the end of the day, he plugs his monitor into a modem and feeds the data to a hospital computer which will print out hard copy for examination.

The arrhythmia monitor is an ideal illustration of a heretofore impractical biomedical device, according to project engineer Joe Walters, Jr., "This microprocessor technology is clearly opening a new area because there's no minicomputer around capable of being reduced to a box this size (2" x 6" x 10") and this power (3.5 watts)."

However, recognizing arrhythmias is just one of the microprocessor's tasks. A clock enables recording of the time intervals between arrhythmias. Algorithms also classify different types of arrhythmias and compress data for storage.

Although ECG waveforms are easily susceptible to mathematical analysis, Walters admits he hasn't quite yet mastered the trick of converting "clinical judgement" into an acceptable algorithm. Constitutional biological differences between patients illustrates one of the vexing variables. That is, what looks like arrhythmias in one patient may be close to normal in another. compounding that fact with the different possible types of arryrhthmias means that the arrhythmia algorithm must not only analyze different waveforms, but additionally recognize the arrhythmia as significant in context with the normal heartbeats. Also, extraneous biological impulses feeding into the ECG sensors create problems, such as triggering the monitor to mistakenly store the impulses in memory. One solution, Walters notes, is beefing up the current 4K memory to 16K or even higher. This would allow the use of STOIC and provide the extra capacity to store the extraneous impulses.

Walters also has plans of making the unit interactive with the patient. For instance, after the unite detects an arrhythmia, a buzzer can alert the patient to answer a series of preprogrammed questions presented on a small LCD display. Giving the patient a choice of "Yes," "No" or "I don't know" buttons to push, typical questions might be: "Are you dizzy?" or "Are you having angina pains?" Correlating these answers with the different types of arrhythmias creates more medically useful information.

Computerizing Pulmonary Function Testing

Another unit under development involves a combination whole body plethysmograph (lung volume capacity) and respiratory gas analysis system. Project engineer Niel Dowling says previous plethysmographs, if they've been computerized at all, usually shared time on a minicomputer. "We want to have a processor dedicated to the task to produce a cheaper, more compact system," he explains.

Effective measurement of a pulmonary system includes measuring lung capacity, lung elasticity and CO_2 and O_2 transfer efficiency, as well as how these factors change within the time of an exercise period. Dowling says the microprocessor using analytic equations (e.g., Boyle's Law) can compute lung capacity straightforwardly. Or by comparing two sets of figures (e.g., lung gas ratios and blood gas ratios), the microprocessor derives medically important information on the gas-transfer efficiency of the lungs. Currently, integrated respiratory gas analysis systems and plethysmographs are not mass produced and can cost up to $50,000 counting minicomputer support, according to Dowling. but he believes a dedicated microprocessor system could cut the current cost in half. Field testing of a prototype should begin in Boston's Peter Bent Brigham Hospital this summer.

Measuring Eye Movements To Detect Balance Disorders

Disorders of the inner ear leading to dizziness or loss of balance sometimes are diagnosed indirectly. One procedure, called electronystagmography, positions a patient on a motorized chair that rotates and tilts. Concurrently, eye movements are monitored and analyzed, since inner ear balance disorders reveal themselves in eye velocities by an integrated response called the ocular-vestibular reflex.

Project engineer John Tole says electrodes placed at the eye corners can measure differences in electrical potential caused by eye movement. Again, these eye movements are susceptible to the type of mathematical analysis microprocessors happily perform. But, just as with the ECG monitor, Tole explains that patients with abnormal characteristics (e.g., unusual head thickness or weaker neurological responses caused by extreme age) can test the flexibility of the software. So far, the algorithms are standardized for a typical middle-age patient with normal neurological response. Additionally, the microprocessor sequences all chair movements and records the chair and eye movements on a time scale because some of the reflexes seem to have a delayed reaction effect.

Measuring Blood Flow

Developing a thermal probe that directly measures blood flow in living tissues is BECCI's fourth project. By placing an electrically heated needle-like probe within the tissue or organ, sensitive measurements of the rate at which the tissue absorbs heat from the probe are made. Comparing these "heat-sink" values, in the presence of blood flow, with standardized values of tissue conduction, in the absence of flow, leads to calculations of the blood flow which carries heat away from the probe.

Project engineer John Volvano says the instrument is due for field testing this summer at the Walter Reed Army Institute of Research near Washington D.C. Aside from an easily correctable but unforseen problem of shielding the sensitive electronic components, Volvano believes the software and hardware is near perfection.

Dr. H. Frederick Bowman, director of BECCI's thermal probe project, says the probe has a number of potential uses. One may be the post-operative monitoring of surgical patients and another the monitoring of transplanted organs to assess disorders stemming from restricted blood flow. Knowledge of low flow rates (known as "shock") are important in patient care.

Bowman also explained that changing the instrument's software enables the probe to monitor the concentration of other fluids. This can be important in the emerging field of cryopreservation— where donor organs are stored for future transplantation. Using a cryopreservative "biological antifreeze" to prevent tissue destruction, the probe could monitor the freezing and thawing rates and "antifreeze" concentration levels for each organ system—all of which have to be meticulously recorded to discover the optimum rate.

Cheaper but powerful computer components are obviously finding a home in biomedical instrumentation. And with a little imagination, the hand-held "body-function analyzer" used by *Star Trek's* Dr. McCoy may not seem to be so impossible after all.

Meet Mickie
The Well Mannered Micro

Nigel Bevan,
Department of Industry,
National Physical Laboratory

Patients of a doctor in West Kensington may be surprised on their next visit to be asked to see not their GP, but Mickie — the Medical Interviewing Computer. Mickie has introduced the microprocessor to the doctor's surgery, and this GP is one of the first users. How would you view the prospect of a consultation with a microprocessor? Perhaps (like me) you would look forward to it with eager anticipation. Many people, however, may be more apprehensive. For the ordinary member of the public familiar with the faceless monster that sends £1,000,000 gas bills, the introduction of a computer in the role of doctor might appear to be yet another step in the relentless depersonalization of society.

The human touch

However, Dr Chris Evans, whose team at the National Physical Laboratory developed Mickie, was very conscious of the need for computers to be able to interact personally with people, so Mickie is a very polite computer.

Imagine that on your next visit to the doctor you are asked to meet Mickie. You sit down in front of a screen on which Mickie says "Please press the YES button to start". The receptionist draws your attention to the box with 3 buttons labelled "YES", "NO" and "DON'T KNOW", and then leaves the room. Perhaps you hesitate, but you are alone with Mickie and as soon as you pluck up courage to press the button the conversation is under way.

Mickie is no faceless monster. He is as polite and reassuring as the most friendly doctor, and takes you carefully through your medical history and symptoms. Nor does Mickie actually replace the doctor, but assists in obtaining a more thorough medical background than a busy doctor normally has time for. When you see the doctor he will have the summary prepared by Mickie, and so can use his limited time to examine in detail the most important symptoms.

How has Mickie reached this stage of development? When the project started in the early 70s it used the Honeywell time-sharing service. (Although dialled up locally, the computer was located in Cleveland USA!). However even the best time-sharing services mysteriously die from time to time, leaving a mystified patient, and a doctor with no summary. Fortunately the reduction in computer costs soon made it possible to transfer the programs, already written in BASIC, to a mini-computer at the NPL (a DEC PDP 11 - 10), which with minor modifications could provide a highly reliable dial up service for 2 to 3 users. With the rapid evolution of microprocessors the next inevitable step was to transfer the programs to a suitable micro-computer system, namely Mickie.

The programs which originally required a powerful computer with fast disks, now run quite happily on a Motorola 6800 microprocessor with 20K bytes of memory, and dual drive mini-floppy disks. The whole system, complete with VDU, printer and response box is being marketed by Computer Workshop for £2,700.

What this really demonstrates is that you can now do almost anything with a micro running a comprehensive version of BASIC and file I/O. So how did we implement medical history taking on Mickie?

Mickie evolves

The earliest programs looked rather like those found in the back of most personal computing magazines. However as the sophistication of the interviews grew, so did the size of the programs required to implement them, until they outstripped the capabilities of even the mightly Honeywell computer service.

The solution was to separate the logic of the program from that of the interview text, a method which adapted well to the need to transfer it to a smaller system. This approach has 2 important advantages. First, the program is much smaller, since the text resides on disk and is read in as required. Furthermore, while the systems programmer worries about debugging BASIC, the doctor can concentrate on specifying the flow of the questions.

Take a simple example of the sort of questions a doctor might ask:

Assuming the patient is responding with a YES or NO button, this might produce the program:

```
10    PRINT "Do you get the pain every day";
20    INPUT A $(1) : IF A $(1) ="Y" GOTO 40 : IF A $(1) =
      "N" GOTO 60
30    GOTO 20 : REM OTHER INPUT COULD BE CHECKED
      HERE
40    PRINT "Is it continuous";
50    INPUT A $(2) = GOTO 80
60    PRINT "Do you get it more than once a week";
70    INPUT A $(3)
80    . . .
```

Note that at the end of the program the contents of the array A $ can be used to produce a summary. However the same text can be much more easily specified in a form we have dubbed "Questext":

```
*
1, 2, 3
Do you get the pain every day
*
2, 4, 4
Is it continuous
*
3, 4, 4
Do you get it more than once a week
*
4  . . .
```

Here the format is:

```
*
Block number, Branch address for YES, Branch address for NO
Text of block . . .
*
Next block number . . .
```
(See Flowchart p.35)

In the example above, Mickie will display the text of the first block, and then pause for the patient to answer the question. If the answer is YES Mickie will branch to block 2, and if NO to block 3. This system really amounts to no more than a numbered flowchart, and is quickly learned by non-computer people.

Although Questext is a language in its own right, it is very easily implemented by writing a BASIC program which reads the file containing Questext line by line. One BASIC program can then read any number of text files.

Here is a simplified example of a BASIC driver program which reads Questext from file 1:

Reprinted with permission from *Personal Computing World*, December 1978.

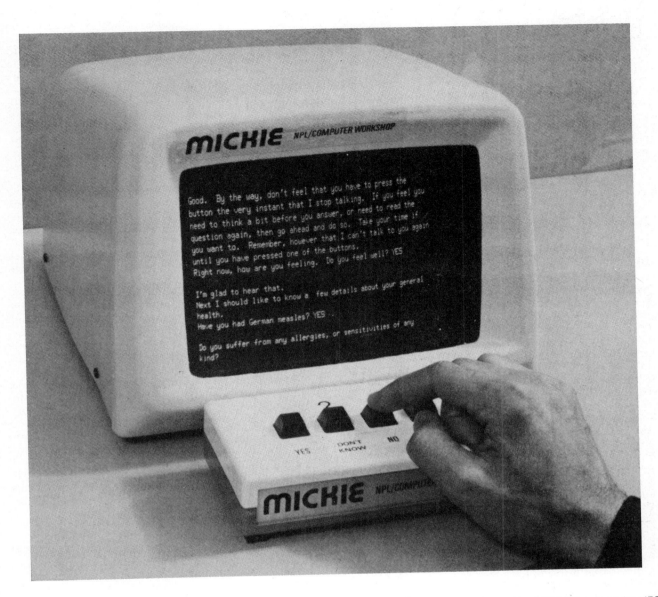

```
10   S = 1
20   READ £1,L $: IF < >"*" GOTO 20
30   READ £1,B,Y,N
40   IF B < >S GOTO 20
50   READ £1,L $: IF L $< >"*"
     THEN PRINT L $: GOTO 50
60   INPUT A $(B)
```

S = search block
find next *
next block no
wrong block?

print text
get response

```
70   IF A $(B) = "Y" THEN S = Y : GOTO 20    check for YES
80   IF A $(B) = "N" THEN S = N : GOTO 20    check for NO
90   GOTO 60                                 try again
```

This type of program can easily be adapted to cater for more than 2 answers, and the text can contain special items which are used to generate the doctor's summary.

Simplified Interaction

It should be apparent that Mickie has simplified the man-computer interface at 2 levels, since neither the doctor nor the patient needs to know anything about computers. The doctor has only to specify a logical sequence of questions which are numbered as blocks, and the patient has only to give simple YES or NO answers to the questions.

Several studies have been made of patients' reactions to medical interviewing by computer. The most notable result is the speed at which people adapt to interacting with the computer. Even the most nervous individuals are soon enthusiastically pressing the buttons, and many comment on how friendly the computer is. In fact patients often say they prefer to be interviewed by the computer rather than the doctor. The reason for this seems to be that many people feel ill at ease in the doctor's presence, worried that they may be wasting his time. Sitting in the doctor's surgery is an intimidating

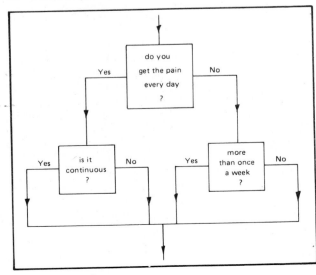

Crown Copyright

situation over which they have little control. With the computer, however, patients soon learn that they control the rate of the interview. Mickie projects a sympathetic personality, and always waits patiently while they think about his questions.

Given that patients are more relaxed in Mickie's presence, how good is Mickie at his job? Does he gather accurate information? Evidence for this comes from a research project in Glasgow where patients with a drink problem were interviewed either by the doctor, or by computer. When the results were analyzed, it was found that on average patients who saw the doctor only admitted to drinking half as much as those interviewed by computer! This supports the impression given by patients that they have difficulty speaking freely with the doctor.

Mickie was designed originally to gather the background medical history required by doctors investigating specific complaints, and has been used in out-patient clinics specializing in abdominal pain, ante-natal care, chest diseases and industrial health. However, Mickie has found wider application in other areas. The West Kensington GP has many young patients living away from their families, and there is often a complex relationship between the symptoms they report and their social background. He found that using Mickie to gather the medical and social history not only provided the information he required, but also enabled patients to reflect on their situation, so that by the time they saw him they were ready to discuss the aspects which particularly troubled them.

Questioning Text

The Mickie approach can be generalized to practically any interactive situation, hence the name for the text format, Questext, indicating "Questioning Text". One example is a training program used by the Fire Research Station to demonstrate the best way to escape from a fire. They designed a mechanically presented flowchart to illustrate how hotel guests can best escape from a fire. Transferred to Mickie this became a rivetting simulation of the possible courses of action open to you when, in the middle of the night, you are woken in your room by what sounds like a distant fire. You are taken through the options available step by step. For instance, do you get dressed, try to phone the reception desk, or look out of the door? Unwise or delayed decisions lead to a fiery death (followed by a post-mortem explaining your errors!)

Questext is in fact very well suited to a variety of Computer Aided Instruction (CAI) situations. Another example is a program written in a couple of hours by a policeman to train constables in handling road accident situations. A petrol tanker is slewed across the busy A30 injuring the driver, and a cow has wandered onto the road through a broken fence. You are first on the scene, so what is the most important thing to do . . .? (The answer is: stop the traffic!)

In this particular program Questext was adapted to allow plain language responses (e.g. "I would call an ambulance"), which gives more flexibility for users familiar with a keyboard.

One of the great advantages of using a micro programmed in BASIC is that the programs can be very quickly modified to cater for special requirements. Another advantage is that the disk operating system which runs BASIC can also support an EDITOR, which makes it very easy to modify the text in the light of experience.

Using Mickie for these sort of applications raises a more general question. It could be argued that many of the programs could be implemented just as effectively but far more cheaply in printed form (like a Programmed Instruction text), either read to the patient by a nurse, or used directly. The reasons for using a (comparatively) expensive computer are quite subtle, but nonetheless important.

For the person preparing the text it is possible to generate and test a program on the computer without the usual difficulties associated with typing, correcting and reproducing. As already mentioned, it is then very easy to make improvements and additions as required. There is none of the usual danger of the text becoming frozen at an early and inadequate stage of development.

For the user the advantage is that he can become wholly absorbed in the interaction, without having to concentrate on keeping his place on the page and finding the next appropriate section. Although this might not sound very difficult, in practice it greatly detracts from the ability of the user to become involved in the learning or questioning process.

For the doctor. Mickie can produce a neat printed summary of the patient's medical history. Extracting this information from a printed questionnaire would be a tedious process.

The future

What then is the future of Mickie? With the DHSS funding an initial trial of 6 Mickies, the prospects look bright for Mickie to increasingly lighten the load of the overburdened doctor. With the new generation of personal computers, there is no reason why Mickie should not further shrink in size and price. If a slight degradation in performance is acceptable, Mickie could be run on cassette based systems, and it won't be long before bubble memory may provide the best solution!

Looking to the wider applications of the Mickie approach, the possibilities are quite exciting. NPL has already experimented with a dental program to advise the general public whether their toothache requires immediate attention or can wait for a convenient appointment.

There is no reason in principle why this should not be extended to the general medical field. GPs currently suffer from patients who at one extreme go to see them with the slightest headache, and at the other refuse to admit there is anything wrong with them till they are about to collapse. A Mickie program could be designed which both reliably identified common trivial ailments (of the 'take an aspirin' variety) and also drew attention to more important symptoms requiring urgent medical attention.

This is not to suggest that doctors will be replaced, but rather that they will be complemented. What we can look forward to is a future in which medical health is improved by the wide availability of Mickie type programs. These will provide early screening of the straightforward complaints, leaving doctors free to deal with the more intractable cases.

Talking and Braille calculators serve the blind—for a high price

JIM McDERMOTT

A vocabulary of 24 words is designed into this talking calculator for the blind by Telesensory Systems.

The readouts of a Monroe 1920 calculator are deciphered by a μP to control a 35-word vocabulary in this Wespro talking-calculator system.

Developing calculators for the blind is more than a matter of presenting the keyed-in information and calculated answers in a form that does not have to be read visually. Calculators that talk and calculators that produce Braille outputs—tactile or on tape—are being developed to fill that need. But one major problem is to interface calculator-display signals with audio or Braille-output systems at a reasonable price. Current calculator prices range from a few hundred to over a thousand dollars. Incorporating microprocessors into these systems promises to substantially reduce costs—but in future designs.

Another problem is that developers of calculators for the blind are separated into two camps—those who believe in talking calculators, and those who are convinced that a Braille-tape readout is the optimum design. While one or the other may be better for a given application, neither is the best solution for all applications.

Survey gets results

A principal contributor to talking-calculator technology is Telesensory Systems, Inc., Palo Alto, with its $395 Speech Plus Hand-held, standard four-function calculator (see photo). The Speech Plus, which has a 24-"word" vocabulary, incorporates features rated high in a predevelopment survey of 180 blind persons throughout this country.

One big problem with most Braille systems, the survey revealed, is that there is no way to verify that the correct data have been entered. For this reason, the number or other key functions such as plus, minus, and times are pronounced by the Tele-sensory unit whenever the appropriate keys are depressed.

Another preference revealed in the study is for a keyboard arranged like that of a Touch-Tone telephone, rather than the standard calculator arrangement. The Speech Plus unit incorporates the telephone format.

The Speech-Plus calculator has a three-chip architecture (see block diagram). A calculator chip drives a visual LED display and sends speech-command signals to a speech synthesizer. The synthesizer uses two custom LSI circuits, one of which is a 16-k MOS ROM. The other is a dedicated Texas Instruments microcontroller that, upon command by the calculator chip, fetches control data from the ROM.

Sound is produced from the ROM data. Speech sounds are made up of digital bits that each make up an increment of an audio analog signal. The control chip converts the digital information into the audio signal via an on-chip d/a converter.

Calculator language can be changed simply by replacing the ROM. Both German and Arabic vocabularies are now available from newer ROMs.

A student model of the Speech-Plus is being developed by the American Printing House for the Blind, Louisville, KY. Whereas Speech-Plus gives all answers with decimal points, the Printing House model does not. It also operates at a one-third slower speech

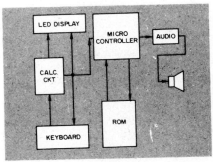

The speech synthesizer of the Telesensory calculator uses a custom microcontroller that converts the output of a special ROM to voice signals.

rate so that the user may make Braille notes if desired.

Speech board is available

The speech board of the Speech-Plus calculator has been made available for $95 to designers working on calculators for the blind. A more recent "Standard Vocabulary" board ($179) with 64 words, including volts, amps, dc, ac, and numbers up to 999,999, is also available. In October, a 64-word ASCII character set will be available for the same price.

A standard Monroe 1920 scientific calculator has been interfaced with the Telesensory-calculator speech board to produce a vocabulary of 35 words and word-beep or word-buzz sound combinations. The Monroe 1920 has over 25 scientific functions, 10 memories and scientific notation.

Produced by consultant Larry Waldron, who heads Wespro Industries, 442 Kasson Rd., Syracuse, NY, the calculator provides a voice output for each keypress and reads the output display after each calculation, or on demand.

Developed for Tim Cranmer, director of the Division of Special and Technical Services of the Kentucky State Bureau for the Blind in Frankfort, KY, the Wespro unit is now being used at Kentucky's state universities. It sells for $920. A statistical talking-calculator version is available using the Monroe 1930.

"What I've done is hang a speech-bus outboard of the Monroe machine," says Waldron. "The machine is a typical calculator because it has multiplexed digital readouts. The strobes for the display also multiplex the keyboard entries.

"I used a MOS Technology 6502 to monitor all of the lines coming out of the machine because this microprocessor is low-cost and simple to use. It's the intelligence that deciphers the keyboard entries and readouts. The 6502 interfaces directly with the TSI speech board which uses a 6-bit code."

The interface system uses MOS Technology's 6530 interface chip, plus two 1702 PROMs, Waldron notes. "This

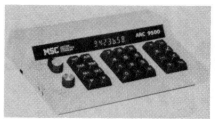

Keys are categorized into three groups for two-hand operation in this Master Specialties voice-output calculator.

combination simplifies the system design by giving me hardware features in software." For example, Waldron had trouble with noise on the interconnection cable between the calculator and his adapter. So he polled the lines with software and waited until the lines settled down and were valid.

To tell the blind user that the calculator is on though not in use, Waldron put in software to count keyboard scans. When a defined number of scans have been counted without any key activity, the calculator gives a "beep" that is in the speech-board vocabulary. This costs nothing in hardware—just some 15 or 20 bytes of software, according to Waldron. "The whole program takes up the two 1702 PROMs, or a total of 512 bytes of ROM."

HP calculator talks

Also developed for Cranmer is a telephone system that interfaces the

powerful Hewlett-Packard 9825A calculator with the Telesensory calculator speech board. Operated by blind women, the system is used to store the telephone numbers of staff and faculty at the University of Kentucky and at the University of Louisville.

The HP calculator is connected to the talking board through the IEEE 488 Interface Bus, according to designer Deane Blazie, vice president of Maryland Computer Services, Belair, MD.

"We buy the interface card from HP and we design from the end of that terminator to the voice board," says Blazie. "We've found that we can store 10,000 names on tape and get an average access time from the HP machine of from 6 to 10 seconds. The principal problem was getting a program to efficiently retrieve the names at random."

There is another problem. "We're currently marketing these systems for $8500 per 10,000 names," says Blazie. "We're considering redesigning a whole system based on a microprocessor and thus getting the cost way down. We're taking a serious look at the MOS Technology 6502 and the Z-80 microprocesssor."

Calculator has lifelike voice

Another talking calculator generates a more lifelike voice than that produced by the Telesensory unit—the ARC 9500 Audio Response calculator by Master Specialties Co., Costa Mesa, CA.

"We try to duplicate a complete waveform," says Ali Malekzadeh, project manager of electronic products and designer of the $565 calculator. The Telesensory system pieces together an audio waveform.

"We know there are a lot of redundancies in our system that make our processor more complex," Malekzadeh goes on. "But the object was to come up with a system that could use 'off-the shelf CMOS' rather than special custom chips." Another goal was to incorporate the most-wanted features in audio machines as determined by a Master Specialities survey of blind people—and at a low cost.

The more redundant technique was chosen because in addition to producing a more human-sounding voice, it is easy to implement and low-cost.

The ARC 9500's keyboard design differs from the Speech Plus's. For one thing, it is engineered for multifinger entry—more like a desk-top machine, Malekzadeh points out.

The vocabulary, however, contains

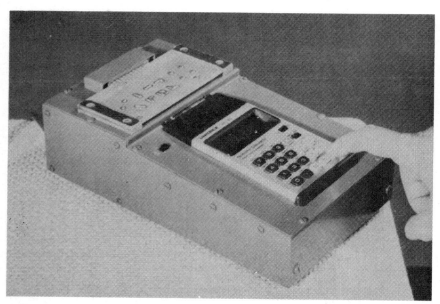

Stationary, tactile Braille readouts are part of a special PC board on this low-cost calculator designed at the National Research Council of Canada. Tones generated by touching the PC elements indicate the digits in the display, a decimal point, or overflow.

only 16 words. A vocal readout is provided for the digits entered and displayed and for the plus, minus, times, divide-by and equals keys. Functions such as $1/x$, x^2, square root and percent give a readout of the answer, but without audio confirmation of the key depression.

Three modes of operation have been incorporated into the Master Specialties unit: Learn, Fast and Calc. In the Learn mode, the key is locked out after each entry so that a beginner may hear one entry completely before making a sequential one.

In the Fast mode, the operator can make entries rapidly. But he won't get any audio verification of the digits, only the operational functions, such as times, divided by and equals.

In the Calc mode, the machine operates like a standard calculator. An audio output is possible only by pressing a repeat key.

In any of the modes the operator can verify what's in the display by pressing a repeat button.

Finger thinking

Unfortunately, some blind individuals can easily lose track of figures when doing complex problems on a talking calculator. Indeed, how effectively a blind person uses a talking calculator greatly depends on how that person thinks. While some can think better aurally, others can think better "visually" or—with their fingers—in Braille.

For the tactile thinkers, hard-copy output from a Braille calculator is a better answer, according to Tom Benham, a blind engineer who heads Science for the Blind Products, Bala-Cynwyd, PA. Benham has integrated a Kingspoint-44 scientific calculator into an $895 system that prints the answer in Braille on ½-in. paper tape. Two newer machines will be available shortly.

"We've had no problems with the Braille printer," he says. "But we've learned that signals feeding the displays of calculators must be cleaned up before they can be used to operate such a printer. We take an existing system and wire it into a calculator and bring out the seven-segment signals. We feed these signals into a ROM that's been programmed to convert them to four-dot Braille printouts."

Because of slow printer speed, however, the Braille signals are clocked at a much slower rate than the calculator signals. The Braille dots are made during a 0-to-32 string of counts. Counts 0, 1 and 2 make one set of dots, 7, 8 and 9 moves the paper, and so on in a fairly complicated sequence.

Even legally blind people who don't read Braille can use his Braille calculator, Benham insists. "Learning to read the full Braille system is a long process. But learning to read the 10 digits shouldn't take anyone more than a half-hour."

Cost must come down

But no matter which method a blind person uses to get information from calculators, he still must hurdle a tre-

A Braille readout is provided on this calculator by the American Foundation for the Blind. It has a variable speed control that enables the user to read as slowly as one digit every four seconds. It sells for $425.

mendous barrier—cost. That's the opinion of Jim Swail, an engineer who has been without sight since the age of four. According to Swail, a research engineer in the medical engineering section of the National Research Council of Canada in Ottawa, the least expensive four-function machine for the blind costs $375. A sighted person can buy an equivalent for under $10.

Hoping to narrow this price gap, Swail has developed a calculator system that uses off-the-shelf components and has no moving parts. The price should be around $100, Swail believes.

A combination of touch and sound is employed to produce the digital readout. In Swail's prototype unit (see photo), a Unitrex calculator is mated with his readout system, a PC Braille board at the top of the instrument.

Two horizontal rows of Braille numbers, extending from the left to the center of the board, represent the eight locations of the calculator-display digits. The matrix of dots used to read the displayed digits is at the right of the board, with a single dot below to indicate the decimal point.

Numbers 0 through 9 are formed by means of four-dot combinations in a 2 $\times$ 2 dot matrix. These dots are also part of the PC-board pattern.

The dots are touched sequentially with the tip of a finger. But only those dots that are involved in forming the Braille shape of the number being displayed on the read-out will activate a 300-Hz tone in an on-board loudspeaker. Other dots remain silent when touched.

To read an answer, one finger is placed on the digit position to be read while another explores the readout matrix for the dots that will produce the 300-Hz tone—actually the refresh rate of the calculator.

An overflow is indicated by a refresh-rate tone that sounds continuously until the overflow is cleared. A 100-Hz tone indicates that the function key has been depressed.

Field trials have indicated that the Swail calculator is easy to use. With a little practice, Swail says, an answer can be read in about half a second per digit. The National Research Council of Canada is seeking a manufacturer for the product.

A $100 talker, too

Meanwhile, a talking calculator for $100 seems feasible to Doug Maure, director of engineering for research and technological development at the American Foundation for the Blind in New York City. He points to a recent Motorola development that may lead the way—the XC3417 and XC3418 ICs, which comprise what is called a continuously-variable-slope delta modulator/demodulator. A low-cost way to digitize a serial stream of voice data is provided by this system, according to Maure.

Coupling low-cost efficient digitizing techniques made possible by the Motorola devices with 16-k ROMs that can be obtained for about $6 in reasonable quantities puts the $100 price tag within range, Maure insists. "We need to find somebody that can adapt an existing calculator chip, or even modify the chip to get the outputs necessary to directly feed or address a ROM that would in turn address the Motorola

A system that allows a blind person to work as a long-distance operator is the outgrowth of a calculator for the blind designed at MIT. Information from 82 switchboard keys is fed to a Motorola 6800, which converts it to 12-character Braille messages at this Little Rock, Arkansas, installation.

devices."

The Foundation, which was started by Helen Keller, is not a commercial organization, Maure explains. "We try to interest commercial organizations in developing products of this sort. If no one else can supply a product, we will develop it."

Indeed, two Braille calculators have already been produced and marketed by the Foundation. One is a $325 five-function device with an eight-digit vis-ual display and a single-digit Braille display that can be used to sample the calculator's eight digit positions at varying speeds. A similar scientific unit sells for $425 (see photo).

Another Foundation objective is a microprocessor-based voice system, with several interchangeable custom I/O chips and ROMs that could be plugged into it. These chips and ROMs would permit the voice system to be used with calculators, electronic thermometers and clocks, and a variety of other such devices.

Efforts to design calculators for the blind are not confined to the U.S. and Canada. A variety of talking and Braille calculators are also being produced in West Germany, Switzerland, Sweden and France. Descriptions of these machines as well as the addresses of several of their suppliers can be found in "The International Guide to Aids and Appliances for Blind and Visually Impaired Persons," available for $3 from the American Foundation for the Blind, 15 W. 16th Street, New York, NY 10011. This publication also describes calculators for the blind available in the U.S. as well as many other kinds of aids.

A discussion of technical problems involved in interfacing calculators with Braille devices is found in "Powerful Calculators for the Blind," ED No. 5, Mar 1, 1977, p. 54. ■■

Smart Electronic Games and Video Games

David H. Ahl

In this year's crop of games you'll find more versatility, more choice, and more smarts for less money.

After the Toy Fair last February, it was obvious that the biggest growth category in the toys and games industry in 1978 would be in electronic and video games. Now that the prototypes that were shown last February are on the store shelves, it's time to do our annual round up of the new, the old, the good and the mediocre.

Many of the games below were reviewed in depth on our pages during 1977 and 1978. In those cases the issue and page number are noted at the end of the capsule description. Other games without an issue noted were tested only briefly for this round up.

In still other cases, we only saw the prototypes and can't vouch that the production models on store shelves will live up to the starry-eyed claims made last February at the Toy Fair or in June at the Consumer Electronics Show. These are identified by **"NT"** (Not Tested) following the name of the game.

No round up like this is ever complete. In some cases we deliberately left out a game (saying nothing at all was the nicest thing we could do with some new entries). In other cases, we just weren't aware that the product existed and/or information arrived after presstime.

In any event, shop around for variety and price. And try things out before you buy to make sure it will hold your interest or the interest of the person for whom it's a gift.

Manual Games

Zone X

Will Invicta ever give us a chance to recoupe (from Master Mind) before they bring out another challenging logic game? Zone X, their newest addition, is an interesting derivation of the Master Mind premise. The zone-breaker uses a pegboard to guess the target point set by the zonemaker on his marker grid. This is not an easy game!

Zone X, complete with searchboard, marker grid, pegs, marker, and eraser.

(A $25 bonus goes to the author of the best computer version of Zone X received by March 1, 1979 in addition to the normal game/article payment. Send listing, run, description and SASE. How about a graphics version for the Apple, TRS-80, or PET?)

Press Ups

Another Invicta game which we got in England some time ago but is finally available in the U.S., Press Ups is a fast-moving logic game. Each player has ten colored pegs, five at each side of the 7 x 7 board. Yellow pegs in the rest of the board are neutral. Players take turns pressing down one peg which must be adjacent to a previously pressed peg trying, on each move, to guide the direction of play toward his colored pegs.

[Did you ever wonder who those exotic models are on the Invicta boxes? You guessed it — they're all Invicta employees in the various plants. — DHA]

(Yet another $25 bonus for the best computer version of Press Ups received by March 1, 1979!)

Super Master Mind

Super Master Mind is a step above Master Mind as it has 8 different colors (Master Mind has only 5). Speedy

computer calculations indicate there are over 59,000 possible answer combinations (according to Invicta, I only came up with 40,320, but I was never much of a mathematician). To add to the challenge, leave an empty space in the "answer code" and watch what happens (you go bananas!).

Grand Master Mind

A game like Grand Master Mind is enough to make you swear off Master Mind games forever, or perhaps become permanently addicted. If you've played previous Master Mind games and thought them difficult, try this one. You are allowed 10 tries to guess the colors, and for a new twist, you also guess shapes. Master Mind aficionados will find this a welcomed addition to their collection.

Smart Electronic Games

Coleco Amaze-A-Tron

This clever little maze game may be played alone or with a partner. The computer gives a starting and finishing point on a 25-square grid. You move a plastic marker and try to find the correct path from start to finish. A short musical tune plays when you hit a correct square; a wrong move gets a "raspberry" sound. It takes a few plays to get the hang of it, but once you do, it's addictive. The tunes are pleasant

and plenty loud to be heard in a noisy room of kids. "Solitaire Maze" is simple enough for a 6-year old, "Blind Alley — Back to Start" is a challenge to an adult.

Blue and white plastic case 4½ x 6¾ x 1½ in. Uses one 9-volt battery. Retail approx. $23.

Coleco Quiz Wiz

Quiz Wiz is a small electronic device which stores the answers to 1001 multiple choice questions. Armed with a booklet of 1001 questions (there are seven such books on subjects like sports, people, history, television, music and books, mathematics and trivia) you punch in the question number and your answer. Quiz Wiz gives you a green light and high tone if you're correct, a red light and low tone if you're not. We found the tones barely audible in a moderately noisy room so you have to watch the lights. To some adults it seemed like too much button pushing, but kids loved it. Ages 6 and up.

Maroon vinyl binder/case, 9½ x 4 x 1½ in. Uses one 9-volt battery. Retail approx. $20. Quiz booklets $3.

Coleco Digits

Yet another electronic Bagels/ Master Mind similar to Milton-Bradley's Comp IV (except Digits only uses 4-digit mystery numbers). Two skill levels.

White plastic 6 x 4 x 1½ in. Uses one 9-volt battery. Retail approx. $18.

Milton Bradley Simon

Simon, a computer update of the age old game, Simon-Says, is, without a doubt, one of the best party games to hit the market this year. It is a large disc with four different color plates. Simon lights up the plates and you follow his lead by playing back the proper color and sound sequence. The music is loud enough to hear at parties and the lights bright enough for inside use. Three different solitaire and multi-player games and four skill levels make Simon suitable for Age 5 to adult. One possible drawback: the plates aren't bright enough for outside use or in the car (which would be a great way to keep the kids busy while driving on vacation.) However, this drawback is minor if you learn the music associated with each color.

White and colored plastic, 12 in. dia. Uses two D cells and one 9-volt battery. Retail approx. $25.

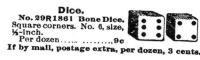

Dice.
No. 29R1861 Bone Dice. Square corners. No. 6, size, ¼-inch.
Per dozen....... ....9c
If by mail, postage extra, per dozen, 3 cents.

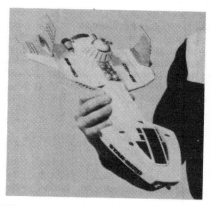

Milton Bradley Star Bird

When Star Bird first flew into the office, most females disliked the Star Wars-style craft, while the males praised it. Having had it in several different environments, this male/female reaction still seems consistant.

A microprocessor detects the attitude of the hand-held plastic plane (climbing, level, or diving) and simulates appropriate engine speeds. It also "fires" lasers with a "realistic" zap sound accompanied by blinking lights.

Various parts detach (escape pods, interceptors, high-speed fighter) and could break in impatient hands, although it is as rugged as any other plastic toy. The Raggedy Ann/Andy school of "kids-make-their-own-fantasy" school of purists won't like Star Bird; most kids (and their fathers) will love it.

Gray plastic with colorful markings, 15 in. long. Uses one 9-volt battery. Retail approx. $15 to $20.

Boris

In this electronic chess game, the amount of time the computer has to process its possible moves is set by the player. Up to 100 hours can be allowed but several seconds is enough to give a challenging game. The pieces, small board, and computer with keyboard and LED readout fit in a walnut box with lid. Boris comments on players' moves via phrases traveling across the LED display. **Boris Master** operates on rechargable batteries and has a memory feature. Suggested retail prices: Boris $299, Boris Master $399. **Boris** is distributed by Chafitz, Inc., 1055 First Street, Rockville, Maryland, 20850.

Chess Challenger X

This is the latest computerized chess game of Fidelity Electronics. The X means ten levels of play where one level roughly corresponds to the microcomputer looking ahead one-half move. Level one requires a few seconds, while level ten requires around several hours for a move. The board is part of the unit while the LED displays and touch pad keyboard are on the side. Features include a beep when its move is complete, and a random choice between moves that

are judged to be nearly equal in value. Suggested retail price is $275.

TI Speak & Spell

Electronic voice pronounces over 200 words, you key in the spelling. It announces when you are right or wrong and displays your score. Games like "Mystery Word" and "Secret Code" add to the fun of learning to spell.

Red plastic, 6½ x 10 x 1½. Uses 4 C-cells. $50. (Sept./Oct. '78, pp 60-61).

TI Spelling Bee

Non-speaking version of Speak & Spell. Comes complete with picture book and fold-up case. Uses 9-volt battery. $30. (Sept./Oct. '78, pp 60-61).

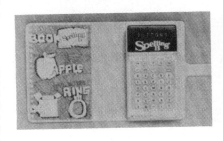

Arithmetic Practice Calculators

Seven of these little calculators are on the market this year, some with built-in games (Dataman), some which keep track of number correct and also

display correct answers (Little Professor, Quiz Kid II), and others that only light up a green or red LED in the case of a correct or incorrect answer. All use one 9-volt battery. Prices from $8 to $25.

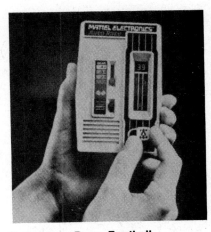

Mattel Auto Race, Football, Missile Attack

In all three games you control a bright light blip which represents your car, player or missile. Computer controlled blips are coming toward you (or you are moving toward them) and you are trying to avoid a collision (in Auto Race) or being tackled (in Football), or you are trying to shoot down enemy missiles. We liked Football best and Missile Attack least. For 1978, Missile Attack has been renamed "Battlestar Galactica Space Alert" perhaps hoping that the new TV show will stimulate sales. Also "Basketball" has been added to the lineup but we've not had a chance to try it.

All come in a handheld plastic case and use one 9-volt battery. Retail range $18-$35. (Jan./Feb. '78, pp 27-29).

Milton Bradley Comp IV

Use the calculator pad to guess a secret 3, 4, or 5-digit number. Comp IV gives you clues (how many digits correct and how many in the correct position). A game with lasting interest.

Plastic console 7½ x 4 x 4 in. Uses one 9-volt battery. Retail range $20 to $40. (Nov./Dec. '77, pp 36-37).

Milton Bradley Electronic Battleship

An electronic version of the manual Battleship game. The electronics mainly provide zippy sound effects. Retail range $30-$50. (May/June '78, pp 47-48).

APF Mathemagician

A teaching calculator which can be "programmed" to provide arithmetic problems on almost any level of difficulty. Mathemagician also has six built-in games which can be played using different plastic overlays. The large size and bright display make it ideal for younger children. Uses 6 C-cells. Retail $39.95. (Mar./Apr. '78, pp 92-94).

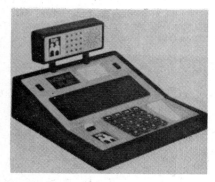

T.E.A.M.M.A.T.E. Game Computer

This device is a battery-operated device with a microprocessor, limited memory, 4 x 4 lamp display, 16 key keyboard, and speaker. It comes complete with 25 simple programs in memory which can be "called" by pressing the appropriate keys on the keyboard. Each program is described in the very complete manual. The "programs" are in a low-level logic rather different than either Basic or machine language. The output is all through the 4 x 4 lamp display which uses a different slide overlay for each one.

Blank overlays are also included so you can write your own.

The second chapter (12 pages) of the manual is an introduction to binary and hexadecimal number systems, computer organization, and elements of a large-scale computer system.

Uses 4 D batteries (which we found should be akaline or extra duty). From Logix Enterprises. Retail $40-$50.

Parker Brothers P.E.G.S.

15 chase and maze games played by inserting pegs into a double-sided electronic board. Makes sound when two pegs are in the same hole on opposite sides of the grid. Sounds innocent enough but once you start playing it begins to get wild! Although aimed at children from 7 to 14, adults had a ball playing "Battle of the Blobs" and "Hostage." Plastic. Uses one 9-volt battery. $15.

Parker Brothers Merlin

Plays 6 games (Tic Tac Toe, Music Machine, Echo, Magic Square, Mindbender, Blackjack 13) with 9 levels of difficulty. We enjoyed "Echo" immensely, trying to echo Merlin's tunes — no one here could echo more than 7 notes correctly. "Magic Square" was quite a challenge also, particularly the "challenge version for experts only." Eleven touch keys; red plastic. Uses 6 AA batteries. $25.

Invicta Electronic Mastermind (NT)

Break the hidden 3, 4, or 5 digit code in this electronic version of Mastermind. LED display tells how many digits are correct and in right position. Handheld. Uses 2 AA batteries. $20.

Video Games

Bally Professional Arcade

Outstanding graphics, 256 colors, nifty 3-function controllers and a nice assortment of game cartridges make this a system well worth considering as a video game system. However, for an extra $50 Bally offers a programming package that includes a Basic cartridge and an excellent printed introduction to the language that does not presume any previous computer experience. The Audio Cassette interface for another $50 allows you to use a standard cassette recorder to save and retrive programs. The ease of using the color, graphics and music (built-in 3-octave music synthesizer) is remarkable, though you probably won't be able to match the complexity of professionally prepared programs. $299. (Sep./Oct. '78, pp 56-59).

Atari Video Pinball

Plays four pinball-type games, two with flippers and two with a moving paddle at the bottom of the screen.

Also two basketball-type games and the incredibly popular Breakout in which you move your paddle to hit a ball to break away six colored walls of bricks at the top of the screen. Fun for the beginner, challenging for the expert. Extremely addictive. Uses 6 C-cells or AC adapter. Retail $55-$75. (Jul./Aug. '78, pp 35-36).

Atari Video Computer System

Perhaps the most comprehensive programmable game playing video system around, this unit has two skill levels, four types of controllers and an enormous library of games. Twenty game cartridges are currently available including Breakout, Indy 500, Blackjack, Starship (maneuver through space), Surround (lay down a maze with an opponent without getting trapped), Air/Sea Battle (planes dropping bombs, submarines launching missiles, shooting gallery), Outlaw, Home Run, Slot Racers, and, of course, Video Olympics (50 Pong-type games and variations). Most cartridges contain 3 to 6 fundamentally different games and 6 to 8 variations of each one.

Retail $165-$200. Cartridges $19 each. (Jul./Aug. '78, pp 37-39).

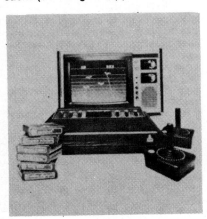

Fairchild Channel F System II (NT)

A redesigned version of the original Channel F, this has four difficulty levels, four time limits, and a unique "freeze" switch which permits interruption of a game with play resumed later (nice if you want to watch TV and play during commercials — or vice-versa). The unique controllers, which we found a bit difficult to get used to, turn, twist, push and pull in eight different ways. Three game cartridges use a numeric keypad controller (Poker, Football and a lunar lander game). Twenty-one other cartridges are availale over a wide range of subjects, some with as many as 284 variations.

Retail $125-$150. Cartridges $20 each.

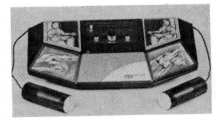

APF Model 500 (NT)

A dedicated video unit with 20 space games including Space War, Space Phasor, Phantom War (invisible space ships) and more. Guided or direct missiles.

Video Sport, TCR-900 PC (NT)

Yet another entry in the programmable price race ($69). This, like the last three products, will probably appear under various private label and store brand names.

Radofin Telesports III (NT)

A Hong Kong entry, Telesports is a low-price ($69 retail) programmable. Comes with 2 joysticks. Seven game cartridges planned with up to 10 games each.

Otron Gamatic 8600 (NT)

Another low price ($69) programmable with two joysticks. Four cartridges as of August. From Korea.

Video Technology Model 501 and Model 2003 (NT)

Two programmable entries in the low price derby (below $70). The 501 is a basic programmable while the 2003 has extended capabilities similar to Video Brain and also high resolution (256 x 256 pixels).

Coleco Telstar Arcade

Of the programmable video games, this is certainly the most tactile. No little knob to steer your racer, but a good size steering wheel and gear shift. And for the target games, a full-size (plastic) pistol. Two remote controls included in the price of the sports cartridge supplement the two built-in ones and allow for four-player competition. Two-level skill control,

Triangular plastic housing approx. 15" on a side. Comes with AC adapter. Bargain priced at $65; cartridges $10 to $15.

Magnavox Odyssey (NT)

Video system featuring a touch-sensitive alphanumeric keyboard as well as the usual joysticks. The keyboard and "computer introduction" cartridge indicate that Magnavox is looking ahead toward a truly programmable computer on the order of the Bally Arcade; but this is still only a game system. Around $180.

BUNAC, the British Universities North America Club, is a non profit-making organisation which arranges charter flights and working holidays to North America for British students. It is run largely by voluntary helpers, most of whom are involved in running the 52 BUNAC clubs on university campuses, but has a permanent staff of seven at its headquarters just off Tottenham Court Road, London.

One of the main tasks of the permanent staff is to process the 2,500 flight reservations they receive each year—a trivial number by British Airways standards, of course, but a different matter for a small staff doing everything by hand.

Until recently, the process involved 11 operations for each passenger, starting with the printing of a metal addressing plate with all relevant details, including that required by the Civil Aviation Authority. In addition, each passenger is contacted in writing five times in the course of dealing with his booking.

Overwhelmed by paperwork

The result was that, at peak periods, the level of paperwork overwhelmed the office. The system worked reasonably well up to about 1,500 flights a year. Above that level, the number of misfilings of records increased and began to create something of a chain reaction.

There were also occasional disasters, such as the time the complete filing system was spilt on the floor.

It was a clear case for computerisation but even so, the BUNAC U.K. general

A computerised reservations system for less than £5,000 sounds like an impossibility. Yet it is something the British Universities North America Club has achieved.

Micro system tackles Jumbo job

JIM BUSH

manager, Jim Buck, says: "Conceptually, we wouldn't have come within light years of computers ourselves. Shortage of funds and total ignorance of computing made the idea virtually unthinkable".

Illumination spread first from a television feature on Tomorrow's World and an article in a Sunday newspaper, detailing computers for as little as £2,000. Impressed, Buck telephoned the BBC to ask for the names of the manufacturer, and it proved to be SWTPC. Then he began searching to see what else was available.

Tracking-down micros in October, 1977 proved to be tricky, especially for someone with little idea of what he was seeking. Buck never discovered who were the other manufacturers. The Business Efficiency Exhibition was full of equipment which was fast, glamorous and very expensive, but nothing was within £1,000

of the cost of the SWTPC hardware.

The process of shopping around, however, provided BUNAC staff with a better insight into the potential of computers. From thinking in terms of little more than a glorified addressing machine, they appreciated other advantages.

Most important of them was security of information, a factor which Buck stresses repeatedly in discussing the system. The idea that information, once entered correctly into the computer, could be guaranteed accurate, and that it could be guaranteed not to be lost, was a revelation. The first time the computer produced a passenger list without a single mistake was a milestone. "Nobody ever had passenger lists as accurate as that", says Buck.

Mental anguish factor

Financial and staff savings, however, were a secondary consideration. BUNAC was able to hire one fewer temporary staff during the three peak months and handled more flights than in the previous year. More important, Buck says, is the saving in "mental anguish" and the long hours of overtime for BUNAC permanent staff.

The decision to buy the computer was taken in November, 1977 and the machine was delivered in February. Systems design and programming was carried out by Tim Beyts of Beyts Logic, to whom BUNAC was introduced by SWTPC. After evaluating BUNAC requirements, Beyts specified a 32K system, with a VDU, twin FD8 disc drives and a Centronics 701 printer. The cost, including software, was about £4,750.

Meanwhile, Buck rushed to buy a Basic manual. He settled on Jerald Brown's *Instant Basic* and recommends it to others who are baffled by the mathematical aspects, which he feels are over-emphasised in most manuals.

As a result, he was able soon to provide

The BUNAC system; 32K processor, twin FD8 discs, printer and VDU.

Reprinted with permission from *Practical Computing*. Vol. 1 Issue 4.

a rough specification of his requirements, in terms of input and output, amendment, enquiry and reporting facilities. The system was operational by March 15.

Data, as before, is taken from passenger reservations and output in the form of booking details in CAA format, passenger lists, address labels and analyses of total bookings. Accounting is reasonably simple, since most charges are fixed and common to all passengers, and was omitted from the original design, though it will probably be added next year.

Data errors are negligible

The passenger file builds up over the season to create a bulky database, occupying three discs. So even a short enquiry or amendment run can take 40 minutes but this is not regarded as a great handicap—the staff proceed with another task.

At present, three of the seven staff have learned to use the computer, though an operator manual is being prepared which will enable anyone, including temporary staff, to carry-out data entry. Data errors on input so far have been negligible. Apart from the built-in validation routines, Buck attributes that to a new-found pride in accuracy which the computer seems to have generated. He speaks of "a small sense of achievement" as each entry is input correctly.

He is also relieved to find that the computer has not deprived him of his "feel" for the way the business is working. Partly because he still deals with much of the data entry himself, he finds he is, for example, still able to decide which would be the best alternative date for a flight which has to be altered, without having to

run through the list of passengers' second choices first.

Goodwill has improved

On the passenger side, he also feels that goodwill has, if anything, improved, though this is difficult to assess with a different set of passengers each year.

BUNAC is sufficiently impressed with its computer to be planning a second system for installation in the States. It will deal with applications for jobs as camp counsellors in BUNAC camps. Although the number of people involved is smaller than the passenger booking system, the problem is complicated by the need to match counsellors' skills and availability to the available jobs.

It is also looking for ways of making use of spare computer time, particularly in the winter months. The club booking season lasts effectively from March to October; the rest of the year, the computer is effectively lying fallow. Anyone with a good use for four months' computer time could contact BUNAC.

Section 5

Microprocessors and Management

The articles in this section review the impact that
microprocessors will have on management and
discuss some of the wider social implications of
the use of microprocessors.

Micro-electronics – some social considerations

by Tony Edwards

Since the first microprocessors and microcomputers came into the market in the early 1970's the bulk of their production has found its way into pocket calculators and TV games.

Now, at last, a growing interest and a focus of attention is being directed toward, not only the use of these microelectronic devices in almost every aspect of life, but also toward the social and economic consequences that will accompany their wide spread application.

It is not an exaggeration to assume that history will describe the last quarter of this century as the beginning of the microelectronic age.

Unlike steam and electricity, its predecessor ages, microelectronics is less concerned with prodigious feats of physical work, instead it is more concerned with the *nature* and the *effectiveness* with which work is done in order to achieve defined objectives.

It is therefore reasonable to assume that a professional body dedicated to the study of work, and to the organisation and methods for achieving it, should occupy a key role in such an age. That is provided that body evolves to meet that new age's challenge.

In essence a challenge that asks how does society intend to use a technological development, which not only adds a new fundamental dimension to the understanding and the effective application of work, but also creates opportunities to identify whole new ranges of feasible objectives, hitherto obscured by traditional thinking. Ranges of objectives which will enable society to broaden the scope of its ambitions and to elevate the horizon of its socio-economic expectations to unimagined levels, or alternatively to plunge itself into ever deepening socio-economic conflict.

The microprocessor and the microcomputer can be used to raise the quality of life to levels not contemplated previously. But, as one might expect, during such a time of fundamental shifts in technology, such devices could also be used in ways that accelerate the fragmenting conflict, which characterizes western society's attitudes toward work, wealth, moral responsibility and socio-economic satisfaction.

In order to preempt the dangers of heightened conflict, especially in business and industry, society through its institutions, and among these I include Parliament, should coordinate its views toward both the economic and the social consequences of living in a microelectronic age, which goes beyond pocket calculators and TV games, to include a harsh reality that will call for restructuring of society's socio-economic attitudes and behaviour as the price to gaining admission to an era that will add new dimensions to living.

In democratic states such as those in which we live the choice, and the responsibility for any course of action we follow, rests with us. Each individual and each institution can go their own way up to some point where eventually they stumble into the electronic age, in conflict with one another. Each damaging the others socio-economic prospects.

Or they can unify their purpose. And in doing so use microprocessors and microcomputers in ways that create a new range of opportunities that can provide socio-economic satisfaction to all sectors of society, without damaging their long term prosperity and within the boundaries of acceptable criteria.

What grounds are there for suggesting that we are on the verge of a microelectronic age, and that society needs to coordinate its institutional concerns for this age?

To get some idea of why we should do this consider the following two brief scenarios. The first largely deals with facts whilst the second deals with some of society's responses to those facts. Together these two demonstrate the social and philosophic truth that decisions do not derive from facts, and are therefore never more than informed opinions, which benefit from critical appraisal. Hence the need for coordinated institutional discussion and action, to improve the socio-economic quality and effectiveness of decisions that deeply affect our future.

First consider this brief technical scenario.

1 A microprocessor consisting of thousands of transistors, fitted onto a silicon chip no more than 0.25 sq cm, containing the arithmetic and logic unit equivalent to a 1960 model powerful computer processor (as big as half a dozen filing cabinets) costs about 50p.

2 The sales rate of integrated circuit chips is growing at 50 per cent per annum. Sales are confidently expected to exceed £6 billion by 1985. As each chip represents encapsulated 'brain power', this amounts to a very substantial addition, to existing human 'brain power'. A situation which will inevitably lead to a large scale invasion by microprocessors and microcomputers, into work areas where human thinking and control has always been employed.

3 In principle it costs little extra to increase the number of circuits, and therefore 'brain power', on a chip from 10 000 to 20 000 or more. The million circuit chip is no longer fanciful, whilst microelectronic thinking sometimes seems to border on the bizarre, when scientists and engineers talk about 'bubble memories with a

density of forty million bubbles per sq inch'.

The microelectronic capability to replace human brain power control of routine and semi routine activities could be unlimited, and is only beginning.

4   Ubiquitous, these devices when placed in tactical areas can control operations, provide information and answers, talk to each other and help to speed up big, mainframe, computer working rates. For technical reasons and for limited software reasons, microprocessors are, at present, an adjunct to mainframe computers. For the time being they are not a threat to their bigger brothers.

But above and beyond all this lies the ability of the microprocessor and microcomputer to eliminate, not only, traditional forms of work, but replace them with new technology that eliminates the need for human thinking and activity.

5   The boundaries to the use of these devices seems to be limited, at present, by human ingenuity — perhaps a reassuring thought — but one that also demands that the professional study of work must evolve into lateral thinking.

One manufacturer is said to have already identified more than 25 000 **different** uses for microelectronic devices.

Against this background consider the following socio-economic scenario.

1   Is the 'Job Killer' revolution on the way?
2   Microelectronics will strengthen centralisation. The alternatives, socialise software, or suffocate society.
3   Microcomputers may help to make us wiser, happier and healthier.
4   The age of individualisation is here, microprocessors open the way to decentralisation.
5   Microprocessors mean mass unemployment.
6   Microprocessors lead to a leisure life.
7   Our children will grow up to face mass unemployment.
8   Microcomputers will provide automatic reading and speaking machines for the blind.
9   Doctors commit their life time medical experience to microcomputer diagnosticians.
10   Speech operated wheelchairs help the handicapped.
11   Microprocessor hearing aids will be embedded in the ears.
12   Micros for automatic typewriters, word processing and satellite 'mailing' of words, will revolutionise office work.
13   West Germany microelectronics manufacturer forecasts 2 million of countrys 5 million typists and secretaries redundant by 1990.
14   Industry must create wealth and sort out the unemployment problems afterwards.
15   EEC country estimates 25 per cent to 30 per cent of banking, insurance and finance employees will be made redundant during the next decade.
16   One EEC country pleads for socio-economic restructuring in face of microprocessor revolution.
17   If the economy grows then automation will help people to meet their expectations. But the world economy is stagnating at less than the required level to reduce unemployment.
18   Government official says we met the challenge of the steam and electricity age and no doubt we will meet the challenge of the microelectronic age.
19   The microcomputer will control the household kitchen processes, and look after family administration in the same way as it will look after business administration.
20   The automated warehouse; from ordering to billing from receiving to issuing, is only one more feasible step toward the automated factory.
21   Industry maintains a low profile on automation and redundancies, to avoid conflict with trade unions. Trade Unions wait and see.
22   Leading moderate trade unionist in an EEC country says 'New investment in industry must be directed toward creating jobs, otherwise rising unemployment will lead to industrial conflict'. Demand for the thirty five hour week has been officially and publicly made to one EEC Government by the major trade unions.
23   In a matter of months computers linked to visual display units bring children to levels of education which they might otherwise never attain.
24   Personal computers are teaching children how to programme computers so they can teach other children.
25   Learning to write a computer programme will soon form an essential part of all liberal education programmes.
26   Microcomputers in the home, linked to a mainframe computer, provide personalized home-school studies.

Give or take a little the probable truth associated with most of these responses, in particular related circumstances, is high. For example, given the right attitudes toward work microelectronics can make people wiser, happier and healthier. Whereas a determined, closed, bureaucratic attitude could lead to these devices 'suffocating society'.

As I have said the choice is with society, and new lateral thinking about that social enigma — work — is the key.

There can be little doubt that the first scenario is close to reality. If work is the key, then before we reach a conclusion we must consider the nature of work and factors that influence it, and describe criteria of its effectiveness.

In a materialistic world, such as ours, work contains social and economic parts, which are represented in socio-economic objectives. Work done by people consists of the sum of human mental and physical activity directed toward the achievement of socio-economic objectives.

Mental activities are governed by the human ego and psychological factors, which are influenced by health, education and leisure pursuits and the socio-economic satisfaction derived from work.

Thus, in terms of doing work, human effectiveness depends on a stable balance being maintained between

a   Health.
b   Education.
c   Work — employment.
d   Leisure.
e   Ego-satisfaction.

Consider these five to be both criteria and objectives of effective work. That is one requires, health, education, employment, leisure and ego satisfaction to do work effectively. Whilst in return for doing work effectively one expects to maintain a stable state of relations between ones health, education, employment, leisure and ego-socio-economic satisfaction. In these circumstances if we damage the criteria we forego the objectives.

Now, an examination of the second scenario shows that many of the responses are contradictory, and could in particular circumstances, lead to the formation of destabilizing social forces. Outright conflict between trade unions and employers being an example.

Examination also shows that these responses could be easily grouped under the five headings representing the criteria/objectives of effective work.

This relationship between the criteria of work effectiveness and the potential for conflict and social instability, means that any ill conceived application of micro-electronic devices will almost certainly be an example of preemption, conflict and self defeat.

The magnitude of the opportunities to change or eliminate, not only the *content* but also the *nature* of work, previously done by people, could if wrongly handled make all the industrial conflicts that have surrounded the professional study of work since Taylor's time, look like a pixies party.

We must begin to broaden, on lateral lines, the way we think about work.

Driven by ego-satisfaction, work is the sum of mental and physical activity concerning ones health, education, employment and leisure. Therefore, a study of work effectiveness must be concerned with the net satisfaction of these criteria, expressed in socio-economic objectives.

Thus, if on the one hand the microelectronic age can offer new dimensions to living, it can on the other hand damage the *net* effectiveness of work. And in doing so release destabilizing socio-economic forces, not only in industry and commerce, but in society in general. In blunt terms, when ego-satisfaction, in work is sufficiently suppressed then ego-frustration leads to irrational behaviour and conflict.

Conflict, which if not arrested depens and eventually attacks the fabric of democratic society.

Therefore I conclude:

1 That the professional study of work must assume new dimensions in order to not only understand the benefits to be derived from microelectronic devices, but also to understand how the criteria of work can be satisfied both inside and outside the factory and office.

2 That failure to adopt new attitudes, toward work, will lead to the self defeat of the use of microelectronic devices.

3 That the microelectronic age is offering an opportunity to competitors, to start even, in a race that faces each business and each country with a fluxed maze of opportunities. From which past failures can be redeemed and present success can be forfeited in failure to understand the multi-dimensional thinking that must evolve with this new age.

4 That past achievement will not guarantee future success.

5 The businesses which grasp the lateral advantages of using the microelectronic age, not merely for short economic gain, but for the long term prosperity to be gained from optimal socio-economic policies; will realize levels of profit that enable them to adopt new policies toward the relationships between cost, profit distribution and investment, that secure the future socio-economic prosperity of both the business enterprise and its employees' community interests. And in doing so contribute to the democratic stability and prosperity of society.

6 That the extent to which society enjoys the almost unbounded benefits of the microelectronic age will depend on:
   a Society's ability to coordinate its approach to this age, through its institutional representatives.
   b The extent to which the professional study of work can be evolved, laterally, to match the needs of the age.

7 That in order to meet its new responsibility the role fulfilled by the professional study of work must move into the corporate areas of business and the central offices of social administration. From which it can relate to the broad criteria of effectiveness.

8 That more and more the 'shop floor' and 'the office' will be the precincts of technology, in which machines controlling machines, are controlled by technologists. The blue collar and white collar will give way to the collarless dust free suit of the microelectronic technologist. Paper and ink in the office will receed into insignificance, whilst routine and semi-routine work, done by people, will vanish.

9 That eventually the true study of work will evolve as the study of objectives and socio-economic satisfaction.
   Whilst work as we knew it will degrade into speed of light impulses controlling the energy supplies for the transformation of resources into products and services.
   However in the meantime there are practical everyday problems, which will not dissolve because we are opening the doors of a new age.
   But it is essential that we understand its lateral consequences, in order that we can make the SAFE, PRACTICAL, PROFITABLE and SOCIO-ECONOMIC transition.

Micro-electronics and employment - a trade union view

KEN GILL

The World is on the threshold of a technological revolution as important as the invention of the wheel, powerlooms, electricity and the assembly line. This derives from two related inventions, firstly that of the computer, and secondly that of a development variously known as the microprocessor, silicon chip, or the integrated circuit.

Commercial interests encourage magic surrounding these developments. This should be removed. A computer in its most common form is little more than a giant filing cabinet containing often hundreds of thousands of pieces of separate information which can be related to each other by a program and which can respond in millionths of a second.

The first computers contained only a few thousand pieces of information and occupied the whole of a large building.

However, the development of the integrated circuit, popularly known as the 'silicon chip' now enables the micro-processor to be made. This, as the name implies, is simply a miniature computer carrying out all the processes of a large machine but which can be placed on a desk or work bench and is expected in a few years time to be containable within a match box.

The dramatic reduction in size has been achieved by creating an integrated circuit on a tiny piece of metal no more than 1/8 in. square and containing within that electrical circuits equivalent in capacity to memory banks of information previously contained on the magnetic tape records of a large computer.

The storage capacity of these chips is measured in 'bits'. The most popular type contains 4096 (4K) separate bits of information. New production plans assume that the international standard is increasing to 16K on the same size chip and the new NEB company, Inmos, plans for a chip containing 64K bits. Some suggest that chips containing a quarter of a million bits are feasible.

Just as computers are getting smaller, so is the price going down. It is estimated that the price of computers is halved every five years and this is likely to accelerate as the silicon chip is further developed.

Like previous technological revolutions the computer and silicon chip will create jobs but equally, as in the first industrial revolution, thousands of jobs will disappear, not just unskilled and semi-skilled, but highly skilled jobs will also be by-passed by the new technology. Engineering will be seriously affected.

To date the silicon chip has destroyed the orthodox watch industry in Germany and has led to Switzerland ceasing to be the pre-eminent watch manufacturer. The electronic calculator produced in millions for a few pounds has displaced electro-mechanical equipment which previously cost several hundred pounds with the consequent loss of thousands of jobs in that sector.

At the present time, the major impact of the integrated circuit has been on that part of the manufacturing industry which previously made electro-mechanical equipment and this now faces job losses through the changeover to electronic components. The telecommunications industry is now moving belatedly from electromechanical to fully electronic public exchanges. The delay in that transfer has already lost the UK most of its traditional world markets. The combination of these two factors, technological change and a slothful reaction to it, has halved employment in the industry and it is believed that when System X is in full production only one manual worker out of four will have been retained. Electronic systems also require less maintenance and has led the Post Office Engineering Union to campaign for a shorter working week.

Not unnaturally the implications of electronics technology has been demonstrated most obviously in the field of computer manufacture itself. Over the last decade the total labour force of ICL in the UK has been reduced from 33 000 to 22 000 and the proportion of manual workers in that total has been reduced from one half to one fifth.

Similar developments are inevitable in the machine tool industry, and in those parts of the electrical industry that traditionally have used electro-mechanical devices eg switch gear and motor control gear.

The increased use of computers on the assembly line will reduce the number of operatives required and require fewer inspectors. Maintenance staff will no longer be required to carry out preventive maintenance because a computer can be programmed to carry out its own. Those maintenance staff left will have to be technologists since the traditional functions required of an engineering craftsman would not be appropriate for maintenance of computers.

The new machinery will not only be suitable for continuous processes, but will be sufficiently flexible to cope with the batch production that is currently very much the prerogative of the small and medium size firms. With the increased cost of equipment the small firms will almost certainly be unable to pay for them; they will go to the wall. The large companies will meet the production loss arising from the collapse of the small firms without necessarily any increase in labour.

Reprinted with permission from Mr. Ken Gill. This article originally appeared in *Management Services* Vol. 22 No. 12.

Equipment is increasingly becoming available that makes the orthodox toolroom irrelevant since tools and dies can increasingly be produced automatically or by-passed completely.

Because of Britain's backwardness in the machine tool technology, equipment is being imported from the United States and Germany. Thus those jobs destroyed by the introduction of new equipment are not being replaced by manufacture of the new equipment. A central demand must be that Britain manufactures the new technology.

A graphic example of the change derived from the new technology is a company like GEC Semi-Conductors where the factory is installed within a research centre, and the production process is carried out by lines of expensive imported equipment overseen by a few non-manual workers. It is a reminder of the current American joke that an electronics company was so successful it was able to move into smaller premises!

Petro-Chemicals and Steel Manufacture already embody some of the new control technology which has eliminated all but a handful of workers. Whilst it is true that the tiny group of maintenance workers that remain may command high salaries because of their importance to the industry, this is no compensation to the thousands of skilled workers displaced.

Technological advances will leave thousands of skilled people redundant. Re-training will be more expensive and difficult for those middle aged workers, like draughtsmen or tool makers, than training for students or school leavers. Disturbing reports are being received that the Government wants educational money associated with the new technology spent not to re-train those currently employed in the industry but used in schools. If this is carried out, scores of thousands of workers will be condemned to the scrap heap of the dole for life. It is essential that the responsibility for meeting the new technology should lie not with the Department of Education but with the Department of Employment and the EITB.

A Government sponsored report issued by the Advisory Council for Applied Research and Development is a damning indictment of employers incompetence: 'As a result (of micro-electronics) we have been overtaken by competitors in fields such as cash registers, food processing equipment, process instruments, machine tools, telephone switching systems, printing machinery and even in ship chronometers. In many of these fields we previously had a dominant position. Moreover, we failed to recognise new opportunities until others produced the products. Examples are calculators, electronic watches and clocks, word processing and television games'. The report goes on, 'On production methods the picture is just as gloomy. Industrial firms are only slowly incorporating new technology such as numerically controlled machine tools into their manufacturing and into production

planning control'. The main conclusion in the report is that every department and agency of the Government including nationalised industries must accept the importance of the new semi-conductor technology. 'We do not suggest that the impact will be substantial immediately, but we believe that over the next ten to fifteen years there will be changes in both manufacturing and service industry which will affect the whole UK economy . . . . 'The technology provides opportunities for developing new products, but unless we incorporate this technology in our products and improve our productivity, our resulting uncompetitiveness will pose a serious threat to the balance of payments', says ACARD.

Some trade union leaders argue that the new technology should be resisted. We have already seen what happens if this occurs. The struggle in Print to resist technology simply led to countless print firms going to the wall and the jobs were lost anyway.

Albert Booth, Secretary of State for Employment, has rightly pointed out that if Britain is to remain an important industrial power it has no alternative but to move as rapidly as possible to accept the new technologies in every field.

If this is accepted then social demands are required on a scale never known before. Technological change need not cause unemployment. Indeed, Britain should welcome developments that could provide higher standards, less boring work, more leisure and more information so that production can be planned more rationally.

At present, however, workers' demands are surprisingly modest. The dramatic reduction in dock employment, for example, led to a 31-hour week, no compulsory redundancy, and voluntary severance pay up to £7,000. But far greater social benefits could have been achievable as part of the cost of introducing the new technology in dock work.

The 1978 TUC passed overwhelmingly an eight point motion calling for public investment and ownership of the basic production in the UK, training and re-training, planned job creation, research into the social consequences, shorter hours, more holidays, early retirement, and co-operation with trade unions abroad. The General Council is preparing a policy statement for a special conference on this subject.

Technology must be our slave and not our master. Our members must be alerted to negotiate on every aspect of the new technology and warn them of those areas of importance of which they may not be immediately aware. The multinational corporations see this technology as a means for greater profits, and greater controls over their employees and the consumer. The union movement see it as more employment and more purchasing power and more leisure for the workers. The massive increase in productivity derived from these developments must go to the benefit of all and not to the few.

Design techniques with microprocessors

National Computing Centre has undertaken a survey into the training needs of microprocessor users. In this article, **Martin Whitbread** outlines the problems to be faced during the specification and control of projects.

Before any design or development activities can take place on a microprocessor project, some essential preparations have to be made. First, the objective of the project, which is really the customer's objective, must be fully documented. It is no use designing the perfect answer to the wrong problem.

Second, various operational, functional and system specifications are needed. Before design and development begins, each and every subsystem should be specified. The relationships of hardware and software must be defined, as should, surprisingly enough, the maintenance and support needed. Difficulties of support may make the design untenable. Finally, a mechanism will be needed to implement changes in specification as they occur and also to feed back any difficulties from the design and development unit. It is only then that a project is ready for design and development work.

The control of microprocessor projects is made easier by the use of comprehensive systems specifications. Mechanisms will be needed to report changes in specifications or design up and down the chain of command.

There are considerable problems of control caused by the very nature of microprocessor activity. There is a need for the skills of hardware design and development and similarly for software production. The careful control of these two and the organization of testing facilities is a full-time task for a project manager. The end result of this is the identification of five skills: project management, systems design, programming, electronics design and electronics assembly.

To take a team made up of these mixed abilities into a totally alien environment would be to court disaster. The novice team will need training, support and above all information. Success centres around the quality of the subsystem specifications and the ability of the project team to carry them through.

Successfully using a microprocessor as a component depends as much on the management and control of the project as on the expertise of the designers. Integrated design techniques are needed to control the mixture of hardware and software.

A balance must be struck between moving too far, too quickly and being overcautious. The very nature of the microprocessor, its cheapness and versatility, means that many companies will be exposing themselves to these problems for the first time. These organizations might feel that they have sufficient grasp of systems and software design to cope with these aspects unaided. There are several reasons why this may not be true. In the current generation of microprocessors, the software has to optimize the use of the processor. The experiences of any inhouse DP staff will probably be in a high-level language run in a multiprogramming environment, a different environment to microprocessing altogether.

Another aspect is software reliability. If an invoicing program fails, it is unfortunate, but can be corrected. In a process control program, however, the results of untidy logic could be expensive if not disasterous.

Microprocessor projects of the future, when VLSI processors are the equivalent of IBM 370s on a chip, may not need such specialized staff as are required now. It will be quite some time before those responsible for hardware and software no longer need at least a working knowledge of each other's discipline.

Despite the falling costs of microprocessor parts and the trend towards cheap utility programs, the cost of a properly equipped development project should not be underestimated. Much more is needed than a few boards and wires. An additional overhead could be the choice of a non-standard facility that adds greatly to the system cost with every enchancement. Choosing a unique bus structure could cost the project dearly, if additional memory boards are needed.

The apparent successful completion of the project: the creation of hardware and software, is not the end of the story by any means. Extensive testing will be needed and maintenance facilities will have to be organized for both hardware and software. This and subsequent articles will cover, in outline, the design approaches that are needed to attempt a successful project. Many people in their early and heady days of microprocessing entertain mistaken ideas that they later come to regret. We all tend to have faith in our own logical ability and this is still true when we write or design software, our confidence remains. But often our grasp of the problem is inadequate and we may not after all be perfect. This produces an imperfect solution to an imperfectly defined problem. No wonder software has bugs!

The very flexibility of software may tempt a designer into loose hardware design in the conviction that it can always be made good with suitable software. At what expense? For a simple illustration of hardware/software tradeoffs, compare the speed of software multiplication with that of hardware in, say, the Texas Instruments 9900. Software sometimes takes more time than can be afforded.

Reprinted for 'Microprocessors and Microsystems' Vol. 2 No. 5. Published by IPC Science and Technology Press Ltd., Westbury House, Bury St., Guildford, Surrey, England GU2 5AW.

The various application areas of microprocessors, which can be classified as

- new products and electronic roles
- minicomputer substitution
- random logic substitution

have led to new approaches in design. A formal approach to design must be preceded by project specification stages of a similar standard. A major interaction is between the producer and the customer. To specify and design what is not wanted is an intellectual exercise which will not pay the bills. For a minimal project, where the producer and customer are one and the same, the early stages of specification are likely to be ignored. This is quite common, but what is often forgotten is that nothing is static, and the results of the designer's labours may well be inherited by a puzzled and frustrated colleague who may then have to repeat the exercise. This is a common experience in DP where one-off programs, undefined and undocumented, abound. Even the one-man designer should produce an operational specification.

As mentioned already, there is a need for all parties to understand the project objectives. The following sections list the specifications needed to maintain effective control of a project and to ensure that what is specified and designed is what is wanted.

Care must be taken to ensure that any changes in specification filter quickly to the designer, otherwise at the very minimum a hurried software rewrite will result.

CUSTOMER OBJECTIVE

The customer may only be aware of the problem and display a degree of uncertainty as to the solution. Various alternatives may have to be proposed and their implications made clear. As it is the potential user's needs that are important, all discussions should be based on them. Having defined the problem and proposed a solution, that solution should be defined in terms of its *operational specification* and requirement.

OPERATIONAL SPECIFICATION

The solution should be defined in the customer's terms. The contractual positions of the customer and supplier should be defined. This should include software indemnities, copyrights and the operational environment of the product. The form and performance of the product will need defining. Key functions, software security, restarts and the many other factors that may concern the user should be clearly defined at this stage. Care should be taken with the product performance specification. Rash promises could mean painful recriminations before the contract is completed. Transalating the customer's solution into the supplier's solution results in the *operational requirement*.

OPERATIONAL REQUIREMENT

This is the technical heart of the product specification. All inputs and outputs should be defined along with the relationships between them. The possibility of later enhancement, say, to add additional channels, should be stated. Now that a definition of input and output is available, a program of tests can be specified that will form the acceptance tests for the system. The physical environment of the system, the type of chassis, sensitivity to temperature, humidity and vibration should all be defined. These will have a

direct bearing on costs, as components to military specification may be needed pushing hardware costs up by a factor of two or three. An estimate of costs could be made at this stage, provided all the components are known entities and not paper tigers. Many chips are announced that never see the light of day.

The way in which the system is to be supported should also be set out. This should include documentation of hardware and software maintenance and training user staff. Once the operational requirements of the product have been defined to the satisfaction of both customer and supplier, the *functional specification* can be developed.

FUNCTIONAL SPECIFICATION

A better estimate of costs and timescale can now be given. The individual functions of the system can be identified and costed in both time and money. However, some experimental work may be needed to determine these. A high-speed communications link using special-purpose chips may well require a test system to prove the design.

When the functions of the system are defined, the design of the system to perform these functions can be specified.

SYSTEM DESIGN SPECIFICATIONS

The specifications describe the manner in which the functions of the system are performed, and in a further stage of analysis, the manner in which the functions of the various subsystems are performed. The functions of an A/D converter, within a monitoring system, could be defined as a subsystem. The very specification of subsystems allows the actual process of detailed design work to proceed. In parallel with the system design specification the *system support specification* must be prepared

SYSTEM SUPPORT AND MAINTENANCE SPECIFICATION

Anticipated realiability and maintenance needs should be documented. Details of customer training and documentation needs should also be ascertained, together with the final specification for the product acceptance test. Now before any software has been written or any hardware assembled, other than function testing, the system is prepared on paper. From the customer's objective down to the performance of the subsystem, a working set of documents has been prepared. The project is now ready for the design and development of hardware and software.

Parallel with the normal rounds of discussion, decision making and finally design and development, documentation is needed (Figure 1). Nothing must be left to chance either at the specification stage or later. If risks are taken they may have to be paid for. Remember Murphy's First Law: Whatever can go wrong, will go wrong, at the worst possible moment. For instance, power supply, chip reliability and incorrect usage introduce three sources of possible failure, which can produce seven combinations of error.

Software will also need careful handling. Using inadequate development aids, it is possible to spend six months doing six days' work. This has already happened in several projects. Techniques for software development and the aids available will be described in later articles.

Some specification stages require the creation of a pro-

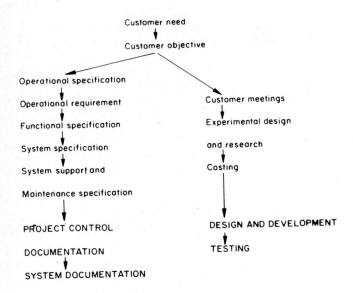

Customer need

Customer objective

Operational specification

Operational requirement

Functional specification

System specification

System support and

Maintenance specification

PROJECT CONTROL

DOCUMENTATION

SYSTEM DOCUMENTATION

Customer meetings

Experimental design

and research

Costing

DESIGN AND DEVELOPMENT

TESTING

Figure 1. Project documentation

cedure for the final product. Hardware and software debugging procedures will be needed. In particular there is the problem of interfaces and just how standard is a 'standard' interface.

The whole spectrum of specification design and development of a microprocessor project will pose many new problems for the uninitiated. Simple projects with short-term goals and the minimum of complexity or risk should be attempted first. Information is a major resource in this environment.

Manufacturers' information and the published works of others are essential reading. This is not a static environment, new ideas and facilities are becoming available to the designer that can mean the difference between a project's success or failure. Six months spent with a £200 evaluation kit can be equated with six days on a £2 000 microcomputer. A proper development system and a logic analyser can be even more help, but associated with the purchase of any such equipment must come formal training courses.

SKILLS

Among the new problems presented by the use of microprocessors is the novel mix of skills required. There is a need for

- management
- systems design
- programming
- electronics design
- electronics assembly

These skills might exist in one man, but he is unlikely to be able to cope alone with anything other than a small-scale project. A good working team would comprise five staff, each with one of these skills.

Because of the rapidly changing microprocessor environment it may be found that certain subsystems can be implemented by different mixtures of hardware and software. This hardware/software tradeoff is becoming increasingly important as more and more specialized chips and boards are becoming available. This, however, presupposes that these are compatible with the system. The much maligned S100 internal computer bus has provided easy access to a large number of specialized boards, so many users must be grateful for this standard despite its inadequacy.

The larger chip manufacturers are producing chips for controlling communication links, keyboards, floppy discs and many other tasks. The software needed to backup one of the hardware units is generally small compared with that needed if, for example, TTL buffers and latches are used. For asynchronous communication, the bit handling and timing would all be in software. By using a UART chip 100 bytes of software is reduced to about 30 bytes. This however is compensated for by a rise in hardware costs for this function by a factor of about 20.

The choice of processor is also a problem. It is better to use a familiar processor, providing it can meet the requirements. This may seem an over-conservative attitude in a dynamic environment, but there are reasons The development and testing equipment may well be suitable for a single manufacturer's range of chips. Using new chips could present problems of documentation and support. The manufacturer may not be able to offer training with the brand-new chip. Yesterday's certainty is a safer bet than tomorrow's possibility. It is also possible to stay in the same architectural family while moving up in power from say, the 8080A, to the Z80. The 'future shock' of such a move would not be as great as moving to a radically . different processor.

However, if the system is one that will need an operating system or extensive software support; the DEC LSI11 or the MicroNova from Data General should be considered. These processors carry much of the support originally provided for their manufacturers' minicomputer ranges.

HARDWARE

A major hardware consideration is the level at which to begin. There are three levels, with many variations in between

- component level
- board level
- chassis level

At the component level, the processor can be assembled from bit-slices or be a complete computer on a chip. The simple path is the middle way: to use a commonly available processor with a 4-, 8- or 16- bit word. This processor must be readily available on the market and not a 'paper tiger'; well supported with both hardware and documentation. Such approaches avoid disaster and disillusion, particularly for novice users.

Using a single-board computer bypasses several subsystem tasks; the major tasks are the efficient use of the board, its interfaces and the software associated with it.

In many cases, additional boards are available that will carry out tasks like A/D conversion. Putting the single-board computer, the interface cards and power supply together creates the chassis-level operation.

When the chassis is bought, with or without peripherals, the major task is creating the software. This makes the product unique. Correspondingly, the skills of the project team would be weighted in this direction.

As the subsystem specifications are drawn up, so the tradeoffs between hardware and software, become apparent. This is a problem of project control: the debate could be a long one unless the number of people involved is minimized. This is essentially an interaction between the designers of subsystems, who are normally working independently.

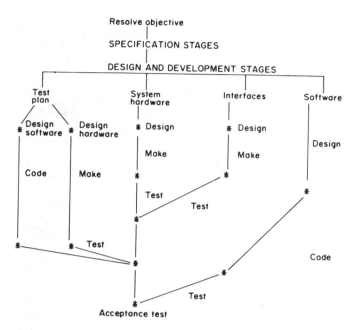

Figure 2. Critical path for specification design and development

MAINTENANCE

Already the maintenance requirements of the system will have been specified, although the exact mechanism may yet to be worked out. Whether equipment should be allowed to run to failure and then repaired or whether preventative maintenance is to be carried out, will affect the design of test points and test equipment. In the former case, replacement on failure and expert attention in a workshop is called for, while in the latter, onsite testing by skilled technicians is needed. Suspect components in the latter case can be replaced at board level. Maintenance is a much neglected area in microprocessor projects, and should really be regarded with much greater importance. The questions of the testing and maintenance of software will be covered in later articles.

TESTING

Another subject that needs more emphasis is hardware testing, and it will be covered in more detail later. A typical critical path network is shown in Figure 2. Notice that the test plan is equal in importance to the other paths. Preparing test hardware and software is no menial task to be passed to a trainee. The success of the project will stand or fall on the excellence or otherwise of the testing. However, it may not be possible to test all combinations in a system. What then is to be done? First, the system should be inherently safe for the user. Isaac Asimov's Laws of Robotics should be applied: do not preserve the system at the expense of the operator; it may sound obvious, but when the designer is concerned with the system and not the operator, things may get out of perspective. The hardware and software should be proven to the best of the team's ability. This may sound like the chicken and egg problem, and it is. A useful test technique is that of voting: taking three unknowns *A*, *B* and *C* and testing the combinations such that *A* is suspect if it fails alongside both *B* and *C*.

The computer is fabricated and tested alone before being run with the interface. The same would apply for additional hardware subsystems. It is not uncommon for later tests on the processor, in combination with other subsystems, to fail because of lack of processing power. Failure to anticipate the power needed may result in a great deal of needless time spent adapting the software. Another point arises here. By now the interactions between hardware and software will have been resolved on paper. Further interaction will no doubt take place and lead to better optimization. To allow this to continue to any great extent will be to delay the whole project. It cannot be overstressed that the hardware/software division of skills can be the Achille's heel of the programme. To divide the work between the disciplines before the functional specifications of each subsystem are decided will mean almost certain failure.

INTERFACING

Things can easily go wrong with interfacing. Even the type of modem to be used in a straightforward communications link can cause problems. If the customer is using equipment different from that available in the test area, weeks of aggravation can be caused, particularly when the installing engineer does not realize this. An example occurred in the communications interface of a system. It was tested with a local synchronous line drive but installed with a GPO modem; the resulting chaos was caused by the different clocking requirements of the two systems. It was not an equipment failure, it was a project-control failure. Software is not just a prickly problem, it is a minefield. Most microprocessor-based systems are staffed by engineers who have previously had little software experience. This situation is improving, albeit gradually. The level of software used is a problem. Coding in hexadecimal might feel better for the engineer than assembler or beyond, but the number of debugged lines a day is the final criterion. At assembler level, between 10 and 30 debugged lines a day can be expected. For a 3k program this represents 100 mandays or thereabouts. Of course, an experienced man can produce a high output of software for a short period, when a trainee may stumble along for months. Software design and testing is covered in a later article.

ACTIVITIES

Attention should now be turned to the activities of the individuals on the team. Figure 3 shows the typical team of five and their responsibilities over an unspecified timescale. The possible occurrence of events is shown, obviously the limitations on activities are that things cannot be built before they are designed and they cannot be tested before they are built. The design of test facilities must also follow the system design otherwise what is being tested is the unknown.

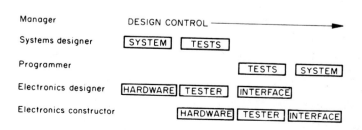

Figure 3. Pretesting activities

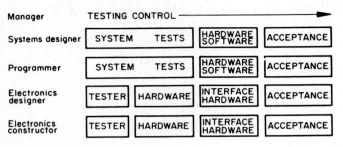

Manager	TESTING CONTROL ——————————————————▶			
Systems designer	SYSTEM TESTS	HARDWARE SOFTWARE	ACCEPTANCE	
Programmer	SYSTEM TESTS	HARDWARE SOFTWARE	ACCEPTANCE	
Electronics designer	TESTER	HARDWARE	INTERFACE HARDWARE	ACCEPTANCE
Electronics constructor	TESTER	HARDWARE	INTERFACE HARDWARE	ACCEPTANCE

Figure 4. Testing activities

The design of test facilities for microprocessors represents a great problem. That is why the programs outlined contain a measure of test hardware. A microprocessor is functionally equivalent to a computer and as such is an extremely complex device. The type of extended acceptance tests given on a mainframe cannot be afforded on a microprocessor, that is why a unit of test hardware is suggested in an attempt to exercise all the options.

Unlike the mainframe, the micro does not come ready assembled, unless a system above chassis level is to be used. This results in the problems of design and of using a mixture of skills. Conceptually, the problems of testing software that may be released in thousands of units of ROM, are very great. Microprocessors have advantages of flexibility over hardwired systems and the possibilities of parallelism in the project provide opportunities for a shorter lead time, provided the project is well controlled.

It will not be easy, and the first few projects will be the worst.

Standards in microcomputer system design

Standards concern all designers and users of microsystems. **Martin Whitbread** describes the interface, instrumentation and communications standards available and gives case studies

The subject of standards should concern all those who design or use microcomputer systems. Interface standards are of prime concern, particularly internal bus standards. The S100 bus dominates the personal computer market, but it has serious drawbacks and other buses are being considered.

Instrumentation buses for microcomputers present problems of cost and manufacturer support. CAMAC is a well supported system, but in its parallel form is probably too expensive for most microcomputers. The IEE-488-75 bus is already available and is well supported.

Communications interfaces on microcomputers owe everything to minicomputer and mainframe systems. The ubiquitous RS-232-C has been improved in the specifications RS-422/3. Better definition for internal and instrumentation buses are in preparation and offer the hope of easier system design.

Before deciding to adopt any particular standard in a project, there are some questions that need to be asked:

- What is gained by using a particular standard?
- What is lost by using it?
- How well defined is it?
- How well accepted is it?
- Who supports it?
- For how long is it likely to remain a standard?
- Are details available and from whom?

All of these questions should be asked of any potential standard. Take the basic unit itself — the microprocessor. There are no accepted standards for the processor, only the *de facto* standard of the Intel 8080. This is a standard by usage, and is one of the reasons why the 8080 code appears as a subset on other processors. This results in several processors of the same word-length that can run the 8080 instruction set, and a newly announced series of 16-bit processors, with upward conversion from that same 8-bit series. Thus, code written for the original 8080 can in theory run on the whole range. This upward compatibility also applies to the Motorola 6800 series. This processor also has a great following.

BUS STANDARDS

When MITS first produced the Altair 8080-based microcomputer, it is doubtful if they realised the impact that the design would have. The Altair 100-line bus was taken up by other manufacturers to provide memory and peripheral interface boards for what was proving to be an expanding market.

This bus — the S100 — is now being discussed as a standard. One of the advantages in using an S100 based system is the vast number of boards, for all manner of purposes, available to the user. These include:

- memory cards
- interface boards
- heuristic boards
- peripheral control boards
- TV display control boards
- clocking/timing facilities

The S100 is practical and will function well in most situations. These are the advantages. The disadvantages are well known, and, with hindsight, could have been avoided. It is too late to change the S100: if it is changed it will no longer be standard.

One of the major problems with the S100, and a potentially costly one, is the adjacent locations of the +5V (pin 51) and 18V (pin 52) power supplies. If a board is removed or replaced with the power on, there is every chance of 18V getting to pin 51. Every single chip using the regulated +5V coming indirectly from this pin, may be wrecked.

The clock lines and a number of control lines are too close for comfort. The sharp rise-and-fall characteristics of these signals could produce spurious signals on other lines. This must be allowed for, in the design of the board itself.

The bus also predates the use of the system-controller chip with the Intel 8080 (8228). As a result, unnecessary control lines are allowed for. Other pins provided are:

- 8 pin data input
- 8 pin data output
- 16 pin address bus
- 3 power lines
- 8 interrupt lines
- 39 control lines

An ideal bus would prevent a board being run up the wrong way, by providing some kind of cutoff. Carefully arranging power and ground pins would help prevent some of the problems described earlier.

The data-transmission facilities are interesting. The normal 8080 bidirectional bus has given way to two unidirectional buses. This appears to waste 8 pins, but otherwise there is no real disadvantage. The 16 address lines are simply a buffered address bus and attract no further comment here.

Power on the S100 is supplied unregulated, to each board. The alternative is to regulate at a central source.

Reprinted for *'Microprocessors and Microsystems'* Vol. 2 No. 6. Published by IPC Science and Technology Press Ltd., Westbury House, Bury St., Guildford, Surrey, England GU2 5AW.

The method used simplifies the distribution of power, but means that multiple regulators have to be used. This system is particularly suitable where various boards are likely to be used, as each board can receive voltages adjusted to its needs.

There is another bus that is used in several microcomputers: the SS50. As the name implies, only 50 lines are used. The S100, however, dominates the scene and the Intel 8080, Zilog Z80, Motorola 6800 and Mos Technology 6502 processors have all been used on it.

There is a movement to design a new standard and at least one with assured LSI interfacing has been proposed already[1]. Without the kind of support the communication interfaces described later receive, however, it is difficult to see how the results of so much labour put into other proposals can take root, let alone bear fruit. Other efforts are being made and the Mullard Space Laboratory, at University College London is actively canvassing all interested parties at the moment.

The Intel Multibus has also been proposed as a standard. This has the advantage of being able to support a multiprocessor configuration, with up to 15 processors slaved to a single master. An 86-pin structure, with 16 address lines and 16 bidirectional data lines, it has met with opposition as being 'too complex' by some and 'too simple' by others. There are spare pins on this bus but these have been reserved for use by Intel. They will be defined shortly, some will expand the memory-addressing capability, so that the 16-bit 8086 will run on it.

INTERFACE STANDARDS

The standardization of external interfaces has been more successful. Those currently available on microcomputers are spinoffs from mini and mainframe standardizations. Apart from being an obvious evolutionary step, it has the added advantage of providing connection between various types of computers.

A better understanding of some of these interfaces and some guidance through the maze of references given by various standards authorities is needed. Table 1 shows some of the interfaces available on microcomputer systems and provides a brief description of each.

RS-232-C is a relatively short-range interface, defined by the EIA (Electronics Industries Association) for bit-serial asynchronous communication. It was defined in 1969 and is well supported by many manufacturers. The maximum length of a communications link using RS-232-C is limited to 15.3m (50 ft); the speed of bit transfer is also limited to 20 kbit/s. The speed and range have been extended in RS-422 and 423. RS-423 defines a balanced line operating with a maximum transmission rate of 10 Mbit/s over a distance up to 1220m (4000 ft).

Binary 0s and 1s are defined in RS-232-C by voltages of greater than +3V and less than −3V respectively. With the 20mA current-loop system, the passage of that current through a pair of wires represents a binary 1, while a negligible current flow represents a binary 0. As with RS-232-C, the speed of transmission is relatively slow.

The V24 interface is perhaps the best known and documented of them all[2]. Its use is for transmission of data via modems, over public networks.

The instrumentation bus IEEE-488-75 is an example of a manufacturer's standard that has been both commercially and technically accepted. The various standards references are given in Table 2. This bus is referred to by the various references given at different times. It is a paradigm for any standard. There are manufacturer's national and international references and they do not always appear in the same document.

Patents are a problem for standards authorities and in the case of the IEEE-488-75 there appears to be a manufacturer's patent on the handshake lines that coordinate the asynchronous data transfer. This patent does not inhibit the use of the bus; licences are issued to all applicants wishing to use it.

There are a total of 16 lines in this bus, 8 bidirectional data lines, 5 general interface-management lines and 3 central byte-transfer lines (handshake). There is an upper limit of 15 instruments that can be connected to the bus, with a distance restriction of 20 m without an additional bus driver. A load is needed every 2 m.

This bus is capable of high-speed data transmission; a maximum transmission of 1 Mbyte/s can be obtained. Each byte is transferred asynchronously, in parallel. Transfer is initiated by the bus controller setting one of the five interface-management lines true and placing the addresses of all involved stations on the databus. Any one of these stations may then talk to the bus or any number listen. Thus the transfer is half-duplex. The handshake lines function the bus before the old one had been successfully read from it.

A great deal of emphasis has been given to the kind of support that standards receive. An unsupported standard is a contradiction in terms. CAMAC is a well supported interface, having the backing of ESONE, an organization linked to the EEC. It was developed by ERDA (Energy Research and Development Administration), and was designed for use in nuclear establishments as an instrumentation bus. Accordingly the structure of the bus matches this environment and not, it is argued, that of process control or data processing.

CAMAC is not a simple system: a total of 86 lines are employed, using a 24-bit bus. Up to 23 modules can be addressed in one system. The modules themselves are referred to as 'crates' and the interconnecting bus is the 'highway'. The system is designed so that connection into the bus is logically simple; it is the basic system that is complex. This means that a minimal application works out to be very expensive, while additions are both simple and relatively cheap. This will probably prevent any large-scale adoption of this system in microcomputers. However, a serial system has been specified and, if implemented, could result in much more interest being taken by microcomputer manufacturers.

CAMAC is well supported and as such, exemplifies the type of backing that any interface needs from both users and suppliers before it can be considered standard. What

Table 1. Description of interface standards

Interface	Description
RS-232-C	Serial; limited distance and speed
RS-422/3	Serial; improved distance and speed
20 mA loop	Serial; local teletypewriter links
IEEE-488-75	Parallel; local instrumentation and control bus
V24	Serial; data communications on public network
CAMAC	Parallel; specialized instrumentation bus

Table 2. Interface standards: international and national references

Common reference	IEEE	IEC	EIA	CCITT	ANSI	Other
IEE-488-75	488-75	TC66(02)			MC1.1	GPIB/
CAMAC	STD-583					HPIB
RS-232-C			RS232-C			
RS-422			RS-422	V.11(X.17)		
RS-423			RS-422	V.10(X.26)		

is also needed is a single centre of decision concerning technical factors. A standard that is left to six different suppliers to adopt unilaterally will end up as six different standards.

RECORDING STANDARDS

Apart from internal and external bus and interface standards, there are other standards that are adhered to, more or less, on available microcomputers.

Data-recording formats present a problem[3]. The way information is recorded on floppy disc does not appear to have settled to any degree. There are, of course, problems of different recording densities, double or single sided, and a choice of 5in or 8in discs. This presents quite a number of permutations and it is doubtful if the situation will settle down before a new technology replaces it.

Cassette tape does not present so many problems. Here the problem is with the recording standard itself and not with the lack of one. The CUTS (Computer User Tape System) or Kansas City Standard is in common use. In this system a logical 1 is represented by a frequency of 2.4 kHz and a 0 by 1.2 kHz.

These frequencies are generated for recording by dividing an internal 4.8 kHz signal by 2 and 4 respectively. When reading, the frequency is taken from the tape, thus allowing for speed and hence frequency variations. However, this system loads both object and source slowly and there are no error checks, CRC or otherwise.

Other standards that affect the microcomputer user are:

- software
- logic diagrams
- documentation
- Codes of Practice

As far as software is concerned, the major problem is that even something like ANSI COBOL ends up by being a standard plus. Manufacturers cannot resist tacking enhancements onto a standard, making it nonstandard in the process. This is probably done in the belief the users who have written software in the standard form (if they can find one); will upgrade to the enhanced version. This is fine, except that many manufacturers do it and the concept of a standard becomes a nonsense.

Real-time software seems to be getting a better deal, as far as standardization is concerned. There are centrally supported languages like CORAL 66 (supported by the Royal Signals and Radar Establishment, UK) and single implementations of a language, such as RTL-2 on PDP11s, which is in general use at ICI, UK.

At a lower level of complexity, real-time BASIC is being defined and promises to present the engineer with

a useful alternative to assembler for small real-time systems. This is a PURDUE Europe project.

Common-or-garden BASIC suppliers suffer from the standard-plus syndrome described earlier, but some *de facto* standards are appearing. This is because there are only a few major sources of software sold on personal computer systems. More information on this subject can be obtained by following the work of John Coll of Oundle School, Peterborough, UK, who has an intimate knowledge of the situation.

Flowcharting real-time systems has long presented a problem and probably very few attempt it. Program network charts to BS 5476 offer a standard solution to this problem[4].

The technique is to present the relationships between software components irrespective of time. Using a normal flowchart template, a real-time system can be documented in an easily understood form.

As microprocessor applications increase in number and complexity, the need for documentation will occur to most project teams. To some it will come too late. This is not a plea for mindbending bureaucracy, but for ordered and tidy thinking.

Until such time as a recommended Code of Practice is produced for microprocessor projects, it is up to the individual or organization to examine current standards in documentation and decide what they need and why.

The need for recognized standards can be illustrated using simple examples. The following three case studies are based on actual projects. The problems presented to the users in trying to use microprocessors, often for the first time, are shown. The aptitude shown by engineers and designers in the face of this new technology is very heartening.

CASE STUDY 1

This concerned a manufacturer of equipment containing a control element. To remain competitive, the decision was make to introduce some kind of microelectronics control. There was considerable inhouse experience in electronics, but little in microprocessors or software. Obviously the first priority was education. A general familiarity was gained through a one-week course and a number of seminars. With this background it was considered that the hardware would need to range from a chassis-type with a standard bus and the software should be at as high a level as possible, if it were to be tackled inhouse. The hardware choices were seen as:

- Chassis type, using a standard board and control interfaces
- Small computing system with control interfaces
- Specialized microprocessor-based control systems
- Minicomputer with control interfaces

Correspondingly the software options were seen to be:

- Inhouse training/recruitment at assembler level
- High-level control language
- External contract with no feedback
- External contract with feedback and eventual handover to inhouse project team

The ultimate choice was to adopt a manufacturer's board/chassis system. Software was to be written by a consultancy, with increasing handover to inhouse expertise. Initially, software would be written at assembler level.

Thus the user placed himself in the hands of a manufacturer for ensuring that components and boards were compatible. The project team gained increasing software experience by working with a consultancy, and this prevented their getting out of their depth at an early stage.

CASE STUDY 2

In this study, a manufacturer, who this time is concerned with information processing, had to determine the best mix of ingredients. The project was one of directly replacing an existing mainframe system, written in FORTRAN.

The choices for this project were seen as:

- Providing mainframe computing online
- Compiling best-mix tables and loading them into a programmable calculator
- Running FORTRAN on a minicomputer
- Running FORTRAN on a microcomputer with a standard bus structure for memory expansion

It was decided to examine the available microcomputers with FORTRAN compilers and sufficient disc storage. A programme of benchmarking was initiated. The compilation time could be expected to be several magnitudes greater than before, but for this case even slow runtime was not a retrograde step. The computation is being placed where it is needed.

Additional memory and interfaces could be provided if further functions were found for the device.

CASE STUDY 3

This was an office application, where a complex bonus calculation was also subject to change at intervals. The choices open were seen as:

- Using programmable calculators
- Using a terminal
- Using a mainframe
- Programming a small personal computer, programmable in a common version of BASIC

The last choice was made, not because it was cheapest but as the most rewarding in terms of experience in a new environment. The computer bought was one of a popular type with memory-expansion possibilities on the manufacturer's standard bus.

A summary of these three studies, which are all real and current; reveals the need for standards in the user's mind. Particular emphasis was placed by them on a standard bus and software, that could be easily handled. It is the availability of memory and interface cards on the particular standard bus that are the attraction. A bus standard without the manufacturer's backing would probably be ignored.

CONCLUSIONS

So far standards have been examined which range from the *de facto* 8080 processor standard to the possibility of a Code of Practice. The situation is in a great state of flux. There is a need for a sophisticated multiprocessor instrument bus, along the lines of CAMAC, but designed with more than one processor in circuit. Again with multiprocessor use in mind, there is a need for a standard internal bus that has the commercial support of the S100, but is designed for general-purpose use. Lastly there is the high-speed serial link that is defined in RS-422/3. This will probably appear as an optical link and add a new dimension to the problem.

REFERENCES

1 Wells T D, *MODBUS: a standard computer bus structure* Admiralty Surface Weapons Establishment, Portsmouth, Hants, UK TR78003 (1978)

2 *Handbook of data communications* NCC (1975) Chapter 7, p 157

3 Borer, A J 'Data-recording formats' *Microprocessors* Vol 2 No 3 (June 1978) pp 123–129

4 Coan, D R A 'Program network charts' *Comput. Bull.* (June 1977)

Software development and system testing techniques

There is no substitute for investment in development aids. **Martin Whitbread** describes the currently available methods of developing software and testing hardware.

Microcomputer software and development techniques are evolving rapidly. Text editors and debugging aids are becoming increasingly available, particularly on inexpensive hardware. A revolution will probably take place soon, with the appearance of complete development systems costing less than £1000.

Software design methods are very much in vogue and the need for structure and documentation in microcomputer software cannot be overstressed. Which level of software to use is a problem that must be solved in the early days of system specification. The solution is often hybrid, composed of high-level code calling on lower-level assembler for fast or complex computations.

System testing aids are becoming available with increased power and versatility. Multiprocessor development systems are now available with ICE (in-circuit emulation), a technique of real-time processor emulation that is receiving increased attention.

This kind of support is still not cheap, but the value-for-money is improving rapidly.

Software can easily become the Achilles' Heel of a microcomputer project. Failure to invest in development aids, for both hardware and software, could result in anything from a major project delay to an inefficient and unreliable (hence unmarketable) system.

For the software developer, the message cannot be overstated. A clear objective must be set and the best support possible must be provided. It is no use attempting software development in a medium or large-scale project with equipment more suited to a half-hour tutorial. Nevertheless, it can be done and the determined designer may make a success of the project. The cost in time and reputation as a result of poor design, however, could be enormous.

Single-board evaluation kits are not suitable for software development if man-hours are costed in the project. Keying programs in hexadecimal, with little or no debugging and editing support, is clearly going to tie-up many hours that could be better spent elsewhere.

LANGUAGE

If a microcomputer or a development system is used,

the question of language arises. The choice is more often based on familiarity or personal preference. There are some ground rules that can be followed, however, for choosing between assembler and compiled or interpreted high-level languages:

- For a low-volume moderate-to-slow system, use an interpretative or compiled language; this allows rapid development at the cost of memory
- For a fast low-volume system use assembler, a very efficient compiler or a high-level/assembler hybrid
- For all high-volume systems, use assembler.

These rules are based on current processor speeds and memory costs. An increase in processor speed by a factor of two or three, or a leap in the memory density/cost ratio, will allow high-level and interpretative languages to be used in many more systems.

For high-volume systems, the overhead on memory, imposed by the relative inefficiency of current compilers, would inflict a heavy burden on the manufacturer. This extra cost must be compared with the one-off overhead of development in assembler.

For higher-level microcomputer languages, there are two classifications that can be applied. First, there are languages such as FORTRAN and BASIC that occur universally in the computing environment and thus have a certain amount of momentum. Second, there are specialized microcomputer languages which, although they sometimes owe something to larger system languages, are really dedicated to microcomputer work: MPL, PL/M, PL/Z and MicroFORTH are examples. The position of CORAL 66 should not be ignored, it is available on many microprocessors.

The more popular languages, BASIC and FORTRAN do not normally provide bit-level operation of inputs and outputs. These operations must be placed in subroutines, written in assembler.

Naturally the more specialized microcomputer language should have these facilities. Their main drawback is that they are only available for one or a limited number of processors:

- MPL on Motorola;
- PL/M on Intel;
- PL/Z on Zilog;
- MicroFORTH on RCA Cosmac and Intel 8080

Reprinted for '*Microprocessors and Microsystems*' Vol. 3 No. 1. Published by IPC Science and Technology Press Ltd., Westbury House, Bury St., Guildford, Surrey, England GU2 5AW.

What should also be noted is the rapid emergence
of PASCAL on microcomputers. It has been reported
that PASCAL will be the only high-level language
supported on Motorola's new processor, the 68000,
available in 1979–80.

DOCUMENTATION

Whatever language is used, the software produced
will need to be documented. This applies particularly
to real-time systems. Documentation is regarded
with disdain by many and sometimes there is the
simple resort to the useless expedient of keeping the
original coding sheets. What should be kept is an
annotated version of the latest source listing. Once
a security copy of the source program has been taken,
the coding sheets should be destroyed.

The structured design of the software is a subject
for a paper in its own right. Suffice to say that this
structure should be modular and every effort should
be made to familiarize the software development
team with modular programming techniques. An
important part of the documentation will be
descriptions of relationships between these modules;
the conditions on entry and exit are critical to
future amendments.

In the early stages of design, it is often useful to
include some temporary modules, whose sole function
is to aid the development stages and provide diagnostics.
These can be removed in the final editing stages.
It is better to design them into the system, rather
than patch them in later.

Only primitive diagnostics are available on many
current assemblers and compilers. This situation is
improving rapidly however, and those available
with current operating systems, including the popular
CP/M from Digital Research, provide very useful
facilities. An element of do-it-yourself may still be
needed, to provide the kind of in-depth testing that
microcomputer projects inevitably need.

Software generation can be an unwelcome chore,
particularly when using systems based on paper tape
or cassette tape. If the project team is large enough,
a junior could well be delegated this task to release
valuable hours of effort elsewhere.

DEBUGGING

In the absence of a development system or diagnostic
software other techniques can be used to develop
and debug software:

- Software is written with interrupts (breakpoints)
  at critical test points
- In areas where the code is complex and liable
  to be extended, blocks of code that have no
  effect are left (NOP or register *n* to register *n*)
- Writing is done in modules which have a clearly
  defined condition at entry and exit. These can
  be tested individually, nested into 'test-bed' code.

These are just some items that are being used. The
permutations in testing can be mindbending. In
some circumstances a separate processor should be
used to simulate the real world. This processor

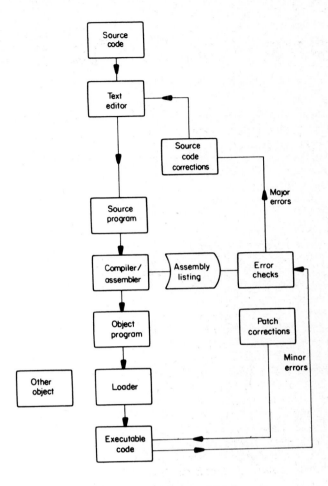

Figure 1. Development system procedures

would not only provide input but also monitor and
record or display the output. The legitimate
combinations of signals need to be carefully defined
and illicit combinations filtered out by software or
hardware. This may sound obvious, but failure to
do so will release a system on the world with a
time bomb ticking away inside. Such a system
might be used in a potentially dangerous situation
and, consequently, present a hazard to both life
and property.

The need for proper development systems
cannot be overstated, and there is a pattern to the
development of software using these systems
(Figure 1).

Once the initial coding sheets have been used
to program entry, they have no further use unless
of course there is no system printer. The listing
produced on the development system is the working
documentation. Care must also be taken with the
recorded program; a fault in the recording
mechanism could mean a lengthy session of rekeying.
There is no substitute for taking security copies.

After compilation, there are two alternative
procedures: one patching in small alterations
for minor changes, and editing the source text for
major changes.

A loader is used to put the object program into
memory. The input to this loader will need to be
from a relocating assembler, if the loader is to
combine several program modules. One of the

problems to be solved by this software is the physical location of variables that are accessed by more than one module.

DEVELOPMENT SYSTEMS

There are several types of development system on which these facilities might be found. In some ways these types represent the various generations of these systems. Perhaps the simplest form such a system can take is a keyboard and processor; with assemblers, text editors and debugging aids held in PROM. Text can be displayed on a TV monitor and the final output of the developed program is through an RS-232-C port to a compatible peripheral. The essence of this type of system, cheap and cheerful as it is, is that it brings powerful software aids to the programmer at minimal cost. It is also worth noting that there are new products coming on to the market in this form and it should be possible to get a basic development system for less than £750 by mid 1979.

More complex systems can be divided into two groups: those with serial file storage on such media as paper or magnetic cassette tape, and those with directly accessible (disc-based) files.

The former often incorporate a teletypewriter, printing at around 10 character/s. Slow printing and tape-reading speeds can result in several hours being consumed in minor amendments and reassembly.

Higher speeds are obviously needed and these can be provided by a fast paper-tape reader/punch and a more sophisticated printer. The obvious move, however, should be towards a disc-based system, providing faster file retrieval, a VDU and a 100—200 character/s printer. This is the current state of development systems as most manufacturers are providing or planning to provide them. PROM programmers and ICE are usually available. ICE provides a link between the development system and the target hardware by replacing the microprocessor. Signals on the system buses are monitored; development system memory and supporting peripherals are also made available to the target. Using ICE for bus monitoring does not rule out the use of a logic analyser, which can analyse and display signals and test devices other than the microprocessor. In time, these facilities will also be available on development systems, particularly on the so-called universal systems.

With the rapid advance of microprocessor devices, it is possible to inhibit progress within a user organization by committing it to an inflexible development system; committing all projects to a particular processor within the useful life of the development system. Manufacturers are, of course, aware of this problem and the general structure of development systems (Figure 2) shows a bus structure that should lend itself to upgrading by card changes. The latest development systems can, in some cases, be upgraded from 8- to 16-bit processors.

Not all development systems are made by microprocessor manufacturers: some are capable of a limited general-purpose operation, with facilities for both 8- and 16-bit processors on the same machine. These are usually very well equipped development

systems, with ICE and PROM programming available as part of the system. Support is normally provided for the popular 8-bit processors: the Intel 8080, Zilog Z80 and the Motorola 6800.

The difficulties of simulating accurately these three processors in a single system are very great. Instead, the policy used is one of emulation; the target processor for the development work is present in the system. This eliminates the subtle kind of errors that could be met using simulation. Two systems that are relevant to this discussion are the Tektronix 8001/2 and the Futuredata Microsystem.

These systems are intended for developing systems on different and in some cases radically different microprocessors. They provide this flexibility to development programmes and will no doubt be a great boon in educational and research establishments. Many projects will, however, have settled for a particular processor or manufacturer and will not necessarily need this flexibility. Indeed it might detract from the programme of work by making noise, distracting the project members, just as the ubiquitous games programs do on commercial microcomputers.

Software development packages are available, as interpreter/compiler combinations or as module test beds. Modularity can exist in a system as a set of subroutines, called directly from a central module. An alternative is for the modules to exist as loosely coupled programs, communicating by clearly defined procedures. A powerful system for modular operation has been developed, known as MASCOT (modular approach to system construction, operation and test). This was developed at the RSRE Malvern.

The reasons for using a loosely coupled modular structure are:

- occurrence of real-time interrupts, causing breaks in running programs
- sharing processor time between many programs that are active simultaneously

Both of these cause breaks in programs that appear to be contiguous in their source forms. MASCOT is geared to providing a systematic and highly disciplined approach to this problem. Basic types of module are defined in terms of source text. These can be compiled, linked and loaded to create executable code. This code can be comprehensively tested under MASCOT and dummy modules can be used to substitute for unfinished or unproven ones.

The software in a MASCOT system consists of a central 'kernel', providing such facilities as interrupt

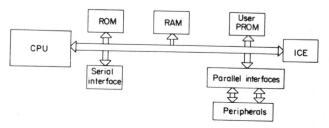

Figure 2. Development system bus structure

handling and processor time control; and MASCOT subsystems which equate to single threads in a multiprogramming system.

MASCOT has great advantages in creating, testing and maintaining real-time software and its value is becoming increasingly recognized; seminars and public courses on its use are now being held.

CROSSPRODUCTS

There are, of course, other ways of developing software. Crossassemblers, crosscompilers and processor simulators can be run on minicomputers, mainframes, timesharing networks and even scientific computers.

Many users have developed their own crossproduct software for developing microprocessor software on inhouse mini or mainframe computers. The quality and reliability of these products may well be unknown and yet they will form the very foundation of the development work. Using the mainframe or mini, cross-software places the designer a conceptual step away from the target processor. This is particularly true with simulators. The simulated processor may differ in many subtle ways from the target processor. Thus the system developed runs a risk of being a theoretical one only; in real life it may not function as designed.

The additional cost of computing time and the availability of the service are major considerations in using crossassemblers and compilers. Development systems are now relatively cheap and are getting cheaper all the time.

Their flexibility and ease of use are positive points in their favour. The additional facilities over crossproduct software of PROM programming and in-circuit emulation, make their purchase by would-be developers essential.

SIGNATURE ANALYSIS

Logic analysis has already been mentioned. There is also the area of field testing for microcomputer systems, which has been much neglected in the past. Portable analysers are now coming onto the market with powerful features, particularly in the area of signature analysis. Like the more static development

systems, they are available from particular manufacturers or in general-purpose form. The basic requirements for such systems are:

- suitcase size and weight
- in-circuit emulation
- signature analysis
- diagnostics
- user written tests
- pulse/frequency measurement

Signature analysis will probably form the basis for future semiautomatic, even online testing. The technique is to inject a predetermined bit-stream into the system and monitor the output.

This output is compressed to produce a short string of numbers or characters, which are then compared with the expected result. Using the right formula, the probability of any two different outputs producing the same signature can be reduced to an almost insignificant degree.

This technique is obviously ideal for preventative maintenance in the field. The main reason for carrying out field test programmes is the cost of returning boards to a central test and maintenance depot. If these boards have a high capital value, a large amount of money will be tied up in nonoperational boards in transit for maintenance. Two examples of current portable test equipment are the Intel Microscope and the Millenium-Microsystem Analyser.

An added complexity to a microcomputer design programme is the growing tendency in certain areas of the market to use bit-slice processors as high-speed emulators of existing processors. The resulting systems are very fast and can, in theory, run programs developed for the original processor. These may be marketed as chassis or board replacements. If they are, they will certainly add a new dimension to system development and testing.

CONCLUSIONS

The message has been repeated many times in many places, there is no substitute for investment in development aids. It is pointless waiting for the next automatic price decrease. Pence gained thus will cost pounds in lost market opportunities.

Further Reading

MICROELECTRONICS (Reprint of Scientific American)
W. H. Freeman 1978

MICROELECTRONICS — THE NEW TECHNOLOGY
Department of Industry, U.K.   H.M.S.O. 1978

AN INTRODUCTION TO MICROCOMPUTERS
Volume 0 — The Beginner's Book.
Osborne and Associates 1978

AN INTRODUCTION TO MICROCOMPUTERS
Volume 1 — Basic Concepts.
Osborne and Associates 1978

AN INTRODUCTION TO MICROCOMPUTERS
Volume 2 — Some Real Microprocessors.
Osborne and Associates 1978

AN INTRODUCTION TO MICROCOMPUTERS
Volume 3 — Some Real Support Devices.
Osborne and Associates 1978

Glossary of Terms

Address

A way of referencing a memory location containing data or program instruction.

Address bus

A physical connection between a processor and computer memory along which addresses are passed so that memory locations can be referenced.

Analogue (or linear)

A system in which the output signal bears a continuous relationship to the input signal, as opposed to the discontinuous relationship exhibited by digital circuits.

Arithmetic logic unit (ALU)

The arithmetic component of the central processor of a computer.

Binary

A digital system where only two levels of signal are used, such as On/Off or High/Low.

Bipolar

Semiconductor devices where the gain is obtained by interaction of positive and negative charge carriers.

Bit

A single binary digit, the basic information unit within a computer. There are two possible values, 0 or 1.

Byte

A unit of information normally comprising 8 bits.

CCD (charge-coupled device)

A device in which information is stored by means of packets of minute electrical charges.

CPU

The Central Processing Unit of a computer, where the computation is controlled and co-ordinated.

Chip (or die)

A small piece of silicon on which is a completely unpackaged semiconductor device — a transistor, diode or integrated circuit.

Code

The representation of information.

Compiler

A program used to convert a high-level language to a low-level language.

Diffusion

A process by which selected chemicals, called dopants, are enabled to enter the crystalline structure of semiconductor materials to change the electrical characteristics.

Digital

A system that handles information as numbers.

Discrete device

A single-function packaged component; for example, a diode or a transistor.

FET (field effect transistor)

A transistor controlled by voltage rather than current. The flow of current through a channel controlled by the effect of an electric field resulting from the voltage applied to an area called the gate. Only one type of charge carrier is involved.

Hexadecimal

A number system based on 16, i.e. 0, 1, 2, 3, 4, 5, 6, 7, 8, 9, A, B, C, D, E, F, 10, 11, 12.

Hybrid

A small electronic module in which passive elements and interconnections are formed by thin- or thick-film techniques on a substrate to which the active devices (for example, transistors) may be added, usually in chip form.

Integrated circuit

A semiconductor device containing circuit elements which are manufactured in a single piece of material and which are indivisibly connected to perform a function.

Interpreter

A program which directly executes instructions in a given language. The most commonly used language in this form is BASIC.

LCD display

Display utilising liquid-crystal technology.

LED display

Display utilising light-emitting diodes.

LSI (large-scale integration)

A term generally applied to integrated circuits containing from 100 to 5,000 logic gates or 1,000 to 16,000 memory bits.

Linear

See Analogue.

Logic

The system in which on/off conditions at the inputs of digital circuits provide related on/off signals at the outputs.

MOS (metal-oxide-silicon)

See FET.

MSI (medium-scale integration)

A term generally applied to integrated circuits containing from 20 to 100 logic gates or less than 1,000 memory bits.

Mask

A photographic plate on which is printed the integrated circuit pattern required for a single step of the silicon wafer fabrication process.

Memory

A device which stores digital information. In semiconductor memories data may be stored in the form of electrical charges or as voltage or current levels.

Micro-electronic devices

The generic term for electronic components or circuits made to very small dimensions.

Microprocessor (MPU)

An LSI circuit design that provides, in one or more chips, similar functions to those contained in the central processing unit of a computer. It interprets and executes instructions and usually incorporates arithmetic capabilities.

N-channel (see also MOS)

A type of field-effect transistor structure in which the conducting channel is n-type (negative) semiconductor material. N-channel devices operate at higher speed than p-type (positive) devices.

Object Code

Low-level code, usually ready to run on a processor.

Octal

A number system, similar to hexadecimal but based on the number 8.

PROM (programmable read-only memory)

A memory into which information can be written after the device is manufactured, but thereafter cannot be altered.

Peripheral

Any device connected to and controlled by a computer.

RAM (random access memory)

A memory in which information can be entered into or retrieved from any storage position.

ROM (read-only memory)

A memory into which information is written during the manufacturing process and which thereafter cannot be altered.

SSI (small-scale integration)

A term applied to integrated circuits containing from one to twenty logic gates.

Semiconductor

A material in which the electrical conductivity lies between that of conductors and insulators. It also has a crystal structure whose atomic bonds allow the conduction of current by either positive or negative carriers when the appropriate dopants are added.

Solid state

The area of physics which deals with materials in their solid form. All silicon semiconductors are solid-state devices.

Structured Programming

A methodology of designing computer programs.

Transistor

An active semiconductor device with three electrodes (emitter, base and collector). Used as a switch or as an amplifier.

VLSI (very-large-scale integration)

A term applied to integrated circuits containing a minimum of 5,000 logic gates, or more than 16,000 memory bits.

Wafer (or slice)

A thin disk of semiconductor material, usually silicon, in which many semiconductor devices are fabricated at one time. The devices are subsequently separated and assembled in individual packages.

Yield

A measure of the efficiency of a production process determined by the ratio of the number of acceptable devices completed to the number of devices started.

Acknowledgements/ Details of Contributing Journals and Magazines

The Publishers should like to thank the following publishers, magazines and journals for giving permission to reproduce articles. Subscriptions to these magazines and journals may be taken out at the addresses detailed below.

BUS AND COACH MOTOR TRANSPORT, IPC Transport Press Ltd, Dorset House, Stamford Street, London, SE1 9LU, England.

THE COMPUTER PORT, 926 N. Collins, Arlington, Texas 76011, USA.

CONTROL ENGINEERING, 1301 S. Grove Avenue, Barrington, IL 60010, USA.

CREATIVE COMPUTING — UK Subscriptions (£13 p.a.), 27 Andrew Close, Stoke Golding, Nuneaton, CV13 6EL, England.

CREATIVE COMPUTING — USA Subscriptions ($15 p.a.) and elsewhere ($23 p.a.), P O Box 789-M, Morristown, NJ 07960, USA.

THE ECONOMIST, 25 St. James Street, London, SW1A 1HG, England.

ELECTRONIC DESIGN, Hayden Publishing Company Inc., 50 Essex Street, Rochelle Park, NJ 07662, USA.

ELECTRONICS AND POWER, The Institution of Electrical Engineers, P O Box 8, Southgate House, Stevenage, Herts., SG1 1HQ, England.

ELECTRONICS WEEKLY, IPC Electrical-Electronic Press Ltd, Dorset House, Stamford Street, London, SE1 9LU, England.

THE ENGINEER, Morgan-Grampian (Publishers) Ltd, 30 Calderwood Street, Woolwich, London, SE18 6QH, England.

ENGINEERING, Design Council, 28 Haymarket, London, SW1Y 4SU, England

INTERFACE AGE, 16704 Marquardt Avenue, P O Box 1234, Cerritos, CA 90701, USA.

MACHINERY AND PRODUCTION ENGINEERING (Subscriptions £24 p.a.), 4 Aldworth Grove, London, SE13 6HJ, England.

MANAGEMENT SERVICES, Institute of Management Services, 1 Cecil Court, London Road, Enfield, Middlesex, EN2 6DD, England.

MEASUREMENT AND CONTROL, Journal of the Institute of Measurement and Control, 20 Peel Street, London W8, England.

MICROPROCESSORS AND MICROSYSTEMS, IPC Science and Technology Press Ltd, Westbury House, Bury Street, Guildford, Surrey, GU2 5AW, England.

OSBORNE & ASSOCIATES INC., Post Office Box 2036, Berkeley, CA 94702, USA.

PERSONAL COMPUTER WORLD, 62A Westbourne Grove, London W2, England.

PERSONAL COMPUTING, LP Enterprises, 313 Kingston Road, Ilford, Essex, IG1 1PJ, England.

PRACTICAL COMPUTING, 2 Duncan Terrace, London, N1 8BJ, England.

PRODUCTION ENGINEERING, Penton Plaza, Cleveland, Ohio 44114, USA.

SIMULATION, The Society for Computer Simulation, Post Office Box 2228, La Jolla, California 92037, USA.

Thanks are also given to the following individuals for permission to reproduce articles.

Dr Martin Healey, Department of Electrical and Electronic Engineering, University College, Cardiff, Wales.

Mr Nigel Bevan, National Physical Laboratory, Teddington.

Mr K. Gill, General Secretary, Amalgamated Union of Engineering Workers, Technical, Administrative and Supervisory Section.